THE MACHINERY OF FREEDOM

THE MACHINERY OF FREEDOM

GUIDE TO A RADICAL CAPITALISM

SECOND EDITION

DAVID FRIEDMAN

Open Court

La Salle, Illinois

OPEN COURT and the above logo are registered in the U.S. Patent and Trademark Office.

© 1973 and 1978 by David D. Friedman. © 1989 by Open Court Publishing Company.

First printing 1989.

Printed and bound in the United States of America.

Library of Congress Cataloging-in-Publication Data

Friedman, David D.
   The machinery of freedom: guide to a radical capitalism/David Friedman.—2nd ed.
     p. cm.
   Bibliography: p.
   Includes index
   ISBN 0-8126-9068-0.—ISBN 0-8126-9069-9 (pbk.)
   1. Liberty. 2. Individualism. 3. Property. 4. Free enterprise.
I. Title.
   JC585.F76 1989
   323.44—dc19   89-31411
                                                   CIP

This book is dedicated to

Milton Friedman
Friedrich Hayek
Robert A. Heinlein,
from whom I learned

and to
Robert M. Schuchman,
who might have written it better

Capitalism is the best. It's free enterprise. Barter. Gimbels, if I get really rank with the clerk, 'Well I don't like this', how I can resolve it? If it really gets ridiculous, I go, 'Frig it, man, I walk.' What can this guy do at Gimbels, even if he was the president of Gimbels? He can always reject me from that store, but I can always go to Macy's. He can't really hurt me. Communism is like one big phone company. Government control, man. And if I get too rank with that phone company, where can I go? I'll end up like a schmuck with a dixie cup on a thread.

LENNY BRUCE

Why can't you see?
We just want to be free
To have our homes and families
And live our lives as we please.

DANA ROHRABACHER
WEST COAST LIBERTARIAN TROUBADOUR

Contents

PREFACE TO THE SECOND EDITION

Most of this book was written between 1967 and 1973, when the first edition was published. I have made only minor changes to the existing material, in the belief that the issues and arguments have not changed substantially over the past 15 years. In some cases the reader will find the examples dated; Chapter 17, for example, was written when Ronald Reagan was governor of California. Where this seemed to be a serious problem I have updated examples or added explanatory comments, but in most places I have left the original text unaltered. Most current examples will not remain current very long; hopefully this book will outlast the present governor of California as well.

I have followed the same policy with regard to numbers. Figures for the number of heroin addicts in New York or U.S. Steel's share of the steel industry describe the situation as of about 1970, when the first edition was being written. When looking at such numbers, you should remember that prices and nominal incomes were about a third as high in 1970 as in 1988, when this preface is being written. Numbers that are purely hypothetical ("If a working wife can hire an Indian maid, who earned _____ dollars a year in India . . . "), on the other hand, have been updated to make them more plausible to a modern reader. The appendices have also been updated, mostly by my friend Jeff Hummel.

These are all minor changes. The major difference between this edition and the first is the inclusion of eight new chapters, making up Part IV of the book.

One thing I should perhaps have explained in my original preface, and which has puzzled some readers since, is the apparent inconsistency among the chapters. In Chapter 10, for instance, I advocate a voucher system, in which tax monies are used to subsidize schooling, but in Part III I argue for a society with no taxes, no government, and therefore no vouchers.

Part II of the book is intended to suggest specific reforms, within the structure of our present institutions, that would produce desirable results while moving us closer to a libertarian society. A voucher system, which moves us from schooling paid for and produced by government to schooling paid for by government but produced on a competitive market, is one such reform. In Part III I try to describe what a full-fledged anarcho-capitalist society might look like and how it would work. Part III describes a much more radical change from our present institutions than Part II while Part II describes how the first steps of that radical change might come about.

One reason for writing a book like this is to avoid having to explain the same set of ideas a hundred times to a hundred different people. One of the associated rewards is discovering, years later, people who have incorporated my ideas into their own intellectual framework. This second edition is dedicated to one such person. I cannot honestly describe him as a follower or a disciple, since most of our public encounters have been debates; I believe that his best-known views are wrong and possibly dangerous. He is merely someone who starts out already knowing and understanding everything I had to say on the subjects of this book as of 1973, which makes the ensuing argument very much more interesting.

For which reason this second edition is dedicated to Jeffrey Rogers Hummel.

PREFACE TO THE FIRST EDITION

My political views seem natural and obvious—to me. Others find them peculiar. Their peculiarity consists largely of carrying certain statements, familiar enough in political oratory, to their natural conclusions.

I believe, as many say they believe, that everyone has the right to run his own life—to go to hell in his own fashion. I conclude, as do many on the left, that all censorship should be done away with. Also that all laws against drugs—marijuana, heroin, or Dr. Quack's cancer cure—should be repealed. Also laws requiring cars to have seat belts.

The right to control my life does not mean the right to have anything I want free; I can do that only by making someone else pay for what I get. Like any good right winger, I oppose welfare programs that support the poor with money taken by force from the taxpayers.

I also oppose tariffs, subsidies, loan guarantees, urban renewal, agricultural price supports—in short, all of the much more numerous programs that support the not-poor—often the rich—with money taken by force from the taxpayers—often the poor.

I am an Adam Smith liberal, or, in contemporary American terminology, a Goldwater conservative. Only I carry my devotion to laissez faire further than Goldwater does—how far will become clear in the following chapters. Sometimes I call myself a Goldwater anarchist.

These peculiar views of mine are not peculiar to me. If they were, I would be paying Harper and Row to publish this book, instead of Harper and Row paying me. My views are typical of the ideas of a small but growing group of people, a 'movement' that has begun to attract the attention of the national media. We call ourselves libertarians.

This book is concerned with libertarian ideas, not with a history of the libertarian 'movement' or a description of its present condition. It is fashionable to measure the importance of ideas by the number and violence of their adherents. That is a fashion I shall not follow. If, when you finish this book, you have come to share many of my views, you will know the most important thing about the number of libertarians—that it is larger by one than when you started reading.

ACKNOWLEDGMENTS

Most of the material in Chapters 12–15, 17–20, 22, 23, and 25 first appeared in *The New Guard* in slightly different form. Most of Chapter 34 was originally published in *The Alternative*. Chapter 10 was written for the Center for Independent Education and later published in *Human Events*. My thanks to all of the editors and publishers involved for permission to use the material here.

Chapter 38 was originally published, in considerably different form, in the *Libertarian Connection*; since, in that peculiar journal, authors retain ownership of what they write, I need not thank the editors for permission to use the material here. I instead thank them for generating useful ideas and maintaining a convenient and productive forum.

Chapter 47 first appeared in *Frontlines*, vol. 2, No. 6, March 1980.

Thanks are also due to those who read and commented on my manuscript: Emilia Nordvedt, Larry Abrams, and especially Milton Friedman. Also, for sporadic criticism and general forbearance, to Diana.

INTRODUCTION

From Ayn Rand to bushy anarchists there is an occasional agreement on means called libertarianism, which is a faith in laissez-faire politics/economics. . . . How to hate your government on principle.

SB, THE LAST WHOLE EARTH CATALOG

The central idea of libertarianism is that people should be permitted to run their own lives as they wish. We totally reject the idea that people must be forcibly protected from themselves. A libertarian society would have no laws against drugs, gambling, pornography—and no compulsory seat belts in cars. We also reject the idea that people have an enforceable claim on others, for anything more than being left alone. A libertarian society would have no welfare, no Social Security system. People who wished to aid others would do so voluntarily through private charity, instead of using money collected by force from the taxpayers. People who wished to provide for their old age would do so through private insurance.

People who wish to live in a 'virtuous' society, surrounded by others who share their ideas of virtue, would be free to set up their own communities and to contract with each other so as to prevent the 'sinful' from buying or renting within them. Those who wished to live communally could set up their own communes. But nobody would have a right to force his way of life upon his neighbor.

So far, many who do not call themselves libertarians would agree. The difficulty comes in defining what it means to be 'left alone'. We live in a complicated and interdependent society; each of us is constantly affected by events thousands of miles away, occurring to people he has never heard of. How, in such a society, can we meaningfully talk about each person being free to go his own way?

The answer to this question lies in the concept of property rights. If we consider that each person owns his own body and can acquire ownership of other things by creating them, or by having ownership transferred to him by another owner, it becomes at least formally possible to define 'being left alone' and its opposite, 'being coerced'. Someone who forcibly prevents me from using my property as I want, when I am not using it to violate his right to use his property, is coercing me. A man who prevents me from taking heroin coerces me; a man who prevents me from shooting him does not.

This leaves open the question of how one acquires ownership of things that are not created or that are not entirely created, such as land and mineral resources. There is disagreement among libertarians on this question. Fortunately, the answer has little effect on the character of a libertarian society, at least in this country. Only about 3 percent of all income in America is rental income. Adding the rental value of owner-occupied housing would bring this figure up to about 8 percent. Property tax—rental income collected by government—is about another 5 percent. So the total rental value of all property, land and buildings, adds up to about 13 percent of all income. Most of that is rent on the value of buildings, which are created by human effort, and thus poses no problem in the definition of property rights; the total rent on all land, which does pose such a problem, is thus only a tiny fraction of total income. The total raw material value of all minerals consumed, the other major 'unproduced' resource, is about another 3 percent. There again, much of that value is the result of human effort, of digging the ore out of the ground. Only the value of the raw resources in situ may reasonably be regarded as unproduced. So resources whose existence owes nothing to human action bring to their owners, at the most, perhaps one-twentieth of the national income. The vast majority of income is the result of human actions. It is created by identifiable groups of people, working together under agreements that specify how their joint product is to be divided.

The concept of property allows at least a formal definition of 'letting alone' and 'coercing'. That this definition corresponds to what people usually mean by those words—that a libertarian society would be free—is by no means obvious. It is here that libertarians part company with our friends on the left, who agree that everyone should be free to do as he wishes, but argue that a hungry man is not free and that his right to freedom therefore implies an obligation to provide food for him, whether one likes it or not.

The book is divided into four sections. In the first, I discuss property institutions, private and public, and how they have functioned in practice. In the second, I examine a series of individual questions from a libertarian viewpoint. In the third, I discuss what a future libertarian society might be like and how it could be achieved. The final section contains new material on a variety of topics added in the second edition.

The purpose of this book is to persuade you that a libertarian society would be both free and attractive, that the institutions of private property are the machinery of freedom, making it possible, in a complicated and interdependent world, for each person to pursue his life as he sees fit.

PART I

In defense of property

A saint said "Let the perfect city rise.
Here needs no long debate on subtleties,
Means, end,
Let us intend
That all be clothed and fed; while one remains
Hungry our quarreling but mocks his pains.
So all will labor to the good
In one phalanx of brotherhood."

A man cried out "I know the truth, I, I,
Perfect and whole. He who denies
My vision is a madman or a fool
Or seeks some base advantage in his lies.
All peoples are a tool that fits my hand
Cutting you each and all
Into my plan."

They were one man.

In DEFENSE OF PROPERTY

The concept of property is funda-
mental to our society, probably to any workable society. Opera-
tionally, it is understood by every child above the age of three.
Intellectually, it is understood by almost no one.

Consider the slogan 'property rights vs. human rights'. Its
rhetorical force comes from the implication that property rights are
the rights of property and human rights the rights of humans;
humans are more important than property (chairs, tables, and the
like); consequently, human rights take precedence over property
rights.

But property rights are not the rights of property; they are the
rights of humans with regard to property. They are a particular
kind of human right. The slogan conjures up an image of a black
'sitting in' in a southern restaurant. That situation involves conflict-
ing claims about rights, but the rights claimed are all property
rights. The restaurant owner claims a right to control a piece of
property—his restaurant. The black claims a (limited) right to the
control of part of the same piece of property—the right to sit at a
counter stool as long as he wants. None of the property claims any
rights at all; the stool doesn't pipe up with a demand that the black
respect its right not to be sat upon.

The only assertion of rights *of* property that I have run across is
the assertion by some conservationists that certain objects—a
redwood tree, for instance—have an inherent right not to be
destroyed. If a man bought land on which such a tree stood,
asserted his right to cut the tree down, and was opposed by a
conservationist acting, not on any right of his own, but in defense
of the rights of the tree, we would truly have a conflict between
'human rights' and 'property rights'. That was not the situation
envisioned by those who coined the phrase.

That one of the most effective political slogans of recent decades is merely a verbal error, confusing rights to property with rights of property, is evidence of the degree of popular confusion on the whole subject. Since property is a central economic institution of any society, and private property is the central institution of a free society, it is worth spending some time and effort to understand what property is and why it exists.

Two facts make property institutions necessary. The first is that different people pursue different ends. The ends may differ because people follow their narrow self-interest or because they follow differing visions of high and holy purpose. Whether they are misers or saints, the logic of the situation is the same; it remains the same as long as each person, observing reality from the distinct vantage point of his own head, reaches a somewhat different conclusion about what should be done and how to do it.

The second fact is that there exist some things which are sufficiently scarce that they cannot be used by everyone as much as each would like. We cannot all have everything we want. Therefore, in any society, there must be some way of deciding who gets to use what when. You and I cannot simultaneously drive the same car to our different homes.

The desire of several people to use the same resources for different ends is the essential problem that makes property institutions necessary. The simplest way to resolve such a conflict is physical force. If I can beat you up, I get to use the car. This method is very expensive, unless you like fighting and have plenty of medical insurance. It also makes it hard to plan for the future; unless you're the current heavyweight champion, you never know when you will have access to a car. The direct use of physical force is so poor a solution to the problem of limited resources that it is commonly employed only by small children and great nations.

The usual solution is for the use of each *thing* to be decided by a person or by some group of persons organized under some *set of rules*. Such *things* are called property. If each thing is controlled by an individual who has the power to transfer that control to any other individual, we call the institution private property.

Under property institutions, private or public, a person who wishes to use property that is not his own must induce the individual or group controlling that property to let him do so; he must persuade that individual or group that its ends will be served by letting him use the property for his ends.

With private property, this is usually done by trade: I offer to use my property (including, possibly, myself) to help you achieve your ends in exchange for your using your property to help me achieve mine. Sometimes, but less often, it is done by persuading you that my ends are good and that you should therefore pursue them; this is how charities and, to some extent, families function.

In this way, under private property institutions, each individual uses his own resources to pursue his own ends. Cooperation occurs either when several individuals perceive that they more easily can achieve a common end jointly than individually or when they find that they more easily can achieve their different ends by cooperating through trade, each helping the others achieve their ends in exchange for their helping him achieve his.

Under institutions of public property, property is held (the use of things is controlled) by political institutions and that property is used to achieve the ends of those political institutions. Since the function of politics is to reduce the diversity of individual ends to a set of 'common ends' (the ends of the majority, the dictator, the party in power, or whatever person or group is in effective control of the political institutions), public property imposes those 'common ends' on the individual. "Ask not what your country can do for you; ask rather what you can do for your country." Ask not, in other words, how you can pursue what you believe is good, but how you can pursue what the government tells you is good.

Consider a particular case where the effects of public and private property can be compared. The printed media (newspapers, magazines, and the like) are produced entirely with private property. Buy newsprint and ink, rent a printing press, and you are ready to go. Or, on a cheaper scale, use a Xerox machine. You can print whatever you want without asking permission from any government. Provided, of course, that you do not need the U.S. Post Office to deliver what you print. The government can use, and occasionally has used, its control over the mails as an instrument of censorship.

Broadcast media (radio and television) are another matter. The airwaves have been designated as public property. Radio and television stations can operate only if they receive permission from the Federal Communications Commission to use that property. If the FCC judges that a station does not operate 'in the public interest', it has a legal right to withdraw the station's license, or at least to refuse to renew it. Broadcasting licenses are worth a great deal of money; Lyndon Johnson's personal fortune was built on a broadcasting empire whose chief asset was the special relationship between the FCC and the majority leader of the Senate.

Printed media require only private property; broadcast media use public property. What is the result?

Printed media are enormously diverse. Any viewpoint, political, religious, or aesthetic, has its little magazine, its newsletter, its underground paper. Many of those publications are grossly offensive to the views and tastes of most Americans—for example, *The Realist,* an obscene and funny humor magazine that once printed a cartoon showing 'One Nation under God' as an act of sodomy by Jehovah on Uncle Sam; *The Berkeley Barb,* a newspaper that has the world's most pornographic classified ads; and the Black Panther publication that superimposed a pig's head on Robert Kennedy's murdered body.

The broadcast media cannot afford to offend. Anyone with a license worth several million dollars at stake is very careful. No television station in the United States would air the cartoons from a random issue of *The Realist.* No radio would present readings from the classified section of the *Barb.* How could you persuade the honorable commissioners of the FCC that it was in the public interest? After all, as the FCC put it in 1931, after refusing to renew the license of a station owner many of whose utterances were, in their words, "vulgar, if not indeed indecent. Assuredly they are not uplifting or entertaining." "Though we may not censor, it is our duty to see that broadcast licenses do not afford mere personal organs, and also to see that a standard of refinement fitting our day and generation is maintained."

The *Barb* does not have to be in the public interest; it does not belong to the public. Radio and television do. The *Barb* only has to be in the interest of the people who read it. *National Review,* William Buckley's magazine, has a circulation of about 100,000. It is purchased by one American out of two thousand. If the other 1,999 potential readers think it is a vicious, racist, fascist, papist rag, that's their tough luck—it still comes out.

The FCC recently ruled that songs that seem to advocate drug use may not be broadcast. Is that an infringement of freedom of speech? Of course not. You can say anything you want, but not on the public's airwaves.

When I say it is not an infringement of free speech, I am perfectly serious. It is not possible to let everyone use the airwaves for whatever he wants; there isn't enough room on the radio dial. If the government owns the airwaves, it must ration them; it must decide what should and what should not be broadcast.

The same is true of ink and paper. Free speech may be free, but printed speech is not; it requires scarce resources. There is no way that everyone who thinks his opinion is worth writing can have everyone in the country read it. We would run out of trees long before we had enough paper to print a hundred million copies of everyone's manifesto; we would run out of time long before we had finished reading the resultant garbage.

Nonetheless, we have freedom of the press. Things are not printed for free, but they are printed if someone is willing to pay the cost. If the writer is willing to pay, he prints up handbills and hands them out on the corner. More often, the reader pays by subscribing to a magazine or buying a book.

Under public property, the values of the public as a whole are imposed on the individuals who require the use of that property to accomplish their ends. Under private property, each individual can seek his own ends, provided that he is willing to bear the cost. Our broadcast media are dull; our printed media, diverse.

Could this be changed? Easily. Convert the airwaves to private property. Let the government auction off the right to broadcast at a particular frequency, frequency by frequency, until the entire broadcast band is privately owned. Would this mean control of the airwaves by the rich? No more than private property in newsprint means newspapers are printed only for the rich. The marketplace is not a battlefield, where the person with the most money wins the battle and takes the whole prize; if it were, Detroit would spend all its resources designing gold cadillacs for Howard Hughes, Jean Paul Getty, and their ilk.

What is wrong with the battlefield analogy? To begin with, the market does not allocate all of its resources to the customer with the most money. If I am spending $10 on widgets and you are spending $20, the result is not that you get all the widgets, but rather that you get two-thirds of them and I get one-third. Nor, in general, is the amount of a given product bought by one customer subtracted from what is available to another—one person's gain need not be another's loss. When I was the only customer for widgets, only $10 worth of widgets (eight widgets at $1.25 apiece) was produced. When you appear with $20, the first effect is to drive up the price of widgets; this induces the widget manufacturers to produce more widgets, and soon there are enough for me to have my eight, and you have to have your sixteen. This is less true for the airwaves, which are, in one sense, a fixed and limited resource, like land. But, as with land, a higher price effectively increases the supply by causing people to use the existing quantity more intensively. In the case of airwaves, if the price of a frequency band is high, it becomes profitable to use improved equipment, to squeeze more stations into a given range of frequencies, to coordinate stations in different areas more carefully so as to minimize 'fringe' areas of interference, to use previously unused parts of the spectrum (UHF television, for instance), and eventually to replace some broadcast stations with cable television or radio.

Another error in the picture of the marketplace as a 'rich man take all' conflict is the confusion between how much money a man has and how much he is willing to spend. If a millionaire is only willing to pay $10,000 for a car, he gets exactly the same amount of car as I get if I am willing to pay the same amount; the fact that he has a million dollars sitting in the bank does not lower the price or improve the quality of the car. This principle extends to radio. Howard Hughes *could* have spent a billion dollars to buy up radio frequencies, but unless he was going to make money with them— enough money to justify the investment—he would not. There were, after all, many far cheaper ways for him to provide entertainment for himself.

What does this imply for the fate of the airwaves as private property? First, the proportional nature of market 'victory' would make it virtually impossible for any rich man or group of rich men to buy the entire broadcast spectrum and use it for some sinister propagandistic purpose. In such a project, they would be bidding against people who wanted to buy frequencies in order to broadcast what the listeners wanted to hear and thus make money (whether directly, as with pay television, or indirectly, as with advertising). Total advertising on the broadcast media amounts to about $4 billion a year. Businessmen, bidding for the ownership of broadcast bands in order to get their cut of that money, would surely be willing, if necessary, to make a once and for all payment of many billions of dollars. Suppose the radio band has room for a hundred stations (the present FM band has room for at least 50, and the AM band has room for many more). In order for our hypothetical gang of machiavellian millionaires to get control of all one hundred stations, they must be willing to pay a hundred times as much as the competition. That would be something in the neighborhood of a trillion dollars, or about a thousand times the total worth of the richest individuals in the country. Suppose, instead, that they can raise about $10 billion (the total worth of the richest ten or twenty Americans) and roughly match the amount that the businessmen who want the stations for commercial purposes are willing to pay. Each group gets 50 frequencies. The businessmen broadcast what the customers want to hear and get all the customers; the hypothetical millionaires broadcast the propaganda they want the customers to hear and get no customers, and ten or twenty of the richest men in America go bankrupt.

It seems clear that the airwaves would be bought for commercial purposes by businessmen who want to broadcast whatever their customers want to hear, in order to make as much money as possible. Very much the same sort of people who own radio stations now. Most stations would appeal to mass tastes, as they do now. But, if there are nine stations sharing 90 percent of the listeners, a tenth station may do better by broadcasting something different and thus getting all of the remaining 10 percent, instead of a one-tenth share of the great majority. With one hundred stations, the hundred and first could make money on an audience of 1 percent. There would therefore be specialty stations, appealing to special tastes. There are now. But such stations would no longer be limited by the veto power that the majority now exercises through the FCC. If you were offended by what you heard on the station owned by *The Berkeley Barb*, there would be only one thing to do about it: turn to a different station.

The media provide a striking example of the difference between the effects of public and private property, but it is an example that shows only part of the disadvantage of public property. For the 'public' not only has the power to prevent individuals from doing what they wish with their own lives, it has a positive incentive to exercise that power. If property is public, I, by using some of that property, decrease the amount available for you to use. If you disapprove of what I use it for, then, from your standpoint, I am wasting valuable resources that are needed for other and more important purposes—the ones you approve of. Under private property, what I waste belongs to me. You may, in the abstract, disapprove of my using my property wastefully, but you have no incentive to go to any trouble to stop me. Even if I do not 'waste' my property, you will never get your hands on it. It will merely be used for another of *my* purposes.

This applies not only to wasting resources already produced, but to wasting my most valuable property, my own time and energy. In a private-property society, if I work hard, the main effect is that I am richer. If I choose to work only ten hours a week and to live on a correspondingly low income, I am the one who pays the cost. Under institutions of public property, I, by refusing to produce as much as I might, decrease the total wealth available to the society. Another member of that society can claim, correctly, that my laziness sabotages society's goals, that I am taking food from the mouths of hungry children.

Consider hippies. Our private-property institutions serve them just as they do anyone else. Waterpipes and tie-dyed shirts are produced, underground papers and copies of *Steal This Book* are printed, all on the open market. Drugs are provided on the black market. No capitalist takes the position that being unselfish and unproductive is evil and therefore that capital should not be invested in producing things for such people; or, if one does, someone else invests the capital and makes the profit.

It is the government that is the enemy: police arrest 'vagrants'; public schools insist on haircuts for longhairs; state and federal governments engage in a massive program to prevent the import and sale of drugs. Like radio and television censorship, this is partly the imposition of the morals of the majority on the minority. But part of the persecution comes from the recognition that people who choose to be poor contribute less to the common ends. Hippies don't pay much in taxes. Occasionally this point is made explicit: drug addiction is bad because the addict does not 'carry his share of the load'. If we are all addicts, the society will collapse. Who will pay taxes? Who will fight off foreign enemies?

This argument becomes more important in a socialist state, such as Cuba, where a much larger fraction of the economy is public property. There, apparently, their equivalent of hippies were rounded up and sent off to work camps to do their share for the revolution.

George Bernard Shaw, an unusually lucid socialist, put the matter nicely in *The Intelligent Woman's Guide to Socialism and Capitalism*.

> But Weary Willie may say that he hates work, and is quite willing to take less, and be poor and dirty and ragged or even naked for the sake of getting off with less work. But that, as we have seen, cannot be allowed: voluntary poverty is just as mischievous socially as involuntary poverty: decent nations must insist on their citizens leading decent lives, doing their full share of the nation's work, and taking their full share of its income. . . . Poverty and social irresponsibility will be forbidden luxuries.
>
> Compulsory social service is so unanswerably right that the very first duty of a government is to see that everybody works enough to pay her way and leave something over for the profit of the country and the improvement of the world [from chapters 23 and 73].

Consider, as a more current example, the back to the land movement, as represented by *The Mother Earth News*. Ideologically, it is hostile to what it views as a wasteful, unnatural, mass consumption society. Yet the private property institutions of that society serve it just as they serve anyone else. *The Mother Earth News* and *The Whole Earth Catalog* are printed on paper bought on the private market and sold in private bookstores, alongside other books and magazines dedicated to teaching you how to make a million dollars in real estate or live the good life on a hundred thousand a year.

A NECESSARY DIGRESSION

A few pages back I asserted that an individual who works hard under institutions of private property gets most of the benefit. This is directly contrary to socialist ideas about exploitation, which I discuss in Chapter 8. It also contradicts the common belief that when an individual becomes more productive, most of the benefit goes to others. This belief is behind much of the public support for state-supported schooling, government subsidies to individual firms, and the like. It would require a fair-sized economics text to deal thoroughly with this question (I suggest several in the Appendix), but a careful examination of a single example may make it easier for the reader to think out the logic of other examples for himself.

Suppose there are one hundred physicians, each charging $10 for a visit. At that price the number of visits patients wish to make to doctors is the same as the number the doctors wish to have made. If that were not the case—if, for instance, there were people willing to pay $10 for a visit but the doctors were booked up—the price would change. Doctors would be able to raise their prices and still keep their appointment books filled. At a higher price, some customers would decide to visit doctors less often. The demand for medical services would fall with rising price until it was equal to the amount of service the doctors were willing to supply at that price.

I decide to become the hundred and first physician. The total supply of medical service is increased. The price at which supply equals demand falls; doctors get only $9.90 per visit. Have I greatly benefited society in general? No. Consider the visits to doctors that would have occurred without me. For each of these, the patient is now ten cents richer, but the doctor is ten cents poorer; on net, people are no better off. Consider the extra visits to doctors that people make because of the lower price. These people must have considered an extra visit to the doctor worth less than $10 or they would have made it at the old price. They must consider it worth more than $9.90 or they would not make it at the new price. Therefore the patients profit on the extra visits by between zero and ten cents per extra visit—the difference between what they pay for it and the value they place on it. But I, the new doctor providing the extra service, make $9.90 for each visit, thus getting most of the benefit from what I produce. In effect, I produce a service worth between $9.90 and $10 and sell it for $9.90.

If the total number of physicians were much larger than one hundred (as it is), the decrease in the price of a visit resulting from the addition of one more physician would be far lower. The nearer this change is to zero, the nearer the new doctor comes to getting 100 percent of what he produces.

As this example suggests, the essential error in the idea that the benefit of one person's productivity goes mainly to others is that it ignores the salary the productive person gets. In a well-functioning private-property society, salary—the amount for which a person can sell what he produces—corresponds closely to the real value of that product to the people who consume it.

This argument depends on my accepting what the patient is willing to pay as the true value to him of what he is getting—a principle that economists call 'consumer sovereignty'. Suppose, in a particular case, that I reject that principle. I believe that most people stupidly underestimate the importance of staying healthy and that a man who is only willing to pay $10 to visit the doctor is really getting something worth $20—he just doesn't know it. I conclude that a doctor receives only half as much as he produces.

The same principle works the other way. If I believe that sitting at a bar getting drunk is an idiotic way to spend an evening, I conclude that bartenders are paid far more than they are 'really' worth because their patrons incorrectly believe that the bartender is performing a valuable service. In both cases, my belief that someone produces more or less than he is paid comes from my refusal to accept the judgment of the person who uses the product as to the value of what he is getting. Naturally, the socialist or the bluenose always assumes that if the state decides what people 'should' want, it will, since his values are 'right', decide his way.

No such argument can imply that everyone who produces is underpaid, for that would mean that people underestimate the value of everything. But each thing is valued in terms of other things; money is merely a convenient intermediary. If I think a visit to the doctor is worth 'only' $10, I mean it is worth only as much as the other things I could buy with that amount. If I am undervaluing the doctor's visit, I must be overvaluing the other things.

Love is not enough

In more and more cases . . . politics and politicians not only contribute to the problem. They *are* the problem.

JOHN SHUTTLEWORTH,
The Mother Earth News.

One common objection to private property is that it is an immoral system because it relies on selfishness. This is wrong. Most people define *selfishness* as an attitude of caring only for oneself and considering other people's welfare of no importance. The argument for private property does not depend on people having such an attitude; it depends only on different people having different ends and pursuing them. Each person is selfish only in the sense of accepting and following his own perception of reality, his own vision of the good.

This objection is also wrong because it poses false alternatives. Under any institutions, there are essentially only three ways that I can get another person to help me achieve my ends: love, trade, and force.

By love I mean making my end your end. Those who love me wish me to get what I want (except for those who think I am very stupid about what is good for me). So they voluntarily, 'unselfishly', help me. Love is too narrow a word. You might also share my end not because it is my end but because in a particular respect we perceive the good in the same way. You might volunteer to work on my political campaign, not because you love me, but because you think that it would be good if I were elected. Of course, we might share the common ends for entirely different reasons. I might think I was just what the country needed, and you, that I was just what the country deserved.

The second method of cooperation is trade. I agree to help you achieve your end if you help me achieve mine.

The third method is force. You do what I want or I shoot you.

Love—more generally, the sharing of a common end—works well, but only for a limited range of problems. It is difficult to know very many people well enough to love them. Love can provide cooperation on complicated things among very small groups of people, such as families. It also works among large numbers of people for very simple ends—ends so simple that many different people can completely agree on them. But for a complicated end involving a large number of people—producing this book, for instance—love will not work. I cannot expect all the people whose cooperation I need—typesetters, editors, bookstore owners, loggers, pulpmill workers, and a thousand more—to know and love me well enough to want to publish this book for my sake. Nor can I expect them all to agree with my political views closely enough to view the publication of this book as an end in itself. Nor can I expect them all to be people who want to read the book and who therefore are willing to help produce it. I fall back on the second method: trade.

I contribute the time and effort to produce the manuscript. I get, in exchange, a chance to spread my views, a satisfying boost to my ego, and a little money. The people who want to read the book get the book. In exchange, they give money. The publishing firm and its employees, the editors, give the time, effort, and skill necessary to coordinate the rest of us; they get money and reputation. Loggers, printers, and the like give their effort and skill and get money in return. Thousands of people, perhaps millions, cooperate in a single task, each seeking his own ends.

So under private property the first method, love, is used where it is workable. Where it is not, trade is used instead.

The attack on private property as selfish contrasts the second method with the first. It implies that the alternative to 'selfish' trade is 'unselfish' love. But, under private property, love already functions where it can. Nobody is prevented from doing something for free if he wants to. Many people—parents helping their children, volunteer workers in hospitals, scoutmasters—do just that. If, for those things that people are not willing to do for free, trade is replaced by anything, it must be by force. Instead of people being selfish and doing things because they want to, they will be unselfish and do them at the point of a gun.

Is this accusation unfair? The alternative offered by those who deplore selfishness is always government. It is selfish to do something for money, so the slums should be cleaned up by a 'youth corps' staffed via 'universal service'. Translated, that means the job should be done by people who will be put in jail if they do not do it.

A second objection often made to a system of private property is that resources may be misallocated. One man may starve while another has more food than he can eat. This is true, but it is true of any system of allocating resources. Whoever makes the decision may make a decision I consider wrong. We can, of course, set up a government bureau and instruct it to feed the hungry and clothe the naked. That does not mean they will be fed and clothed. At some point, some person or persons must decide who gets what. Political mechanisms, bureaus and bureaucrats, follow their own ends just as surely as individual entrepreneurs follow theirs.

If almost everyone is in favor of feeding the hungry, the politician may find it in his interest to do so. But, under those circumstances, the politician is unnecessary: some kind soul will give the hungry man a meal anyway. If the great majority is against the hungry man, some kind soul among the minority still may feed him—the politician will not.

There is no way to give a politician power that can be used only to do good. If he gives food to someone, he must take it from someone else; food does not appear from thin air. I know of only one occasion in modern peacetime history when large numbers of people starved although food was available. It occurred under an economic system in which the decision of who needed food was made by the government. Joseph Stalin decided how much food was needed by the inhabitants of the Ukraine. What they did not 'need' was seized by the Soviet government and shipped elsewhere. During the years 1932 and 1933, some millions of Ukrainians died of starvation. During each of those years, according to Soviet figures, the Soviet Union *exported* about 1.8 million tons of grain. If we accept a high figure for the number who starved—say, eight million—that grain would have provided about two thousand calories a day to each of them.

Yet there *is* something in the socialist's objection to capitalism's 'misallocation', something with which I sympathize esthetically, if not economically.

Most of us believe in our hearts that there is only one good and that ideally everyone should pursue it. In a perfect centrally planned socialist state everyone is part of a hierarchy pursuing the same end. If that end is the one true good, that society will be perfect in a sense in which a capitalist society, where everyone pursues his own differing and imperfect perception of the good, cannot be. Since most socialists imagine a socialist government to be controlled by people very like themselves, they imagine that it will pursue the true good—the one that they, imperfectly, perceive. That is surely better than a chaotic system in which all sorts of people other than the socialists perceive all sorts of other goods and waste valuable resources chasing them. People who dream about a socialist society rarely consider the possibility that some of those other people may succeed in imposing their ends on the dreamer, instead of the other way around. George Orwell is the only exception who comes to mind.

A third objection made to private property is that men are not really free as long as they need the use of other men's property to print their opinions and even to eat and drink. If I must either do what you tell me or starve, the sense in which I am free may be useful to a political philosopher but it is not very useful to me.

That is true enough, but it is equally true of any system of public property—and much more important. It is far more likely that there will be one owner of all food if things are owned by governments than if they are owned by private individuals; there are so many fewer governments. Power is diminished when it is divided. If one man owns all the food, he can make me do almost anything. If it is divided among a hundred men, no one can make me do very much for it; if one tries, I can get a better deal from another.

INTERLUDE

I have talked in the abstract about "private property" and "public property" and have argued for the superiority of the former. But in existing societies, 'capitalist' as well as 'communist', there is a mixture of public- and private-property institutions. I may own my car, but the government owns the streets. How far can the idea of private property be pushed? Are there some tasks that must be done but that, by their nature, cannot conceivably be done privately and must therefore continue to be done by government?

I believe not. I believe that although there are certain important tasks which for special reasons are difficult to do under institutions of total private property, these difficulties are in principle, and may be in practice, soluble. I hold that there are *no* proper functions of government. In that sense I am an anarchist. All things that governments do can be divided into two categories—those we could do away with today and those we hope to be able to do away with tomorrow. Most of the things our government does are in the first category.

The system of institutions I would like to see achieved ultimately would be entirely private—what is sometimes called anarcho-capitalism, or libertarian anarchy. Such institutions would be, in some respects, radically different from those we now have; how they might work is discussed at some length in the third section of this book.

After reading the next few chapters, the reader may reasonably wonder why, if I do not expect anarcho-capitalism to produce anything much like historical capitalist societies, I bother to defend the historical record of those societies. Some anarcho-capitalists do not. They concede the justice of many of the usual attacks on 'capitalism', but argue that everything would be different if we could get rid of government.

That is a cop-out. Human beings and human societies are far too complicated for us to have confidence in a priori predictions about how institutions that have never been tried would work. We can and should attempt to distinguish those elements in historical capitalist societies that were produced by institutions of private property from those that were produced by government intervention. Having done so, we must base our belief that institutions of private property will work well in the future on the observation that those institutions, to the extent they existed, worked well in the past.

4

Robin hood sells out

Ask not what the government can do for you.
Ask what the government is doing to you.

Many people who agree that private property and the free market are ideal institutions for allowing each person to pursue his own ends with his own resources reject complete laissez faire because they believe that it leads to an unjust, or at least undesirable, distribution of wealth and income. They concede that the market responds to the demands of consumers, expressed by their willingness to pay for what they want, in a much more sensitive and efficient fashion than the political system responds to the demands of voters, expressed by their votes. But they claim that the market is 'undemocratic' because the number of 'votes'—that is, the number of dollars available to be spent—varies widely from person to person. Therefore, they argue that the government should intervene in the market to redistribute wealth and income.

This argument correctly regards the free market as having its own internal logic, producing results, such as an unequal distribution of income, independent of the desires of its supporters. It incorrectly treats the political process as if it had no corresponding internal logic of its own. The argument simply assumes that political institutions can be set up to produce any desired outcome.

Suppose that one hundred years ago someone tried to persuade me that democratic institutions could be used to transfer money from the bulk of the population to the poor. I could have made the following reply: 'The poor, whom you wish to help, are many times outnumbered by the rest of the population, from whom you intend to take the money to help them. If the non-poor are not generous enough to give money to the poor voluntarily through private charity, what makes you think they will be such fools as to vote to force themselves to give it?'

That would have been a crushing argument one hundred years ago. Today it is not. Why? Because people today believe that our present society is a living refutation of the argument, that our government is, and has been for many years, transferring considerable amounts of money from the not-poor to the poor.

This is an illusion. There are some government programs that give money to the poor—Aid to Families With Dependent Children, for instance. But such programs are vastly outweighed by those having the opposite effect—programs that injure the poor for the benefit of the not-poor. Almost surely, the poor would be better off if both the benefits that they now receive and the taxes, direct and indirect, that they now pay were abolished. Let us consider some examples.

Social Security is by all odds the largest welfare-type program in America; its annual payments are about four times those of all other welfare programs combined. It is financed by a regressive tax—about 10 percent on all income up to $7,800, nothing thereafter. Those who have incomes of less than $7,800, and consequently pay a lower amount per year, later receive lower payments, but the reduction in benefits is less than proportional. If the schedule of taxes and payments were the only relevant consideration, Social Security would redistribute slightly from higher-income to lower-income people.

But two additional factors almost certainly reverse the effect. Most Social Security payments take the form of an annuity—a certain amount per year, starting at a specified age (usually 65) and continuing until death. The total amount an individual receives depends on how long he lives beyond age sixty-five. A man who lives to age 71 receives 20 percent more, all other factors being equal, than a man who lives to age seventy. Further, the amount an individual pays for Social Security depends not only on how much he pays in taxes each year but on how many years he pays. A man who starts work at age 24 will pay Social Security taxes for 41 years; one who starts work at age 18 will pay for 47 years. The first, other factors being equal, will pay about 15 percent less than the second for the same benefits. The missed payments come at the beginning of his career; since early payments have more time to accumulate interest than later ones, the effective saving is even greater.

Assuming an interest rate of 5 percent, the accumulated value of the first man's payments, by age 65, would be about two-thirds as much as the accumulated value of the second man's payments.

People with higher incomes have a longer life expectancy. The children of the middle and upper classes start work later, often substantially later, than the children of the lower classes. Both these facts tend to make Social Security a much better deal for the not-poor than for the poor. As far as I know, nobody has ever done a careful actuarial analysis of all such effects; thus one can only make approximate estimates.

Compare someone who goes to school for two years after graduating from college and lives to age 72 with someone who starts work at age 18 and dies at age 70. Adding the one-third savings on payments to the 30 percent gain in receipts (here the interest effect works in the opposite direction, since the extra payments for the longer life come at the end), I estimate that the first individual gets, from these effects, about twice as much for his money as the second. I do not know of any effects in the opposite direction large enough to cancel this.

Social Security is by no means the only large government program that takes from the poor to give to the not-poor. A second example is the farm program. Since it consists largely of government actions to hold up the price of crops, it is paid for partly by taxes and partly by higher food prices. Many years ago, when I did calculations on part of the Agriculture Department's activities, I estimated, using Agriculture Department figures, that higher food prices then made up about two-thirds of the total cost of the part of the farm program I was studying. Higher food prices have the effect of a regressive tax, since poorer people spend a larger proportion of their income on food.

Higher prices benefit farmers in proportion to how much they sell; the large farmer gets a proportionately higher benefit than the small one. In addition, the large farmer can better afford the legal costs of getting the maximum benefit from other parts of the program. Notoriously, every year, a considerable number of farms or 'farm corporations' receive more than $100,000 apiece and a few receive more than $1 million in benefits from a program supposedly set up to help poor farmers.

So the farm program consists of a slightly progressive benefit (one which benefits those with higher incomes somewhat more than proportionately to those incomes) financed by a regressive tax (one which taxes those with higher incomes somewhat less than proportionately to those incomes). Presumably it has the net effect of transferring money from the more poor to the less poor—a curious way of helping the poor. Here again, I know of no precise calculations that have measured the overall effect.

One could list similar programs for many pages. State universities, for instance, subsidize the schooling of the upper classes with money much of which comes from relatively poor taxpayers. Urban renewal uses the power of the government to prevent slums from spreading, a process sometimes referred to as 'preventing urban blight'. For middle-class people on the border of low-income areas, this is valuable protection. But 'urban blight' is precisely the process by which more housing becomes available to low-income people. The supporters of urban renewal claim that they are improving the housing of the poor. In the Hyde Park area of Chicago, where I have lived much of my life, they tore down old, low-rental apartment houses and replaced them with $30,000 and $40,000 town houses. A great improvement, for those poor with $30,000. And this is the rule, not the exception, as was shown years ago by Martin Anderson in *The Federal Bulldozer*.

This is not to deny that poor people get some benefit from some government programs. Everyone gets some benefit from some government programs. The political system is itself a sort of marketplace. Anyone with something to bid—votes, money, labor—can get a special favor, but the favor comes at the expense of someone else. Elsewhere I argue that, on net, very nearly everyone loses. Whether that is the case for everyone or not, it surely is the case for the poor, who bring less to the bidding than anyone else.

One cannot simply say, 'Let government help the poor.' 'Reform the income tax so that rich people really pay.' Things are as they are for reasons. It would make as much sense for the defender of the free market to argue that when he sets up *his* free market it will produce equal wages for everyone.

All of the numbers in this chapter, including the description of the Society Security tax, refer to about 1970; both the tax rate and the maximum income subject to tax have increased substantially since then.

5

THE RICH GET RICHER AND

THE POOR GET RICHER

. . . in proportion as the use of machinery and division of labor increases, in the same proportion the burden of toil also increases, whether by prolongation of the working hours, by increase of the work exacted in a given time, or by increased speed of the machinery, etc.

The lower strata of the middle class . . . all these sink gradually into the proletariat . . . as machinery . . . nearly everywhere reduces wages to the same low level.

The modern laborer, on the contrary, instead of rising with the progress of industry, sinks deeper and deeper below the conditions of existence of his own class.

MARX AND ENGELS, *THE COMMUNIST MANIFESTO*

Much of the opposition to institutions of private property comes from popular beliefs about the effects such institutions have had in the past, beliefs largely unsupported by historical evidence. Marx was scientist enough to make predictions about the future that could be proved or disproved. Unfortunately, Marxists continue to believe his theory long after his predictions have been proved false.

One of Marx's predictions was that the rich would get richer and the poor, poorer, with the middle class gradually being wiped out and the laboring class becoming impoverished. In historical capitalist societies the trend has been almost the exact reverse. The poor have gotten richer. The middle class has expanded enormously, and now includes many people whose professions would once have classified them for membership in the laboring classes. In absolute terms, the rich have also gotten richer, but the gap between rich and poor seems, so far as very imperfect statistics make it possible to judge, to have been slowly closing.

Many modern liberals argue that Marx's predictions were accurate enough for laissez-faire capitalism, but that such liberal institutions as strong labor unions, minimum wage laws, and progressive income taxes prevented them from being realized.

A statement about what might have happened is difficult to refute. We can note that both the rise in general standard of living and the decreasing inequality appear to have been occurring fairly steadily, over a long period of time, in a variety of different more or less capitalist societies. The progressive part of the progressive income tax collects very little income (see the Appendix) and has almost no effect on the accumulation of wealth by means of capital gains. The main effect of the minimum wage law seems to be that unskilled workers, who frequently are not worth the minimum wage to any employer, are deprived of their jobs. (This effect is seen in the dramatic rise in the unemployment rate of nonwhite teenagers which consistently follows rises in the minimum wage.) In the previous chapter I argued that liberal measures tend to injure the poor, not benefit them, and to increase, not decrease, inequality. If that has been true in the past, then the increasing equality we have experienced is in spite of, not because of, such measures.

Another version of the same argument is the claim that the great depression was the true expression of laissez faire capitalism and that we were rescued from it by the abandonment of laissez faire in favor of Keynesian policies. The controversy here runs into, not merely a book, but an extensive literature; for some decades it was a central issue of debate among economists. Those who would like to see the anti-Keynesian side will find one variant of it in *The Great Contraction* by Friedman and Schwartz. The authors argue that the great depression was caused not by laissez faire but by government intervention in the banking industry, and that without such intervention it would not have occurred.

Few people believe that capitalism leads inexorably to the impoverishment of the masses; the evidence against that thesis is too overwhelming. But relative inequality is a much harder matter to judge, and many people believe that capitalism, left to itself, produces an increasing inequality of income. Why? Their argument, in essence, is that the rich capitalist invests his money and thus makes more money. His children inherit the money and continue the process. Capitalists get richer and richer. They must somehow be getting their high income from the workers, who 'really produce' the goods the rich man consumes and who must therefore be getting poorer. This argument seemingly implies that the workers get absolutely poorer, but those who make the argument tend to assume that general economic progress is making everyone richer, so the impoverishment is only relative.

The assertion that the capitalist gets his increased income at the expense of the workers ignores the fact that capital is itself productive, a subject I discuss at greater length in chapter 8. The increased productivity resulting from capital accumulation is one of the reasons for general economic progress.

Even if the capitalist invests all the income from his capital and consumes none of it, his wealth will only grow at the rate of return on capital—the interest rate his money can earn. If the interest rate is less than the rate at which the total wages of workers increases, the relative wealth of the capitalists will decline. Historically, the rate of increase in total wages has run about 5 to 10 percent a year, roughly comparable to the interest rate earned by capital. Furthermore, capitalists consume part of their income; if they did not, there would be little point in being a capitalist. Historically, the total share of the national income going to capital in this country has steadily decreased, as shown in the Appendix.

Of course, a truly successful capitalist earns much more than the ordinary interest rate on his capital—that is how he accumulates a fortune. And, having been born to a much lower income, he may find himself unable to consume a substantial fraction of what he makes. But his children are a different story; they have no special talent for earning wealth but a lot of practice in spending it. As have their children. The Rockefellers are a prominent example of the decline of a great family. Its founder, John D. Rockefeller, was an able businessman. His children were philanthropists. Their children are politicians. The purchase of the governorship of two states has not exhausted the fortune built up by the old man, but it must have at least slowed its growth.

Marx not only predicted increasing ruin for the working classes, he also asserted that that ruin was already occurring. Like many of his contemporaries, he believed that the spread of capitalist institutions and industrial methods of production had, by the early nineteenth century, caused widespread misery. This belief is still common. It is based on questionable history and far more questionable logic.

Many people, reading of the long work days and low salaries of nineteenth-century England and America, consider the case against capitalism and industrialism already proven. They forget that those conditions seem intolerable to us only because we live in an enormously richer society and that our society became so productive largely through economic progress made during the nineteenth century under institutions of relatively unrestrained laissez-faire capitalism.

Under the economic conditions of the nineteenth century, no institutions, socialist, capitalist, or anarcho-capitalist, could have instantly produced what we would regard as a decent standard of living. The wealth simply was not there. If a socialist had confiscated the income of all the capitalist millionaires and given it to the workers, he would have found the workers little better off than before. The millionaires made far more than the workers, but there were so many more workers than millionaires. It required a long period of progress to produce a society rich enough to regard the conditions of the nineteenth century as miserable poverty.

More thoughtful people charge that conditions during the Industrial Revolution, especially in England, should be condemned, not in contrast to our present standard of living, but in contrast to earlier conditions. This was the belief of many English writers of the time. Unfortunately, few of them knew much about English life of the previous century; their attitude can be gathered from Engels's euphoric description of the eighteenth-century English working class.

> They did not need to overwork; they did no more than they chose to do, and yet earned what they needed. They had leisure for healthful work in garden or field, work which, in itself, was recreation for them . . . they were 'respectable' people, good husbands and fathers, led moral lives because they had no temptation to be immoral, there being no groggeries or low houses in their vicinity, and because the host, at whose inn they now and then quenched their thirst, was also a respectable man, usually a large tenant farmer who took pride in his good order, good beer, and early hours. They had their children the whole day at home and brought them up in obedience and the fear of God. . . . The young people grew up in idyllic simplicity and intimacy with their playmates until they married.

The historical evidence, although imperfect, seems to indicate that during the nineteenth century the condition of the working classes was improving: the death rate fell; the savings of workers increased; consumption by workers of such 'luxuries' as tea and sugar increased; hours of labor fell. Those interested in a lengthier discussion of this evidence may wish to read *The Industrial Revolution* by T. S. Ashton, or *Capitalism and the Historians,* edited by F. A. Hayek.

While the Industrial Revolution was actually occurring, much of the opposition to it came from the conservative landed gentry, who objected that luxuries and independence were corrupting the working classes. It is a curious irony that time has made those gentlemen the intellectual allies—often the directly quoted authorities—of modern liberals and socialists who assail nineteenth-century capitalism for rather different reasons. The modern liberal will claim that it was state legislation, limiting hours, preventing child labor, imposing safety regulations, and otherwise violating the principle of laissez faire, that brought progress. But the evidence indicates that the legislation consistently followed progress rather than preceding it. It was only when most workers were already down to a ten-hour day that it became politically possible to legislate one.

6

Monopoly I: how to lose your shirt

One of the most effective arguments against unregulated laissez faire has been that it invariably leads to monopoly. As George Orwell put it, "The trouble with competitions is that somebody wins them." It is thus argued that government must intervene to prevent the formation of monopolies or, once formed, to control them. This is the usual justification for antitrust laws and such regulatory agencies as the Interstate Commerce Commission and the Civil Aeronautics Board.

The best historical refutation of this thesis is in two books by socialist historian Gabriel Kolko: *The Triumph of Conservatism* and *Railroads and Regulation*. He argues that at the end of the last century businessmen believed the future was with bigness, with conglomerates and cartels, but were wrong. The organizations they formed to control markets and reduce costs were almost invariably failures, returning lower profits than their smaller competitors, unable to fix prices, and controlling a steadily shrinking share of the market.

The regulatory commissions supposedly were formed to restrain monopolistic businessmen. Actually, Kolko argues, they were formed at the request of unsuccessful monopolists to prevent the competition which had frustrated their efforts.

Those interested in pursuing the historical question should read Kolko's books, which deal with the Progressive period, as well as the articles by McGee and Stigler mentioned in the Appendix. McGee discusses the history of Standard Oil, and Stigler examines the question of whether concentration has historically tended to increase. His conclusion is that the degree of concentration in the economy has been relatively stable. It always appears to be increasing, because highly concentrated industries are much more visible than more competitive ones. We are all aware that, sometime between 1920 and the present, General Motors acquired a commanding position in the automobile industry. Few of us realize that during the same period U.S. Steel lost its dominance in the steel industry. For the same reason, we tend to exaggerate the amount of concentration existing at any given time. The areas of the economy which we think of as 'important' tend to be those in which we can identify a single large firm. We rarely consider such 'industries' as the restaurant and bar business, domestic service, or the manufacture of textiles and apparel, each of which is highly competitive and *each* of which employs more people than iron, steel, and automobile manufacturing *combined*.

Whatever the facts about monopoly may be, the belief that competition inevitably tends to produce monopoly is widespread. The remainder of this chapter is devoted to understanding the arguments that support this belief and why they are wrong.

There are three different sorts of monopoly: natural monopoly, artificial monopoly, and state monopoly. Only the first is of any importance in a laissez-faire society.

In most economic activities, the efficiency of a firm increases with size up to some optimum size and then decreases. The increasing efficiency reflects the advantages of mass production. These advantages generally occur only up to some definite level of size; for example, one steel mill is far more efficient than a backyard blast furnace, but making an existing steel mill still larger brings no added advantage—that is why steel mills are the size they are—and two steel mills are no more efficient than one. Increasing size also brings increased cost of administrative bureaucracy. The men at the top get further and further removed from what is actually going on at the bottom and are therefore more likely to make costly mistakes. So efficiency tends to decrease with increasing size once firms have passed the point where they can take full advantage of mass production. For this reason some very large firms, General Motors, for example, break themselves down into semi-autonomous units in order to approximate as nearly as possible the more efficient administrative arrangements of smaller firms.

A natural monopoly exists when the optimum size for a firm in some area of production is so large that there is room for only one such firm on the market. A smaller competitor is less efficient than the monopoly firm and hence unable to compete with it. Except where the market is very small (a small town grocery store, for example), this is a rather uncommon situation. In the steel industry, which is generally regarded as highly concentrated, there are between two hundred and three hundred steel mills, and between one hundred and two hundred firms. The largest four firms (which are by no means the most profitable) produce only half the total output, and the next four produce only 16 percent of total output.

Even a natural monopoly is limited in its ability to raise prices. If it raises them high enough, smaller, less efficient firms find that they can compete profitably. Here Orwell's implicit analogy of economic competition to a contest breaks down. The natural monopoly 'wins' in the sense of producing goods for less, thus making a larger profit on each item sold. It can make money selling goods at a price at which other firms lose money and thus retain the whole market. But it retains the market only so long as its price stays low enough that other firms cannot make a profit. This is what is called potential competition.

A famous example is Alcoa Aluminum. One of the charges brought against Alcoa during the anti-trust hearings that resulted in its breakup was that it had kept competitors out of the aluminum business by keeping its prices low and by taking advantage of every possible technological advance to lower them still further.

The power of a natural monopoly is also limited by indirect competition. Even if steel production were a natural monopoly, and even if the monopoly firm were enormously more efficient than potential competitors, its prices would be limited by the existence of substitutes for steel. As it drove prices higher and higher, people would use more aluminum, plastic, and wood for construction. Similarly a railroad, even if it is a monopoly, faces competition from canal barges, trucks, and airplanes.

For all of these reasons natural monopolies, although they occasionally exist under institutions of laissez faire, do not seriously interfere with the workings of the market. The methods government uses to control such monopolies do far more damage than the monopolies themselves, as I show in the next chapter.

An artificial monopoly is a large firm, formed for the purpose of controlling the market, raising prices, and thus reaping monopoly profits in an area where the conditions for natural monopoly do not exist. When the same effect is produced by an agreement among several firms, the group of firms is called a cartel. Since a cartel has most of the problems of a monopoly in addition to problems of its own, I shall discuss monopolies first.

Suppose a monopoly is formed, as was U.S. Steel, by financiers who succeed in buying up many of the existing firms. Assume further that there is no question of a natural monopoly; a firm much smaller than the new monster can produce as efficiently, perhaps even more efficiently. It is commonly argued that the large firm will nonetheless be able to achieve and maintain complete control of the industry. This argument, like many others, depends on the false analogy of market competition to a battle in which the strongest must win.

Suppose the monopoly starts with 99 percent of the market and that the remaining 1 percent is held by a single competitor. To make things more dramatic, let me play the role of the competitor. It is argued that the monopoly, being bigger and more powerful, can easily drive me out.

In order to do so, the monopoly must cut its price to a level at which I am losing money. But since the monopoly is no more efficient than I am, it is losing just as much money *per unit sold*. Its resources may be 99 times as great as mine, but it is also losing money ninety-nine times as fast as I am.

It is doing worse than that. In order to force me to keep my prices down, the monopoly must be willing to sell to everyone who wants to buy; otherwise unsupplied customers will buy from me at the old price. Since at the new low price customers will want to buy more than before, the monopolist must expand production, thus losing even more money. If the good we produce can be easily stored, the anticipation of future price rises, once our battle is over, will increase present demand still further.

Meanwhile, I have more attractive options. I can, if I wish, continue to produce at full capacity and sell at a loss, losing one dollar for every hundred or more lost by the monopoly. Or I may save money by laying off some of my workers, closing down part of my plant, and decreasing production until the monopoly gets tired of wasting its money.

What about the situation where the monopoly engages in regional price cutting, taking a loss in the area where I am operating and making it up in other parts of the country? If I am seriously worried about that prospect, I can take the precaution of opening outlets in all his major markets. Even if I do not, the high prices he charges in other areas in order to make up for his losses against me will make those areas very attractive to other new firms. Once they are established, he no longer has a market in which to make up his losses.

Thus the artificial monopoly which tries to use its size to maintain its monopoly is in a sad position, as U.S. Steel, which was formed with 60 percent of total steel production but which now has about 25 percent, found out to its sorrow. It has often been claimed that Rockefeller used such tactics to build Standard Oil, but there seems to be little or no evidence for the charge. Standard Oil officials occasionally tried to use the *threat* of cutting prices and starting price wars in an attempt to persuade competitors to keep their production down and their prices up. But the competitors understood the logic of the situation better than later historians, as shown by the response, quoted by McGee, of the manager of the Cornplanter Refining Company to such a threat: "Well, I says, 'Mr. Moffett, I am very glad you put it that way, because if it is up to you the only way you can get it [the business] is to cut the market [reduce prices], and if you cut the market I will cut you for 200 miles around, and I will make you sell the stuff,' and I says, 'I don't want a bigger picnic than that; sell it if you want to,' and I bid him good day and left."

The threat never materialized. Indeed it appears, from McGee's evidence, that price cutting more often was started by the small independent firms in an attempt to cut into Standard's market and that many of them were quite successful. Cornplanter's capital grew, in twenty years, from $10,000 to $450,000. As McGee says, commenting on the evidence presented against Standard in the 1911 antitrust case: "It is interesting that most of the ex-Standard employees who testified about Standard's deadly predatory tactics entered the oil business when they left the Standard. They also prospered."

Another strategy, which Rockefeller probably did employ, is to buy out competitors. This is usually cheaper than spending a fortune trying to drive them out—at least, it is cheaper in the short run. The trouble is that people soon realize they can build a new refinery, threaten to drive down prices, and sell out to Rockefeller at a whopping profit. David P. Reighard apparently made a sizable fortune by selling three consecutive refineries to Rockefeller. There was a limit to how many refineries Rockefeller could use. Having built his monopoly by introducing efficient business organization into the petroleum industry, Rockefeller was unable to withstand the competition of able imitators in his later years and failed to maintain his monopoly.

So far I have been discussing the situation where there is a single monopoly firm. When the monopoly is shared by several firms who make up a cartel, the difficulties may be even greater.

A cartel is strongest in an industry where there is almost a natural monopoly. Suppose, for instance, that the optimum size of a firm is such that there is room for only four firms large enough to be efficient. They agree to raise prices for their mutual benefit. At the higher price the firms, which are now making a large profit on every item sold, would each like to produce and sell more. But, at the higher price, the total demand for their product is lower than before. They must in some way divide up the total amount of business.

A firm that sells more than its quota can greatly increase its profit. Each firm is tempted to 'chisel' on the agreement, to go to special customers and offer to sell them more at a slightly lower price 'under the counter', without letting the other members of the cartel know about it. As such chiseling becomes widespread, the cartel agreement effectively breaks down; this seems to be what happened to many of the short-lived cartels formed at the beginning of this century. 'Chiseling', of course, is what the other cartel members call it; from the standpoint of the rest of us it is a highly desirable form of behavior.

If a cartel manages to prevent chiseling among its members, it, like a monopoly, still has the problem of keeping new firms from being attracted into the industry by the high prices and consequent high profits. Even where there is almost a natural monopoly, such that any new competitor must be very large, this is difficult.

The obvious strategy of the cartel members is to tell any potential competitor that, as soon as he has sunk his capital into constructing a new firm, they will break up the cartel and return to competition. The new firm will then find himself the fifth firm in an area with room for only four. Either one of the firms will go broke or all will do badly. Either way, it does not look like a very attractive speculation.

That strategy will work as long as the cartel does not raise prices much above their market level. When it does, a profitable counter-strategy becomes available. The potential competitor, before investing his capital in building a new firm, goes to the major customers of the cartel. He points out that if he does not start a new firm, the cartel will continue to charge them high prices, but that he cannot risk investing money until he has a guaranteed market. He therefore offers to start the new firm on condition that the customer agrees to buy from him, at a price high enough to give him a good profit but well below the cartel's price, for some prearranged period of time. Obviously, it is in the interest of the customers to agree. Once he has signed up a quarter of the total business, he builds his factories. Either the cartel restricts output still further, keeps its prices up, and accepts the loss of a quarter of the market, in which case the newcomer may eventually expand, or it competes for the customers the newcomer has not already tied up. Since there is only enough business to support three firms, one of the four goes broke.

Although an artificial monopoly or cartel may be able to influence prices slightly, and although it may succeed for a while in gaining additional profits at the cost of attracting new competitors, thus reducing its share of the market, any attempt to drive prices very far above their natural market level must lead to the monopoly's own destruction.

Unfortunately, the same cannot be said of the third kind of monopoly, state monopoly. State monopoly occurs when competition is prevented in one way or another by the government. It is far and away the most important kind of monopoly, both historically and presently. Ironically, one of its most common causes—or at least excuses—has been the attempt to prevent or control monopolies of the first two kinds.

The Post Office is a state monopoly run directly by the government. Competition, at least in the delivery of first-class mail, is forbidden by law. Contrary to common opinion, there have been many private post offices in both American and English history; such post offices have been responsible for many, perhaps most, innovations in the business of carrying mail. At one point in the nineteenth century, illegal private post offices, operating on the black market with wide public support, carried about one-third of all U.S. mail. The United Parcel Service presently offers better service than parcel post and at a lower price, and the business of delivering third-class mail privately is growing rapidly.

The Post Office has often defended its monopoly on the grounds that it needs the money it makes on first-class mail to subsidize the other classes; it claims that private competitors would 'skim the cream of the business' and leave the Post Office to lose money or raise rates on the less profitable classes. And yet private firms are providing better service (guaranteeing delivery by a particular time, for example) than the Post Office, charging considerably less, and making money in precisely the area that the Post Office claims it needs its profits from first class to subsidize.

The history of private post offices and their present status is discussed at some length by William Wooldridge in *Uncle Sam the Monopoly Man*. My main concern is with a less obvious sort of state monopoly, but I cannot leave the subject of the Post Office without making two historical notes.

One of the largest of the private post offices was the American Letter Mail Company, founded by Lysander Spooner, a nineteenth-century libertarian anarchist and author of an anarchist tract entitled 'No Treason: The Constitution of No Authority'. Spooner attacks the contract theory of government like a lawyer arguing a case. He asks precisely when he signed the social contract (specifically, the Constitution), whether, indeed, anyone signed it, and if so, whether the signers had his power of attorney, and, if not, on what basis he can be held bound to it. After dealing with all of the standard arguments he concludes "that it is obvious that the only visible, tangible government we have is made up of these professed agents or representatives of a secret band of robbers and murderers who, to cover up, or gloss over, their robberies and murders, have taken to themselves the title of 'the people of the United States.'" The ALMC was legislated out of existence, but the Post Office, Spooner claimed, imitated his low rates.

My second historical note may be apocryphal; I have never had courage and enterprise enough to check back and verify the story. If it isn't true, it should be. It seems that in the early nineteenth century, when railroads were beginning to become important, some enterprising gentleman conceived the novel idea of using them, instead of horses, to carry mail. Private post offices were at this time already illegal, but the law was not rigorously enforced. The gentleman did very well for himself until the day that he tendered a bid to the U.S. government to carry the government's mail—at one-fifth the price the U.S. Post Office was charging. The Post Office regarded this as going a bit too far and insisted on its rights. The gentleman was put out of business and the Post Office stole his idea.

When a mail truck gets stuck in the mud, third class is what they throw under the wheels.

Stewart Brand

7

Monopoly II: State Monopoly for Fun

AND PROFIT

> A reg'lar pollytician can't give away an' alley without blushin',
> but a businessman who is in pollytics . . . will . . . charge an
> admission price to th' lake front and make it a felony f'r annywan
> to buy stove polish outside iv his store, and have it all put down to
> public improvements. . . .
>
> MR. DOOLEY*

In the United States in this century the predominant form of
monopoly has not been natural monopoly, artificial monopoly, or
direct state monopoly, but state monopoly in private hands. Private
firms, unable to establish monopolies or cartels because they had
no way of keeping out competitors, turned to the government. This
is the origin of the regulation of transportation—the Interstate
Commerce Commission (ICC) and the Civil Aeronautics Board
(CAB). A similar process is responsible for occupational licensing,
which gives monopoly power to many craft unions, among them
the most powerful and probably the most pernicious craft union of
all, the American Medical Association.

The difficulties facing private cartels are nicely stated in
Rockefeller's description, cited by McGee, of an unsuccessful
attempt (in 1872) to control the production of crude oil and to drive
up its price:

> . . . the high price for the crude oil resulted, as it had always done
> before and will always do so long as oil comes out of the ground, in
> increasing the production, and they got too much oil. We could not
> find a market for it.

---

* Mr. Dooley was a fictional Irish barkeeper whose wisdom was popularized by the
American humorist Finley Peter Dunne.

> . . . of course, any who were not in this association were undertaking to produce all they possibly could; and as to those who were in the association, many of them men of honor and high standing, the temptation was very great to get a little more oil than they had promised their associates or us would come. It seemed very difficult to prevent the oil coming at that price . . . .

Rockefeller's prediction was overly pessimistic. Today, although oil still comes out of the ground, federal and state governments have succeeded where the oil producers of 1872 failed. Through federal oil import quotas and state restrictions on production, they keep the price of oil high and the production low. Progress.

It is widely believed that railroads in the late nineteenth century wielded almost unlimited monopoly power. Actually, as Kolko shows, long distance transportation was highly competitive, freight rates were declining, and the number of railroads was increasing until after the turn of the century. One line might have a monopoly for short distances along its route, but a shipper operating between two major cities had a choice of many alternative routes—twenty existed between St. Louis and Atlanta, for instance. Railroad rebates, frequently cited as evidence of monopoly, were actually the opposite; they were discounts that major shippers were able to get from one railroad by threatening to ship via a competitor.

Rail executives often got together to try to fix rates, but most of these conspiracies broke down, often in a few months, for the reasons Rockefeller cites in his analysis of the attempt to control crude oil production. Either the parties to the agreement surreptitiously cut rates (often by misclassifying freight or by offering secret rebates) in order to steal customers from each other, or some outside railroad took advantage of the high rates and moved in. J. P. Morgan committed his enormous resources of money and reputation to cartelizing the industry, but he met with almost unmitigated failure. In the beginning of 1889, for example, he formed the Interstate Commerce Railway Association to control rates among the western railroads. By March a rate war was going, and by June the situation was back to where it had been before he intervened.

By this time a new factor was entering the situation. In 1887, the Interstate Commerce Commission was created by the federal government with (contrary to most history books) the support of much of the railroad industry. The ICC's original powers were limited; Morgan attempted to use it to help enforce the 1889 agreement, but without success. During the next 31 years its powers were steadily increased, first in the direction of allowing it to prohibit rebates (which, Kolko estimates, were costing the railroads 10 percent of their gross income) and finally by giving it the power to set rates.

The people with the greatest interest in what the ICC did were the people in the rail industry. The result was that they dominated it, and it rapidly became an instrument for achieving the monopoly prices that they had been unable to get on the free market. The pattern was clear as early as 1889, when Aldace Walker, one of the original appointees to the ICC, resigned to become head of Morgan's Interstate Commerce Railway Association. He ended up as chairman of the board of the Atchison, Topeka, and Santa Fe. The ICC has served the railroads as a cartelizing agent up to the present day; in addition, it has expanded its authority to cover other forms of transportation and to prevent them, where possible, from undercutting the railroads.

It was in 1884 that railroad men in large numbers realized the advantages to them of federal control; it took 34 years to get the government to set their rates for them. The airline industry was born in a period more friendly to regulation. In 1938 the Civil Aeronautics Board (CAB), initially called the Civil Aeronautics Administration, was formed. It was given the power to regulate airline fares, to allocate routes among airlines, and to control the entry of new firms into the airline business. From that day until the deregulation of the industry in the late 1970s, no new trunk line— no major, scheduled, interstate passenger carrier—was started.

The CAB had one limitation: it could only regulate interstate airlines. There was one major intrastate route in the country— between San Francisco and Los Angeles. Pacific Southwest Airlines, which operated on that route, had no interstate operations and was therefore not subject to CAB rate fixing. Prior to deregulation, the fare between San Francisco and Los Angeles on PSA was about half that of any comparable interstate trip anywhere in the country. That gives us a good measure of the effect of the CAB on prices; it maintained them at about twice their competitive level.

Does this mean that half the money spent on airline fares went to monopoly profits for the airlines? No. The effects of regulation are far more wasteful than a simple transfer. If the fare between two cities is a hundred dollars and the cost to the airline of flying a passenger is fifty, each additional passenger is worth a fifty dollar profit to the airline. Each airline is willing to bear additional costs, up to fifty dollars per passenger, to lure passengers away from its competitors. Without the CAB airlines would compete on price until the fare fell to fifty dollars, thus wiping out the extra profit. With the CAB setting fares, they get the same effect by competing in less useful ways. They may spend money on advertising or fancy meals and fancier stewardesses. They may fly half-empty planes in order to offer the passengers more flights a day. The load factor— the percentage of seats filled—in the American airline industry ran about 50 percent. It would be interesting to analyze the changes in the load factor after deregulation in order to estimate how many of those empty seats were the result of unavoidable uncertainty in demand and how many the result of airlines competing away the monopoly profit they had been given by regulation.

In this complicated world it is rare that a political argument can be proved with evidence readily accessible to everyone, but until deregulation the airline industry provided one such case. If you did not believe that the effect of government regulation of transportation was to drive prices up, you could call any reliable travel agent and ask whether all interstate airline fares were the same, how PSA's fare between San Francisco and Los Angeles compared with the fare charged by the major airlines, and how that fare compared with the fare on other major intercity routes of comparable length. If you do not believe that the ICC and the CAB are on the side of the industries they regulate, figure out why they set minimum as well as maximum fares.

The ICC and the CAB exemplify one sort of government-granted monopoly. Another, of comparable importance, is occupational licensing. The political logic is the same. A law is passed, and political institutions are established, ostensibly to protect the consumers of some product or service. The producers, having a much more whole-hearted interest than the consumers in the operation of those institutions, take them over. They use them to raise prices and prevent competition.

The most notorious example is probably the licensing of skilled workers in the construction trades, such as plumbers and electricians. Licensing is under effective control of the respective craft unions, who use it to keep down the number of workers and to drive up their salaries, sometimes to astonishing levels. In order to maintain such salaries, the unions must keep down the number of workers licensed and must use local laws to keep out unlicensed workers. This has sometimes led to conflict between blacks, who wanted to get into the building trades, and the unions, who wanted to exclude them and everyone else except friends and relations of the present union members. Craft unions also take advantage of building codes, using them to prohibit the adoption of technological advances which might threaten their jobs. Innovation in low-cost construction methods thus is effectively banned from the big cities, where it is most needed.

Of all the craft unions that exploit licensing, the most important is the American Medical Association, which is not usually considered a union at all. Physicians are licensed by the states, and the state licensing boards are effectively controlled by the AMA. That is hardly surprising; if you were a state legislator, whom could you find more qualified to license physicians than other physicians? But it is in the interest of physicians to keep down the number of physicians for exactly the same reason that it is in the interest of plumbers to keep down the number of plumbers; the law of supply and demand drives up wages.

Physicians justify restricting the number of physicians, to others and doubtless to themselves as well, on the grounds of keeping up quality. Even if that were really what they were doing, the argument involves a fundamental error. Refusing to license the less qualified 50 percent of physicians may raise the average quality of physicians but it lowers the average quality of medical care. It does not mean that everyone gets better medical care but that half the people get no care or that everyone gets half as much.

Some of the restrictions the AMA has advocated, such as requiring applicants for medical licensing to be citizens and to take their licensing examinations in English, have a very dubious relationship to quality. They look more like an attempt to prevent immigrants from competing with American doctors. It is interesting to note that during the five years after 1933 the same number of physicians trained abroad were admitted to practice in this country as during the previous five years, despite the large numbers of professional people fleeing here from Germany and Austria during that period. This is striking evidence of the power of organized medicine to limit entry to its profession.

How does the AMA control the number of doctors? Refusing to license doctors after they are trained would create a great deal of hostility among those rejected; that would be politically expensive.

Instead, it relies mainly on the medical schools. In order to be licensed, an applicant must be a graduate of an approved medical school; the states get their list of approved schools from the Council on Medical Education and Hospitals of the AMA. For a medical school, removal from the list means ruin. In the 1930s, when doctors, like everyone else, were suffering the effects of the Great Depression, the Council on Medical Education and Hospitals wrote the medical schools, complaining that they were admitting more students than they could train properly. In the next two years, every school reduced the number it was admitting. Since then the AMA has become less obvious in its methods, but the logic of the situation has not changed.

Many people, faced with the evidence on regulatory commissions and occupational licensure, argue that the solution is to retain the commissions and the licensing but to 'make' them work in the public interest. This is tantamount to arguing that the consistent pattern of almost every regulatory agency and licensing body over the past century is merely accidental and could easily be altered. That is nonsense. Politics does not run on altruism or pious intentions. Politics runs on power.

A politician who can regulate an industry gets much more by helping the industry, whose members know and care about the effects of the regulation, than by helping the mass of consumers, who do not know they are being hurt and who would not know if they were being protected. An astute politician can—as many have—both help the industry and get credit for protecting the consumers. The consumers, whose relationship to the industry is a very small part of their lives, will never know what prices they would have been paying if there were no regulation.

The same principles apply to licensing. Once it exists, it must almost inevitably be taken over by the profession. Who else has either the concentrated interest in how it is done or the special knowledge required to do it? And the interest of the profession is directly contrary to the interest of the rest of us—in favor of keeping down its numbers instead of expanding them.

The subject of this chapter is government monopoly, not consumer protection; I cannot go into the question of what would happen if all forms of professional licensure, including licensure of physicians, were abolished, as I think they ought to be. That question is discussed in some detail in *Capitalism and Freedom*, by Milton Friedman, whose research more than fifty years ago first established the relationship between medical licensing and the high incomes of physicians.

In addition to regulation and licensing, the government also reduces competition somewhat by restraints on trade. For a given size firm, the larger the marketplace the more firms. The American automobile market supports only four manufacturers, but the world market supports many more. By imposing tariffs on foreign cars, the government makes it more difficult for foreign firms to compete and thus decreases competition on the American market. The same is true in many other industries.

There is one more way in which government has encouraged monopoly; surprisingly enough, it was probably unintentional, a side effect of laws designed to help rich tax payers pay lower taxes. If a corporation pays out its profits in dividends, the stockholders must report the dividends as income and pay income tax on them. If the corporation invests the profits internally, increasing the value of its stock, the stockholders may avoid ever paying taxes on the increase and will, at the worst, eventually pay at capital gains rates, which are lower. So as long as capital gains were taxed at a lower rate than income it paid a corporation to invest internally, increasing its own size, even when the result was economically less efficient than giving the money to its stockholders to invest. This tended to make firms grow larger than the size which was optimum from the standpoint of producing goods efficiently. When I first wrote this chapter, I pointed out that the effect would disappear if the tax laws changed in a way that eliminated this tax advantage but that with steeply graduated tax rates capital gains was too valuable a loophole to be surrendered easily. Fourteen years later, the tax reform act of 1986 sharply reduced the top tax rates and eliminated the special treatment of capital gains. One eventual result should be a reduction in the size of inefficiently large firms.

The conclusion of this and the previous chapter, taken together, is clear. Monopoly power exists only when a firm can control the prices charged by existing competitors and prevent the entry of new ones. The most effective way of doing so is by the use of government power. There are considerable elements of monopoly in our economy, but virtually all are produced by government and could not exist under institutions of complete private property.

8

Exploitation and Interest

'Exploitation' is a word often used but rarely defined. In its most literal meaning—I 'exploit' you if I in some way benefit from your existence—it is the reason human society exists. We all benefit from one another's existence. We all exploit each other. That is why we associate with each other. But as the word is usually used, it carries the implication of one person benefiting by harming another, or at least of one person's benefiting unfairly, at the expense of another. This usage may derive from Marx's theory of the exploitation of labor. Whether or not that is its origin, by rebutting this theory I can answer one of the most frequent charges of 'exploitation' made against capitalism and capitalists.

Marx argued as follows: Goods are produced by workers using tools (machines, factories, and so forth). The tools were themselves made by earlier workers. All production is done by workers, either current workers or past workers. But the capitalist claims some of the return from the production. His justification is that he has provided the tools; this is invalid since the tools were actually produced by previous workers. The capitalist who, having contributed nothing to production, takes part of the product is obviously stealing from—exploiting—the real producers, the workers.

The trouble with this argument is that it does not recognize that paying for tools today and waiting for years to get the money back is itself a productive activity, and that the interest earned by capital is the corresponding payment.

Consider a specific situation. A factory built during 1849 produces from 1850 to 1900. Having cost $1 million, it generates for its owner an income of $100,000 a year. This, according to Marx, is either wealth produced by the workers who built the factory, which should go to them, or wealth stolen from the workers working in the factory, who in that case are being paid less than they really produce.

Assume that the workers who built the factory were paid $1 million, the total cost of building it. (For simplicity's sake I will ignore other costs of construction. According to Marx, such costs ultimately can be traced back to the cost of the labor of other workers at an earlier time.) The money provided by the capitalist will be returned to him in the first ten years. After that the income is, from the Marxist standpoint, pure exploitation.

This argument depends on regarding the $1 million paid in 1849, when the work was done, as being 'equal' to $1 million received over the next decade. The workers themselves would not agree with this. They would hardly have done the job if they expected to wait ten years for their pay. If they had been willing and able to work on those terms, the capitalist would indeed have been superfluous; the workers could have built the factory themselves, working for free, received their pay over the next ten years, and continued to receive it for forty years more. It is the function of the capitalist to pay them wages in advance. If he were not available to pay them, the factory would not be built and the goods would not be produced. He himself bears a cost, since he too would rather have the money to do with as he wishes in 1850, instead of having it tied up and released slowly over a period of time. It is perfectly reasonable that he should receive something for his contribution.

Another way of making this point is to say that money represents a bundle of alternatives. If I have ten dollars now, I can either spend it taking my girlfriend to a restaurant, or use it as bus fare somewhere, or . . . . Having additional alternatives is always desirable, since I then have a wider range from which to pick the most attractive. Money is easily stored, so I do not *have* to spend it when I get it; ten dollars today can either be saved until tomorrow and spent on one of the alternatives possible for ten dollars tomorrow, or it can be spent today if I see an alternative more attractive than any I expect to see later. Thus ten dollars today is worth more than ten dollars tomorrow. This is why interest rates exist, why, if I borrow ten dollars from you today, I must give back a little more than ten dollars tomorrow.

The advantage of money today over money tomorrow is tiny, as is the interest accumulated by ten dollars in one day. When the time involved is a substantial portion of a man's life, the difference in value is also substantial. It is not a matter of indifference to me whether I can buy a house for my family today or ten years from now. Nor is the ten years insignificant to the man who lends me the money now and expects to receive something in exchange. The Marxist is wrong to regard interest received by a capitalist or paid by a debtor to a creditor as stolen money. It is actually payment for value received.

The same error is one reason many people consider inheritance unjust. They assume that if a father earns money and leaves it to his son, who lives off the interest, the son is really living *at the expense of* the people around him. As one person with whom I argued this put it, the stock market—shares, bonds, bank accounts, and the like—are merely symbols or facades. One must see through them to the real things that are happening to real objects. This reality is that someone is producing nothing and consuming something and that someone else must be paying for it.

It is his father who pays for it. If the son were literally living on food produced and stored by his father this would be obvious, and few would object. But the situation is really the same when the father chooses to invest wealth instead of consuming it or turning it into stores of food. By buying a factory instead of a yacht, he is increasing the productivity of the society. Workers are able to produce more, using that factory, than they could without it. It is that additional production which feeds his son.

To the true egalitarian, who regards equality as itself a paramount end, this is no defense. Inheritance is unequal, thus unjust. His is a view with which I have no sympathy. I see no reason better than greed for claiming that I 'deserve' a share of someone else's wealth, which I have had no part in producing, when he dies. I see no reason nobler than jealousy for objecting to another man's good fortune in being left an 'unearned' inheritance.

9

I DON'T NEED NOTHING

The word 'need' should be eliminated from the vocabulary of political discourse. It is inextricably bound up with a dangerous oversimplification of reality—the idea that there exist certain values infinitely more important than all others, things I need rather than merely want, and that these 'needs' can be determined objectively.

At first glance, this idea seems reasonable. Is not my 'need' for food, water, and air entirely different from desire for pleasure or comfort? These things are necessary for life; surely life is not merely more important than anything else, but infinitely more important. The amount of food, water, and air required to maintain life is not a matter of taste or preference but of biological fact.

The consequence for my life expectancy of being deprived of food, water, or air may be a matter of biological fact. The value to me of living is not. Staying alive is, for most of us, highly desirable, but it is not infinitely desirable. If it were, we would be willing to sacrifice all other values to it. Every time you smoke a cigarette, every time I drive a little too fast, we are knowingly offering life—a little bit of life, a very small chance of dying now or a large chance of not living quite as long—for a rather minor pleasure.

The person who says, as almost everyone does say, that human life is of infinite value, not to be measured in mere material terms, is talking palpable, if popular, nonsense. If he believed that of his own life, he would never cross the street, save to visit his doctor or to earn money for things necessary to physical survival. He would eat the cheapest, most nutritious food he could find and live in one small room, saving his income for frequent visits to the best possible doctors. He would take no risks, consume no luxuries, and live a long life. If you call it living. If a man really believed that other people's lives were infinitely valuable, he would live like an ascetic, earn as much money as possible, and spend everything not absolutely necessary for survival on CARE packets, research into presently incurable diseases, and similar charities.

In fact, people who talk about the infinite value of human life do not live in either of these ways. They consume far more than they need to support life. They may well have cigarettes in their drawer and a sports car in the garage. They recognize in their actions, if not in their words, that physical survival is only one value, albeit a very important one, among many.

The idea of 'need' is dangerous because it strikes at the heart of the practical argument for freedom. That argument depends on recognizing that each person is best qualified to choose for himself which among a multitude of possible lives is best for him. If many of those choices involve 'needs', things of infinite value to one person which can be best determined by someone else, what is the use of freedom? If I disagree with the expert about my 'needs', I make, not a value judgement, but a mistake.

If we accept the concept of needs, we must also accept the appropriateness of having decisions concerning those needs made for us by someone else, most likely the government. It is precisely this argument that is behind government subsidy to medicine, present and prospective. Medicine, like food, water, or air, contributes to physical survival. The kind and quantity of medical attention necessary to achieve some particular end—to cure or to prevent a disease, for example—is a question, not of individual taste, but of expert opinion. It is consequently argued that the amount of medical attention people 'need' should be provided free. But how much is that? Some 'needs' can be satisifed, and at a relatively low price; the cost of a fully nutritious minimum-cost diet (largely soy beans and powdered milk), for instance, is only a few hundred dollars a year. Additional expenditures on food merely make it taste better—which, it might be argued, is a luxury. But additional medical care continues to bring improved health up to a very high level of medical expenditure, probably up to the point where medicine would absorb the entire national income. Does that mean that we should satisfy our 'need' for medical care by having everyone in the country become a doctor, save those absolutely needed for the production of food and shelter? Obviously not. Such a society would be no more attractive than the 'life' of the man who really regarded his life as infinitely valuable.

The error is in the idea that improved health is worth having at any price, however large, for any improvement in health, however small. There is some point at which the cost, in time and money, of more medical care is greater than the resulting increase in health justifies. Where that point occurs depends on the subjective value to the person concerned of good health, on the one hand, and the other things he could buy with the money, or do with the time, on the other. If medical care is sold on the market, like other goods and services, individuals will consume it up to that point and spend the rest of their money on other things. Through Medicare, government makes the decision; it forces the individual to buy a certain amount of medical care, whether he thinks it is worth the price or not.

A program such as Medicare may also transfer money from one person to another; such an effect is often cited by those who claim that such programs make it possible for the poor to get good medical care that they could not otherwise afford. If so, the transfer should be evaluated separately from the specifically medical part of the program. If transferring money from the rich to the poor is good, it can be done without any program of compulsory medical insurance; if compulsory medical insurance is good, it can be done without any transfer. There is no sense in using the transfer to defend the insurance.

In fact, it is very questionable whether government medical programs transfer money from rich to poor. There is evidence that socialized medicine in Britain has had the opposite effect. The upper-income classes pay higher taxes, but they also, for various reasons, take much greater advantage of the services. In America, Medicare has been tacked onto Social Security, an existing system of compulsory 'insurance' which, as I showed in an earlier chapter, probably transfers income from the poor to the not-poor.

If past experience is any guide, the poor are not likely to get much that they do not pay for and may pay for things they do not get. The principal effect of such programs, on them as on everyone else, is to force them to pay for services that they would not buy willingly because they do not think them worth the price. This is called 'helping the poor'.

Defenders of such programs always argue that the poor are so poor that they cannot afford vital medical care. What this means, presumably, is that they are so poor that in order to pay for even minimal medical care they would have to give up something even more vital—food, for instance. But since the benefits the poor receive are usually paid for by their own taxes, the situation is only made worse; instead of having to give up medical care in order to eat, the poor are commanded to give up eating in order to get medical care.

Fortunately, the situation is rarely that bad. Lurid reports to the contrary, most poor people are not on the edge of literal starvation; evidence indicates that in this country the number of calories consumed is virtually independent of income. If the poor spent more of their own money on doctors, they would not starve to death; they would merely eat worse, wear worse clothes, and live in even worse housing than they now do. If they do not spend very much money on medical care it is because that cost, which they are in an excellent position to evaluate, is too high. If people who have more money wish to donate it to providing medical care to the poor, that is admirable. If they wish to donate the money of the poor, it is not.

PART II

LIBERTARIAN GRAB BAG OR HOW TO SELL THE STATE IN SMALL PIECES

PARANOIA

This man I never saw before
At 3 A.M. breaks down the door
To tell me my aspirin is LSD.
"It says right there on the bottle,
Acetylsalicylic *Acid*."
I tell you doctor, honestly,
It seems like someone's after me.

I don't think fighting is what I'm made for
But this lottery ticket I never paid for
Sold by a pusher known as Sam
Has won me a ticket to Vietnam,
A twelve months, expenses paid, tropical
    vacation
With a funeral, free, from a grateful nation.
But the doctor says I need therapy
For thinking someone is after me.

And then there are things I just can't ignore
Like the little man in our bedroom door
Says we'll be in jail by the end of the night
Unless we turn over and do it right.

Doctor, Doctor, come and see
There's really someone after me.

Then he asks, as he rips off the sheet,
For our marriage license and tax receipt;
Says "you need a license to shoot at a duck
How come you think that it's free to . . . "
Who so blind as will not see;
The state, the state, is after me.

Sell the schools

Riddle of the year: How is a public school like the U.S. Post Office? Answer: It's inefficient, it costs more each year than the last, it is a perpetual subject of complaint about which nothing is ever done. It is, in short, a typical government monopoly.

The Post Office is a legal monopoly; no one else can carry first-class mail for profit. The public school is a monopoly by virtue of the money it receives from state and local governments. In order to compete with it, an unsubsidized private school must be, not merely superior, but so much superior that its customers are willing to forgo their share of that money.

There is a simple solution. Governments should subsidize schooling instead of schools. This could easily be accomplished by a voucher system, under which each student would receive from the state a tuition voucher, redeemable by any qualified school, public, private, or parochial.

The value of the voucher would be the state's per capita expenditure on schooling. Public school systems would have to support themselves on the money brought, in the form of vouchers, by their pupils. Private and parochial schools could, if they chose, supplement the vouchers with additional tuition, charitable donations, or church monies.

The school system would then be open to real competition. An educational entrepreneur who found some way of providing a better education at a lower cost would make money and expand his operations; his competitors, public as well as private, would have to improve or shut down.

Such an entrepreneur would have the best possible incentive to find good teachers and pay them what they are worth. Many different teaching methods would be tried. Those that failed would disappear; those that succeeded would be copied.

The state would have to determine what was a 'qualified' school in order to guarantee that the vouchers were spent on schooling. Some supporters of private education fear that this power would be used to control schools that are now independent. For that reason they either oppose all subsidies to private schools or prefer tax rebates.

The trouble with tax rebates is that they are useless to the poor, who, since they get the worst education of all from the public schools, would be the greatest beneficiaries of a competitive system. If rebates are used, they should be combined with a system of direct vouchers for parents whose tax payments are less than the amount of the rebate.

Even with rebates, the state (or the federal government) decides what qualifies as an 'educational expense'. Even if there is no subsidy at all, there are still compulsory schooling laws; the state decides what is or is not a school. A state which wishes to control its private schools can do so now.

The best solution to this problem would be for any state instituting a voucher system to include, as part of the initial legislation, the provision that any institution can qualify as a school on the basis of the performance of its graduates on objective examinations. In New York, for instance, the law might state that any school would be recognized if the average performance of its graduating class on the Regents exam was higher than the performance of the graduating classes of the bottom third of the state's public schools.

A new school could operate provisionally, accumulating vouchers until its first class graduated. A school dealing with retarded or otherwise disadvantaged children could petition the state for special recognition if it was unable to meet the usual criterion.

Such legislation would be sufficient to prevent parents from setting up fake 'schools' in order to transfer the voucher money to their own pockets. At the same time, it would make it almost impossible for the state to control either the method or content of private schooling.

The state could force schools to teach certain ideas (by putting them on the exam) but could not prevent them from teaching others and would have no control over how they were taught. A teacher who disagreed with the orthodox position could always tell his class that 'this is what the examiners want you to write on the test. On the other hand, what I think is true is. . . .'

A voucher system, with such precautions, would not only prevent the state from controlling the pupils now in private schools, it would also greatly reduce the state's power over students who are now in public schools.

According to a Gallup poll some years ago, 30 percent of parents would send their children to private schools if they were free, and 29 percent would send them to parochial schools. Parochial schools already charge less than the amount the state spends on public schools, so with vouchers they could be free. Present private schools could charge much lower tuition, and a few of them, as well as many of the new schools set up to compete with the public schools, would be free. Thus the number of pupils in schools run by the state would be cut in half.

For those people who view the power of government to make sure that everyone learns the same things in the same way as desirable, this is a disadvantage of the voucher system. For those of us who prefer a free and diverse educational system, it is an advantage.

It is possible that the Supreme Court would forbid the use of vouchers by parochial school pupils, on the grounds that it violated the separation of church and state. Similar legal difficulties have arisen in the past over segregated schooling; in the Prince Edward County, Virginia, case, the court ruled that state aid to private school pupils could not be used as a device to avoid integration. Presumably this would mean that racially segregated schools could not receive voucher funds. If the court made a similar ruling with regard to religious schools, the voucher system could still function, but would be restricted to private schools.

When I first wrote this chapter around 1970, it was unclear what position the court would take on whether it was constitutional to use vouchers for religious schools; when I revised it in 1988 it was still unclear, but the odds that the court would rule them constitutional had improved somewhat, at least in the judgement of a law professor friend of mine who specializes in church-state issues.

Whatever the court rules, is the voucher system in fact an illegitimate subsidy of religion? No. The state is subsidizing parents in the purchase of schooling for their children; they can buy that schooling wherever they wish. For them to use the subsidy to buy schooling from a parochial school is no more a state subsidy of religion than for a welfare client to buy his food at a church bazaar. Of course, the parochial school hopes to achieve its end of teaching religion at the same time that it provides the state what it is paying for: education in secular subjects. Similarly, the church hopes to use its profits from the bazaar to finance religious projects.

One argument sometimes made against a voucher system is that it would subsidize the rich and impoverish the public school system by transferring money to upper-class parents who send their children to private prep school.

Unfortunately for this argument, only about half of 1 percent[1] of all pupils in the U.S. go to private, nonreligious schools (about 250,000). The great majority of pupils in nonpublic schools (about 5.5 million) are in church-related schools, and their parents are frequently poorer, not richer, than the average of the community.

In states where Roman Catholics make up a large percentage of the population, the voucher system would substantially increase the state's educational costs, since the state would have to provide vouchers for children now in parochial schools. But without some form of state aid, the parochial schools may well close down,[2] and the state will have to pay for their pupils anyway.

Furthermore, these are precisely the states where it is now difficult to get money for public schools, since parents whose children are not in the public schools are notoriously unfriendly to new taxes for schooling.

A related objection to the voucher system is that it would increase educational inequalities. Presently, it is said, all children, rich and poor, go to the same public schools. Under a voucher system, poor parents would send their children to public schools or to private schools that subsisted only on vouchers, while richer parents could supplement the vouchers with additional tuition payments and so put their children in better schools.

But under our present system, the school a child goes to is determined by where he lives, and where he lives is largely determined by the income of his parents. Under the voucher plan a ghetto parent who was deeply concerned about his child's educa-

---

[1] This figure, and those following, are from the *Statistical Abstract of the United States: 1967*.

[2] New York *Times*, September 22, page 32; September 4, page 44; June 16, page 1. (1969)

tion might be able to scrape up a thousand dollars a year, or get a small scholarship, add that to the value of his voucher, and so send the child to a good private school. Under the present system he has the choice of either paying $5,000 a year for a good private school or buying a $200,000 house in a suburb with a good school system.

Thus the voucher system, although it does not eliminate class distinctions in education, blurs them. Today a small elite goes to private prep schools, middle-class children go to moderately good suburban schools, and the inner city poor get schools that are often little more than custodial institutions.

Under a voucher system the motivated middle-class parent could afford the differential between the cost of a public school education and a good prep school. Low-income parents who felt that they were being short-changed in the schooling provided to their children would have the option of setting up their own schools, perhaps along the lines of the Harlem Street Academies, or persuading someone to set up private schools for them and financing them with vouchers.

Thus the voucher plan, like other free market mechanisms, provides the ultimate form of decentralization and does so in a way that protects the rights of even small minorities. If 60 percent of one school district's population wants one kind of school, the other 40 percent can take their vouchers and set up their own school. If a local minority is too small to support a school of its own, it can pool its resources with similar groups elsewhere.

When I originally wrote this chapter I predicted that a voucher plan would be adopted in some state sometime in the next few years. I was wrong. There were several attempts to introduce such plans, but they were bitterly and successfully opposed by the educational bureaucracy and the teachers' unions.

That is no reason to give up. It took a long time to get the country into its present situation and it will take a long time to get it out. While attempts to get the government out of the schooling business have so far been unsuccessful, both the ideology of government control and the public's support for the public school system have been growing gradually weaker. I am not willing to make any more predictions, but I can still hope.

For years we have been told that all the public school system needs is more money. For years we have watched its per pupil spending rise, with little visible effect on quality. It is time to try something new.

11

A RADICAL CRITIQUE OF AMERICAN UNIVERSITIES

In [some] universities the teacher is prohibited from receiving any honorary or fee from his pupils, and his salary constitutes the whole of the revenue which he derives from his office. His interest is, in this case, set as directly in opposition to his duty as it is possible to set it. . . . It is the interest of every man to live as much at his ease as he can; and if his emoluments are to be precisely the same, whether he does, or does not perform some very laborious duty, it is certainly his interest, at least as interest is vulgarly understood, either to neglect it altogether, or, if he is subject to some authority which will not suffer him to do this, to perform it in as careless and slovenly a manner as that authority will permit. If he is naturally active and a lover of labour, it is his interest to employ that activity in any way, from which he can derive some advantage, rather than in the performance of his duty, from which he can derive none.

If the authority to which he is subject resides in the body corporate, the college, or university, of which he himself is a member, and in which the greater part of the other members are, like himself, persons who either are, or ought to be, teachers; they are likely to make a common cause, to be all very indulgent to one another, and every man to consent that his neighbor may neglect his duty provided he himself is allowed to neglect his own. In the university at Oxford, the greater part of the public professors have, for these many years, given up altogether even the pretence of teaching.

[In a state or religious university a professor will probably not be allowed] to neglect his duty altogether. All that . . . [his] superiors, however, can force him to do, is to attend upon his pupils a certain number of hours, that is, to give a certain number of lectures in the week or in the year. What those lectures shall be, must still depend upon the diligence of the teacher; and that diligence is likely to be proportioned to the motives which he has for exerting it. . . .

If the teacher happens to be a man of sense, it must be an unpleasant thing to him to be conscious, while he is lecturing his students, that he is either speaking or reading nonsense, or what is very little better than nonsense. It must too be unpleasant to him to observe that the greater part of his students desert his lectures; or perhaps attend upon them with plain enough marks of neglect, contempt, and derision. If he is obliged, therefore, to give a certain number of lectures, these motives alone, without any other interest, might dispose him to take some pains to give tolerably good ones. Several different expedients, however, may be fallen upon, which will effectually blunt the edge of all those incitements to diligence. The teacher, instead of explaining to his pupils himself the science in which he proposes to instruct them, may read some book upon it; and if this book is written in a foreign and dead language, by interpreting it to them into their own; or, what would give him still less trouble, by making them interpret it to him, and by now and then making an occasional remark upon it, he may flatter himself that he is giving a lecture. The slightest degree of knowledge and application will enable him to do this, without exposing himself to contempt or derision, or saying anything that is really foolish, absurd, or ridiculous. The discipline of the college, at the same time, may enable him to force all his pupils to the most regular attendance upon this sham-lecture, and to maintain the most decent and respectful behavior during the whole time of the performance.

The discipline of colleges and universities is in general contrived, not for the benefit of the students, but for the interest, or more properly speaking, for the ease of the masters. Its object is, in all cases, to maintain the authority of the master, and whether he neglects or performs his duty, to oblige the students in all cases to behave to him as if he performed it with the greatest diligence and ability. It seems to assume perfect wisdom and virtue in the one order, and the greatest weakness and folly in the other. Where the masters, however, really perform their duty, there are no examples, I believe, that the greater part of the students ever neglect theirs. No discipline is ever requisite to force attendance upon lectures which are really worth the attending, as is well known wherever any such lectures are given. Force and restraint may, no doubt, be in some degree requisite in order to oblige children, or very young boys, to attend to those parts of education which it is thought necessary for them to acquire during that early period of life; but after twelve or thirteen years of age, provided the master does his duty, force or restraint can scarce ever be necessary to carry on any part of education.

Excerpts from *An Inquiry into the Nature and Causes of the Wealth of Nations,* Book V, part 3, article 2. Written by Adam Smith and published in 1776.

12

THE IMPOSSIBILITY OF A UNIVERSITY

The modern corporate university, public or private, contains an implicit contradiction: it cannot take positions, but it must take positions. The second makes the demand for a 'responsible university' appealing, intellectually as well as emotionally. The first makes not merely the acceptance of that demand but its very consideration something fundamentally subversive of the university's proper ends.

It cannot take positions because if it does, the efforts of its members will be diverted from the search for truth to the attempt to control the decision-making process. If it takes a public position on an important matter of controversy, those on each side of the controversy will be tempted to try to keep out new faculty members who hold the other position, in order to be sure that the university makes the 'right' decision. To hire an incompetent supporter of the other side would be undesirable; to hire a competent one, who might persuade enough faculty members to reverse the university's stand, catastrophic. Departments in a university that reaches corporate decisions in important matters will tend to become groups of true believers, closed to all who do not share the proper orthodoxy. They so forfeit one of the principal tools in the pursuit of truth—intellectual conflict.

A university must take positions. It is a large corporation, with expenditures of tens of millions of dollars and an endowment of hundreds of millions. It must act, and to act it must decide what is true. What causes high crime rates? Should it protect its members by hiring university police or by spending money on neighborhood relations or community organizing? What effect will certain fiscal policies have on the stock market, and thus the university's endowment? Should the university argue for them? These are issues of professional controversy within the academic community.

A university may proclaim its neutrality, but neutrality, as the left quite properly argues, is also a position. If one believes that the election of Ronald Reagan or Teddy Kennedy would be a national tragedy, and a tragedy in particular for the university, how can one justify letting the university, with its vast resources of wealth and influence, remain neutral?

The best possible solution within the present university structure has been, not neutrality, but the ignorance or impotence of the university community. As long as students and faculty do not know that the university is bribing politicians, investing in countries with dictatorial regimes, or whatever, and as long as they have no way of influencing the university's actions, those acts will not hinder the university in its proper function of pursuing truth, however much good or damage they may do in the outside world. Once the university community realizes that the university does, or can, take actions substantially affecting the outside world and that students and faculty can influence those actions, the game is up.

There is no satisfactory solution to this dilemma within the structure of the present corporate university. In most of the better universities, the faculty has ultimate control. A university run from the outside, by a state government or a self-perpetuating board of trustees, has its own problems. A university can pretend to make no decisions or can pretend that the faculty has no control over them, for a while. Eventually someone will point out exactly what the emperor is wearing.

The solution is to replace the corporate university by institutions with an essentially economic rather than political structure, a market instead of a hierarchy. Such a structure is described in the next chapter. In a free-market university, the problem disappears. Market places do not take positions.

Adam smith u.

Some years ago, the student government at the University of Chicago considered a plan under which it would hire one professor who would be selected by a majority vote of the student body. This was advanced as a way to expand the university beyond 'consensus scholarship'. Such a proposal exemplifies the intellectual failure of the New Left. The objective of decentralizing academic power in order to allow controversy and diversity is an admirable one. The means proposed, the choosing of faculty by majority vote, is positively inimical to that objective. 'Democratic' decision making is a means for finding and implementing the will of the majority; it has no other function. It serves, not to encourage diversity, but to prevent it. Intelligent members of the New Left are surely aware of the futility of such a proposal; perhaps that is why they are so reluctant to describe how a society should work. They have not grasped, emotionally or intellectually, the concept of noncoercive cooperation, of a society that lets everyone get what he wants.

Before discussing how a 'free-market university' would work, we must analyze what is essentially wrong with the present system. The lack of student power which the New Left deplores is a direct result of the success of one of the pet schemes of the old left, heavily subsidized schooling. Students in public universities and, to a lesser extent, in private ones do not pay the whole cost of their schooling. As a result the university does not need its students; it can always get more. Like a landlord under rent control, the university can afford to ignore the wishes and convenience of its customers.

If the subsidies were abolished or converted into scholarships awarded to students, so that the university got its money from tuition, it would be in the position of a merchant selling his goods at their market price and thus constrained to sell what his customers most want to buy. That is the situation of market schools, such as Berlitz and the various correspondence schools, and that is how they act.

A university of the present sort, even if financed entirely from tuition, would still be a centralized, bureaucratic organization. In a free-market university, on the other hand, the present corporate structure would be replaced by a number of separate organizations, cooperating in their mutual interest through the normal processes of the marketplace. These presumably would include one or more businesses renting out the use of classrooms, and a large number of teachers, each paying for the use of a classroom and charging the students who wished to take his course whatever price was mutually agreeable. The system thus would be ultimately supported by the students, each choosing his courses according to what he wanted to study, the reputation of the teacher, and his price.

Other organizations might coexist with these. There might be one that did nothing but give examinations in various subjects and grant degrees to those who passed; presumably, teachers would be hired to spend part of their time writing and grading such examinations. Another might perform clerical functions, printing a course catalogue listing courses that were being offered and their prices, or compiling transcripts for those students who wanted them and were willing to pay for them. There might be groups publishing and selling evaluations of teachers and courses, like the 'Confidential Guide' compiled by the *Harvard Crimson*.

There might be research groups, working in the same community in order to allow researchers to supplement their income by teaching and in order to use students as inexpensive research assistants. Some members of the community might be simultaneously teaching elementary courses in a subject and paying other members for advanced instruction. There might be companies providing privately run dormitories for those students who wished to live in them.

The essential characteristic of this scheme is that, like any market system, it produces what the consumer wants. To the extent that the students, even with the assistance of professional counselors and written evaluations of courses, are less competent to judge what they are getting than are the people who now hire and fire teachers, that may be a disadvantage. But it does guarantee that it is the students' interest, not the interest of the university as judged by the university, that determines what teachers are employed.

Under the sort of market system I have described, a majority of students, even a large majority, can have only a positive, not a negative, effect on what is taught. They can guarantee that something will be taught *but not that something will not be*. As long as there are enough students interested in a subject that a teacher can make money teaching it, that subject will be taught, however much other students dislike it. The market system accomplishes the objective of the new left's proposal.

It might be possible to reform our present universities in the direction of such free-market universities. One way would be by the introduction of a 'tuition diversion' plan. This arrangement would allow students, while purchasing most of their education from the university, to arrange some courses taught by instructors of their own choice. A group of students would inform the university that they wished to take a course from an instructor from outside the university during the next year. The university would multiply the number of students by the average spent from each student's tuition for the salary of one of his instructors for one quarter. The result would be the amount of their tuition the group wished to divert from paying an instructor of the university's choice to paying an instructor of their own choice. The university would offer him that sum to teach the course or courses proposed. If he accepted, the students would be obligated to take the course.

The university would determine what credit, if any, was given for such courses. The number each student could take for credit might at first be severely limited. If the plan proved successful, it could be expanded until any such course could serve as an elective. Departments would still decide whether a given course would satisfy specific departmental requirements.

A tuition diversion plan does not appear to be a very revolutionary proposal; it can begin on a small scale as an educational experiment of the sort dear to the heart of every liberal educator. Such plans could, in time, revolutionize the universities.

At first, tuition diversion would be used to hire famous scholars on sabbatical leave, political figures of the left or right, film directors invited by college film groups, and other such notables. But it would also offer young academics an alternative to a normal career. Capable teachers would find that, by attracting many students, they could get a much larger salary than by working for a university. The large and growing pool of skilled 'free-lance' teachers would encourage more schools to adopt tuition diversion plans and thus simplify their own faculty recruitment problems. Universities would have to offer substantial incentives to keep their better teachers from being drawn off into free-lancing. Such incentives might take the form of effective market structures within the university, rewarding departments and professors for attracting students. Large universities would become radically decentralized, approximating free-market universities. Many courses would be taught by free-lancers, and the departments would develop independence verging on autarchy.

Under such institutions the students, although they might have the help of advisory services, would have to take the primary responsibility for the structure of their own education. Many students enter college unready for such responsibility. A competitive educational market would evolve other institutions to serve their needs. These would probably be small colleges offering a highly structured education with close personal contact for students who wished to begin their education by submitting to a plan of study designed by those who are already educated. A student could study at such a college until he felt ready to oversee his own education and then transfer to a university.

It is time to begin the subversion of the American system of higher schooling, with the objective not destruction but renaissance.

14

Open the Gates

Give me your tired, your poor,
Your huddled masses yearning to breathe free,
The wretched refuse of your teeming shore,
Send these, the homeless, tempest-tossed to me;
I lift my lamp beside the golden door.

VERSE ENGRAVED ON THE BASE
OF THE STATUE OF LIBERTY

Until the middle of the 1920s this country followed a general policy of unrestricted immigration; except for some exclusion of orientals, anyone who wanted to come was welcome. From 1905 to 1907, and again in 1910, 1913, and 1914, over a million immigrants a year came. They and their descendants have created a large part of our economic and cultural wealth. It would be hard to find any major public figure willing to argue that this policy was a mistake.

It would be almost as hard to find a major public figure who would advocate a return to that policy. Recent debates have been on how we should allocate and enforce our limited immigration quota among different nationalities, not on whether the quota should exist.

In my opinion, the restriction on immigration is a mistake: we should abolish it tomorrow and reopen the most successful attack on poverty the world has ever seen.

One danger in this policy is that poor immigrants might come with the intent of somehow surviving until they became citizens, and then going on welfare. I therefore include in my proposal the condition that new immigrants should face a fifteen year 'residency' requirement before they become eligible for welfare. I also suggest that the federal and state minimum wage laws be altered so as not to cover new immigrants, or, better yet, be repealed.

We would receive a vast flood of immigrants, probably more than a million a year, possibly several million. Most would come from Asian and Latin American countries. Most would be poor. Many would work as unskilled labor for the first generation, as did most of the previous immigrants. They would bring with them levels of education, nutrition, and health, which would appall our social workers; they would live, by our standards, very badly, but they would live well by their former standards, and that is why they would come.

Unrestricted immigration would make us richer, as it has in the past. Our wealth is in people, not things; America is not Kuwait. If a working wife can hire an Indian maid, who earned a few hundred dollars a year in India, to work for her at six thousand dollars a year, and so spend her own time on a 30 thousand a year job, who is worse off?

As long as the immigrants pay for what they use, they do not make the rest of the society poorer. If increased population makes the country more crowded, it does so only because the immigrants produce wealth which is worth more to the owners of land than the land is worth, and the immigrants are able to use that wealth to buy the land. The same applies to whatever the immigrants get on the free market; in order to appropriate existing resources for their own uses, the immigrants must buy them with new goods of at least equal value.

The immigrants will get some governmental services for which they will not pay directly. They will also pay taxes. Given present conditions, I see no reason to expect that they will cost government more than government will cost them.

The new immigrants will drive down the wages of unskilled labor, hurting some of the present poor. At the same time, the presence of millions of foreigners will make the most elementary acculturation, even the ability to speak English, a marketable skill; some of the poor will be able to leave their present unskilled jobs to find employment as foremen of 'foreign' work gangs or front men for 'foreign' enterprises.

More important than any of these economic effects is the psychological effect on the present poor; they will no longer be the bottom of the barrel, and as Liberals have pointed out with some justice, it is where you are, not what you have, which defines poverty. Mobility will be restored; each generation of immigrants will be able to struggle up to a position from which to look down on their successors.

A policy of unrestricted immigration would bring us more than cheap unskilled labor. It would bring a flood of new skills, not least among them the entrepreneurial ability that has made Indian and Chinese emigrants the merchant classes of Asia and Africa. Once the new citizens become familiar with the language and culture of their adopted country, they will probably work their way into the great American middle class just as rapidly as did their predecessors of eighty years ago.

It is a shame that the argument must be put in terms of the economic or psychological 'interest' of the present generation of Americans. It is simpler than that. There are people, probably many millions, who would like to come here, live here, work here, raise their children here, die here. There are people who would like to become Americans, as our parents and grandparents did.

If we want to be honest, we can ship the Statue of Liberty back to France or replace the outdated verse with new lines, 'America the closed preserve/That dirty foreigners don't deserve.' Or we can open the gates again.

> *Welcome, Welcome, Emigrante*
> *To my country welcome home.*
> BUFFY SAINTE-MARIE

15

Sell the Streets

The slogan 'sell the streets' has long been used as an example of libertarian principles carried to a ridiculous extreme. That it might also be a practical proposal was first suggested to me by the late Robert Schuchman some 28 years ago. At the time, I was not convinced.

Certainly there are practical difficulties in transferring the present system of governmentally owned streets and highways to private hands (although the difficulties are much less for newly created communities, some of which are already being set up with private road systems). The cost of negotiating private contracts to guarantee each homeowner access to his home and to define his legal rights and responsibilities with regard to access roads would be considerable. So are the costs of the present governmentally owned system.

The rush hour problem is a good example. The size of city expressways is determined almost entirely by the peak traffic that they have to bear. The extra cost to the city of an additional driver at 3 a.m. is essentially zero—the roads are there anyway and nobody is using them. The extra cost of an extra driver at rush hour averages out, I am told, to about five dollars per trip. Presently, both drivers are charged essentially the same price, in the form of higher gas costs due to gas taxes. If the roads were privately run, it would pay their owners to encourage off-hour traffic by charging a low price and to discourage people from driving at rush hour by charging them the full cost of their trip.

That cost—five dollars per trip—comes to over two thousand dollars a year, a sizable sum for the average commuter. One way to decrease it would be by changing his working hours. The present custom of having almost everybody work the same nine-to-five day has some advantages (a businessman knows that if he is in his office, his customer probably is too), but it also has severe costs, especially in a crowded city. Fixed resources, such as parks, beaches, restaurants, and roads, are used very irregularly, jammed at certain times and empty at others.

A two thousand dollar a year saving on transportation cost, when added to cheaper parking and such nonmonetary benefits as a quicker trip and less crowded restaurants, would surely be a sufficient incentive to induce some firms to shift their hours of operations, or the hours of some of their employees, from nine-to-five to (say) eleven-to-seven, or even three-to-eleven (p.m.).

The cost of rush hour driving could also be avoided in other ways. Commuters could use cheaper forms of transport—bus, train or car pool. They could move back to the city, or their businesses could move out to the suburbs. In any case, they would be responding to the real cost of their actions, something they are not now forced to do.

How could a private firm charge variable fees? It might use toll booths and vary the rate according to time of day and condition of traffic. It might charge a fixed monthly fee for the right to use its roads at peak load hours and a lower fee for the right to use them only at others times; those who paid one fee or the other could be given identifying license plates, and other arrangements could be made for those customers who used the road less regularly. Different highway companies might have exchange agreements, allowing customers of one to use others at no extra cost.

Using modern technology it would be possible, and relatively inexpensive, to set up a much more detailed system of fees, varying by both where and when you drive. Each car would be equipped with a transponder, a small radio designed to receive the query 'who are you?' and respond with the computer equivalent of 'I am car number 97341'. The technology to do this already exists; it has been used for years to automate toll collection for buses. The information about what car drove where when would be collected in a central computer and drivers billed monthly. If customers were worried that detailed information about their movements might fall into the hands of a jealous spouse or overzealous employer, the system could be set up to keep track of how many road units each car used each day but not when and where; the number of road units charged per mile could still vary with time and place.

The imposition of variable charges is not the only improvement that a profit-making corporation could make. Traffic jams are minor inconveniences to a government bureau; to a private corporation, they mean the loss of a small fortune in potential customers. Traffic jams are not the inevitable result of many people wanting to drive at once. The rate of traffic flow in a jammed expressway, with cars taking up twenty feet apiece and moving at five miles an hour, is far lower than in the same expressway with traffic at 50 miles an hour and each car taking up 60 or 80 feet. A well-operated expressway, with computer control of entrance to keep people out when traffic density got too high or with 'holding lots' into which surplus traffic could be temporarily diverted in order to speed up traffic flow, would get everyone to his destination sooner.

Electronic recording devices, computer-controlled entrances, and three-to-eleven working days sound like science fiction. Private highways would also bring more obvious improvements, some of them long awaited. It would hardly pay a private corporation to clog its highway with repair crews through the rush hour and then send them home, leaving it empty of both cars and workmen at night.

Any of these improvements could, in principle, be made by the socialist institutions now running our highways. None, so far as I know, has been. Meanwhile, our cities continue to clog their highways with heavily subsidized traffic, beg Washington for money, and blame the whole mess on private enterprise.

This chapter was first written in 1969. A two thousand dollar savings in 1969 dollars comes to about six thousand 1989 dollars.

16

99 AND 44/100THS PERCENT BUILT

I have solved the problem of urban mass transit. To apply my solution to a major city requires a private company willing to invest a million dollars or so in hardware and a few million more in advertising and organization. The cost is low because my transit system is already over 99 percent built; its essence is the more efficient use of our present multibillion dollar investment in roads and automobiles. I call it jitney transit; it can most easily be thought of as something between taxicabs and hitch-hiking. Jitney stops, like present-day bus stops, would be arranged conveniently about the city. A commuter heading into town with an empty car would stop at the first jitney stop he came to and pick up any passengers going his way. He would proceed along his normal route, dropping off passengers when he passed their stops. Each passenger would pay a fee, according to an existing schedule listing the price between any pair of stops.

Would this be an efficient transportation system? Yes. Cars are inefficient only because they usually travel three-quarters empty; a full car is competitive with the usual forms of mass transport. Furthermore, cars already exist and are being driven hither and yon in great numbers; the additional cost of jitney transit is merely the cost of setting up the stops and arranging price schedules and the like.

Would commuters be willing to carry passengers? Given certain conditions, which I will deal with later, yes; the additional income from doing so would be far from trivial. Assume a charge of $2 a head. A commuter who regularly carried four passengers each way, five days a week, would make $4,000 a year—no mean sum. He would also convert his automobile, for tax purposes, into a business expense.

There are two difficulties with jitney transit. The first is safety;

the average driver is not eager to pick up strangers. This might be solved by technology. The firm setting up the jitney stops could issue magnetically coded identification cards to both drivers and potential passengers; in order to get such a card, the applicant would have to identify himself to the satisfaction of the company. Each stop would have a card-reading machine, with one slot for the driver and one for the passenger. As each inserted a valid card, a light visible to the other would go on. In a more sophisticated system, the machine could have access to a list of stolen or missing cards; insertion of a listed card would ring a bell in the local police station. The machine might even be able to record the pair of cards; if a driver or passenger were to disappear, the police would know just whom to look for. The cost of such security measures would be trivial compared to the cost of any of the current mass transit schemes. Four hundred jitney stops would blanket Chicago, with one every half mile in each direction. If the sign and the card reader cost $2,500 for each stop, the total cost would be a million dollars.

The other difficulty is political. Many large cities have regulations of one sort or another to control cabs and cab drivers; these would almost certainly prohibit jitney transit. Changes in such regulations would be opposed by bus drivers, cab drivers, and cab companies. Local politicians might be skeptical of the value of a mass transit system whose construction failed to siphon billions of dollars through their hands.

Jitneys are not, as it happens, a new idea. They are a common form of transportation in much of the world. In the U.S. they flourished briefly for a few years after World War I and were then legislated out of existence when the trolly-car companies found they could compete more successfully in the political than in the economic market. You will find the whole story in the article by Eckert and Hilton cited in Appendix II.

Many years ago, I found myself at an airport, en route to the center of the city. Being at the time an impecunious student, I started looking for someone going the same way with whom I could split the cost of a cab. I was stopped by the driver of a limousine who carried passengers into town for a price slightly below cab fare. He gleefully informed me that what I was doing was illegal. I have no doubt that he was right; out-of-town airline passengers, in that city or elsewhere, are not a powerful lobby.

Perhaps I am being too ambitious. Before investing any money, even a measly million dollars, in jitney transit, we might test more modest proposals. As a first step, how about providing airports with signs for the various parts of town; passengers could gather under the sign for their destination and arrange to share cabs.

Don't hold your breath.

17

A FIRST STEP

In the Washington circles where Great Ideas are conceived and circulated before being released upon an unsuspecting public, the idea of metropolitan area government has been circulating for several years. Most big city governments, unlike the governments of towns, villages, and small cities, have been doing a very bad job of providing their citizens with public services and doing it at a very high cost. The idea is that this problem could be solved by making these governments even bigger. New York, which with eight million people has proven virtually ungovernable, would, so this thesis holds, become as easy to govern as West Fairlee, Vermont, if it annexed its neighboring suburbs and expanded itself into a metropolitan monster of 15 to 20 million. This idea was originated by the same genius who discovered that poverty, which is declining, is the cause of crime, which is increasing.

I do not believe that if small governments are good and large governments bad, mammoth governments must be better. The proper lesson to be drawn is that our city governments are already far too large. Those who advocate decentralization as a solution to this problem usually mean administrative reorganization of the city governments. What is needed is decentralization of a more fundamental sort. Our cities should have elected subcity governments, complete with mini-mayors, controlling areas with populations of no more than 100,000. These governments should take over the provision of police protection, schooling, and many other governmental services.

Such governments are not, of course, too small to be practical; the great majority of the American population lives under local governments governing populations of fewer than 100,000—and the great majority of the American population gets better government services at lower cost than those of us who live in big cities. Some services, such as public transportation or city throughways, might best be handled by present city governments; if so, such services should be retained by them. Where the advantages of scale are less clear, in garbage collection, for example, the city government might offer subcities the option of leasing the service from the city.

This decentralization would strengthen local control of education, an objective shared by a wide range of well-meaning people, from black nationalists to anti-busing whites and from William F. Buckley to John Lindsay. Yet it need not prevent children from going to school anywhere they wish; children from one subcity could go to school in another, provided that their own subcity paid an appropriate per capita cost. Such a system is frequently used in rural areas, where some towns cannot afford their own school. Similar arrangements would make possible special schools, such as Bronx Science in New York, run either by the city or by one of the subcities.

Decentralization is equally important for the police force. A major complaint, especially in ghetto areas, is that the police do not protect the residents and are not there to protect the residents, that they are an occupying army sent by City Hall to protect the property of the rich and influential. Local police, hired and paid by local governments, would do their job or lose their jobs. And the job would be easier because the local residents would view police as their employees and protectors, not as their enemies.

There still remains the question of who should collect the taxes. One possibility is for the city to collect all taxes and allocate part of its receipts, on some simple basis, to subcities. Other alternatives would be for the subcities to collect their own taxes or, perhaps more efficiently, for the city to define the tax base and collect the taxes, while each subcity sets tax rates within its borders and receives taxes collected there. One subcity might offer a high level of government services, paid for by a high level of taxes, while another compensated for its low level of services with low taxes.

A radical proposal, if it is to have any immediate effect, must be politic as well as prudent. Decentralization of the cities is politic because city and county governments are creatures of the state government from which they receive their charters. State constitutions can be changed only by the voters of the state, not by

Congress. City charters, in contrast, can be changed only by the state legislature, or with its permission. It happens that most big cities are run by Democrats and located in states run by Republicans. Chicago is the most striking example; others include New York, Los Angeles, Cleveland, and Philadelphia. Under present institutions, a Democratic mayor who controls 60 percent of the votes in a large city controls all of the spending, all of the patronage, all of the power. If the city were broken up by act of the state government, those subcities where Republicans or independent Democrats had a majority would be out of the mayor's hands; even Democratic subcities would be one step further from his direct control. His power would go from 100 percent down to, perhaps, 70 percent, and his opponents would be able to build their own power bases within the subcities he did not control.

Decentralization, in addition to being desirable on its own merits, is also a means for stealing a big city out from under the feet of a Sam Yorty or John Lindsay. Ronald Reagan and Nelson Rockefeller, please note.

This chapter was written in 1969; readers should feel free to substitute current examples.

18

Counterattack

Every day brings news of intrusions by government into the rapidly contracting area reserved to private enterprise. To fans of the *Zeitgeist*, surfers on the wave of the future, the future of capitalism looks as bright as the future of the dodo. They are wrong. The counterattack is moving forward. Wherever there is a government monopoly, there is inefficiency, bad service, and an opportunity for profits. Capitalism is striking back.

The most publicized such monopoly is the Post Office. There the advancing forces of capitalism have forced the government monopoly, in spite of its massive federal subsidy, to take legal action to limit private competitors.

There exists a government monopoly bigger and more inefficient than the Post Office. It is a service industry run so inefficiently that customers frequently wait in line for years before receiving any attention and spend years more waiting for the government to finish a job that should require a week or two. It is not surprising that 80 to 90 percent of the customers give up, go home, and do the work themselves.

I refer, of course, to the service of arbitrating and enforcing private contracts. This service is now performed primarily by the civil courts. It could be performed better by private institutions. Sometimes it is.

Those who compete with the courts in this business are called arbitrators; the largest organization in the business is, I believe, the American Arbitration Association. Corporations, especially those operating internationally and therefore subject to the complications of international law, sign contracts in which they agree that any dispute over the meaning of the contract will be arbitrated by the AAA. Normally, such contracts cover matters where it is more important that a decision be immediate than what the decision is. If such a matter goes to court, both parties will forget what the disagreement was about long before the case is settled. Arbitration provides a faster and cheaper way of resolving such disputes.

Arbitration arrangements without some enforcement mechanism are a satisfactory substitute for the courts when the problem is merely an honest disagreement and the matter being settled is less important than continued good relations between the two parties. In other cases, arbitration may be unsatisfactory if the arbitrator, unlike the court, has no way of enforcing his decisions. If one party refuses to accept a decision, the other's only recourse is to go to court in the hope that the settlement, when it finally comes through, will be of some use to his grandchildren.

A large part of the potential business for arbitration involves contracts for which some enforcement mechanism is needed. An entrepreneur able to provide such enforceable arbitration should be able to make a great deal of money. Billions are spent now on buying the same service from the court system; a good private institution should be able to turn a substantial fraction of those billions into profits.

I can think of two ways in which such enforceable arbitration could be provided without involving the government court system. Both require that arbitration agencies, like present arbitrators, not only have a reputation for being no more corrupt than the courts, but go far beyond this, to the point of being known to be positively honest. There is evidence that corporations with such a reputation will develop if there is a market for them. Some years ago, for instance, American Express assumed someone else's debt, amounting to a substantial fraction of its profits for that year, although it had no legal responsibility to do so. American Express did so because it was arguable that American Express was morally responsible, and since the firm is in the business of producing money (which it does much better than the government, incidentally), its reputation for scrupulous honesty was worth more to the company than the cost of assuming the debt.

The first method of enforcement would be for the two contracting parties to turn over to the arbitration firm a sum equal to the maximum penalty provided for under the contract. The arbitration firm would have complete discretion to do what it wished with the money. In case of a breach of contract, it would allocate an appropriate amount of one firm's money to the other. When the contract expired, it would return the money, plus interest, to the contracting parties, after deducting a prearranged fee. There would be no court-enforced contract between the contracting firms and the arbitrator; there would thus be no legal bar to prevent the arbitration firm from keeping both deposits for itself—once.

The second form of enforcement is already in use, although not by arbitration firms. In its present form it is called a credit rating. Any firm which agreed to have a contract arbitrated and then refused to go along with the arbitration would be 'blacklisted' by the arbitration agency—forbidden to use its services again. Before two firms signed an arbitration agreement, each would first check with all the reputable arbitration agencies to make sure the other firm was not on such a blacklist, since there would be little point in signing an arbitration agreement with a firm that had reneged on such agreements in the past. Thus a blacklisted firm would be forced to make its contract enforceable in the courts instead of by arbitration. With the courts as bad as they now are, the un-availability of the arbitration mechanism would be a serious cost. Thus the threat of blacklisting would be an effective sanction to enforce compliance with arbitrated contracts.

Under such a system there would develop two sorts of firms, those that had virtually all their contracts arbitrated and had a reputation of always abiding by the arbitration and those that used court-enforced contracts instead. The first group would have an obvious competitive advantage. Honesty does pay.

Such free enterprise mechanisms need not be limited to civil cases involving explicit contracts. Many personal injury cases could be covered by arbitration agreements among insurance companies, as could other kinds of civil cases. To some extent this already happens; present insurance companies not only provide the service of pooling their customers' risks, but also provide, by negotiations among themselves aimed at settling out of court and thus avoiding legal costs, a partial substitute for the courts. This job could perhaps be done better by firms whose sole business was such arbitration.

A potential arbitrator has a multibillion dollar market now almost completely in the hands of a government monopoly selling low quality services at an exorbitant price. All you need to go into business is honesty, ingenuity, hard work, and luck.

19

Might have been

Since Apollo 11 opposition to the space program has come almost entirely from critics on the left, who argue that it consumes resources badly needed on Earth. Few of them made that objection to Sputnik. Perhaps they object, not to the space race, but to America winning it, just as many of them oppose, not our intervention in Vietnam, but our choice of sides.

Most conservatives seem now to have accepted, and even embraced, the space program and with it the idea that the exploration of space can only be achieved by government. That idea is false. If we had not been in such a hurry, we not only could have landed a man on the moon, we could have done it at a profit.

How? Perhaps as a television spectacular. The moon landing alone had an audience of 400 million. If pay TV were legal, that huge audience could have been charged several billion dollars for the series of shows leading up to, including, and following the landing. If the average viewer watched, altogether, twenty hours of Apollo programs, that would be about twenty-five cents an hour for the greatest show off earth.

After the landing everyone from Columbia Gas to Stouffers Foods tried to claim the credit. They could have been charged for the privilege. America's annual expenditure on advertising is about $20 billion. What company wouldn't give 10 percent of its advertising budget to be part of the biggest news story since the crucifixion?

The moon rocks, after being studied, could have been auctioned off. So could stamps cancelled on the moon. The astronauts could have staked out a modest territorial claim to everything within a hundred miles of the landing site and sold it. What would you pay for legal title to an acre of the moon? How about billboards on the moon—with a small freight and installation charge?

Is this an evil, commercialized vision that only a filthy capitalist utterly debased by greed could approve? The alternative was to use the state's taxing power to take an average of $500 from every family in the country, willing or unwilling—at the point of a metaphorical gun. Is that better than selling the commercial values of the program to willing customers? Greedy capitalists get money by trade. Good liberals steal it.

A greedy capitalist could have sold the moon landing in 1969 for something over $5 billion. The government spent $24 billion to get to the moon. It costs any government at least twice as much to do anything as it costs anyone else. It would have cost something under $12 billion to produce the Apollo program privately.

But Apollo was a crash program. If we had been in less of a hurry, it would have cost far less. While we were waiting, economic growth would increase the 'price' of the moon and technological progress would cut the cost of getting there. We would have arrived, at a profit, sometime in the seventies.

The American flag, on the moon or anywhere else, is worthless except as a symbol, a symbol of men achieving their ends by voluntary association, cooperating through mutual exchange in a free society. Capitalism. It is in no way honored by spending billions of dollars of tax monies to put a piece of painted metal on the moon.

POSTSCRIPT: **Friedman's law**

Skeptical readers may want evidence for my claim that it costs any government twice as much as it should to do anything. A domestic example is the Post Office; private postal companies make a profit delivering third-class mail at half what the Post Office charges to deliver it a loss. A foreign example is Russia's government-run economy, which invests twice as much of its GNP as we did at a comparable period in our development to achieve the same growth rate. Japan invests privately at the same rate as Russia and gets twice Russia's growth rate.

When this was written, the idea of a private enterprise space program was the sort of thing that only science-fiction writers and very far-out libertarians took seriously. Currently, it is the official policy of the incumbent administration.

20

Is WILLIAM F. BUCKLEY

A CONTAGIOUS DISEASE?

The federal government should pass laws based on the emergency powers taken by the state in plague situations. . . .

WILLIAM F. BUCKLEY, THE UNMAKING OF A MAYOR

What noted conservative advocates jailing people to prevent the spread of their ideas? Would you believe William F. Buckley?

It is Buckley. The issue on which he takes this position is narcotics addiction. He does not state it in these terms, of course. He says, rather, that "narcotics is a contagious disease," whose spread is to be prevented by "quarantining all addicts, even as smallpox carriers would be quarantined during a plague," in other words, by incarcerating addicts to prevent them from addicting others.

He calls narcotics addiction a contagious disease because most addicts acquire the habit from other addicts. This analogy denies free will. Catching a disease requires no cooperation on the part of the victim; he associates with someone who has the disease and gets sick, whether he wants to or not. A 'Typhoid Mary' is quarantined to prevent her from infecting unwilling victims. Narcotics addiction is not, in this sense, infectious. The victim must choose to take the drug. Mr. Buckley, associating with a dozen addicts, would be in no danger of addiction.

Someone who becomes addicted by associating with other addicts has not been forcibly infected. He has seen a behavior pattern and chosen to adopt it. He may do so, as Mr. Buckley says, because he is "psychologically weak or misinformed." Such possibilities exist for any decision—getting married or subscribing to *National Review*. The choice is up to him. His decision, like any act of free will, may be wrong. It is not involuntary. It is conversion or persuasion, not infection. Narcotics addiction is a contagious disease only in the same sense as conservatism and Catholicism. Like narcotics addiction, both are patterns of belief and action which many people regard as harmful to both the 'addict' and his society. Like narcotics addiction, both are spread by the already infected. Mr. Buckley is a carrier of one and perhaps both; to his credit, he has infected many. Does he oppose the incarceration of conservatives and Catholics only because he agrees with their views? Would he favor jailing Galbraith, Bundy, and several Rockefellers as carriers of liberalism, a disease which has done far more damage than drug addiction?

The answer is no. The position Mr. Buckley takes on narcotics addiction is inconsistent with his belief in a free society. Even on the issue of internal communism, where he is most frequently charged by the left with authoritarian views, he justifies internal security laws on the grounds that Communists are trying to impose their system, by force, upon the rest of us. Narcotics addicts are not. He wants to imprison them for acting and persuading others to act in a way injurious mostly to themselves.

Mr. Buckley might not concede that addiction damages mostly the addict; he quotes Mayor Wagner as estimating "the cost to the community in crime, treatment, and added police protection" at a billion dollars a year. If true, this comes to about $20,000 per addict; the city could save money by hiring a policeman to accompany every addict at all times. Whether true or not, it is irrelevant. This is the cost, not of addiction, but of laws prohibiting narcotics. Addicts commit virtually no crimes while actually high on narcotics; they have neither the will nor, usually, the ability. They steal to pay for the next fix. If legal, narcotics would cost a small fraction of their present price, and few addicts would have to engage in large-scale crime to pay the costs, just as few alcoholics do.

Mr. Buckley's answer: "It is not feasible to dispose of the social problem by making drugs generally available under doctor's prescription. A typical addict always desires more of the drug than a responsible doctor, concerned with the addict's physical health, is willing to give him." This assumes that it is the business of the doctor to impose his judgment on the addict. Certainly the doctor should warn the addict of the effect of overlarge doses. If, knowing this, the addict is willing to trade his health or his life for a few years, or months, or minutes of drug-induced ecstasy, that is his affair. Part of freedom is the right of each of us to go to hell in his own fashion.

It sounds brutal to say that an addict should be allowed to kill himself with drugs. Consider the alternative to which Mr. Buckley is driven. Out of a benevolent regard for the addict's health, we limit his consumption of drugs. Because of his desire for more drugs, the addict becomes a danger to us, his benevolent protectors. So we put him in jail and, so far as I can tell from Mr. Buckley's statements, throw away the key. After all, as Mr. Buckley says, "It is practically impossible to 'cure' a narcotics addict who does not desire to be cured."

Mr. Buckley should re-examine his premises when he finds himself casually talking about the difficulty of curing people of things they do not want to be cured of. He has allowed an incorrect analogy to lead him to an intolerable position.

Those who have stumbled into physiological addiction and wish to be cured deserve our sympathy and our charity. Those addicts who do not wish to be cured should be left alone.

This chapter was originally printed as an article in *The New Guard* in April 1969. Buckley replied in the Summer 1969 issue of the same magazine. I rerebutted briefly in the October 1969 issue.

In his syndicated column of March 1985, Buckley announced that he had changed his mind and now favored legalizing heroin and cocaine, a step which "shrewd observers" had "recommended . . . for years". Buckley makes it clear that he still doesn't see anything wrong in principle with government regulation of private moral behavior. He supports legalization because he thinks the government can never win the war on drugs, while prohibition greatly increases violent crime.

21

It's my life

Ninety-five percent of anything is crap.

STURGEON'S LAW

You cannot buy certified raw milk in Illinois. Raw milk is milk that has not been pasteurized; certified raw milk is raw milk produced under such scrupulously sanitary conditions that its bacteria count is *lower* than that of pasteurized milk. Heating milk to pasteurize it denatures the protein and destroys some vitamins and enzymes; some nutritionists argue that pasteurization drastically lowers milk's nutritional value and that raw milk, provided it is sanitary, is much superior to pasteurized milk. It is also, in Illinois, illegal.

There are a number of chemicals that some nutritionists believe are necessary to nutrition in much the same way that recognized vitamins are necessary. Choline and inositol, for instance, are thought to be involved in metabolizing cholesterol, and thus protecting against hardening of the arteries and heart attacks.

According to the label on my bottle of choline, "the need for choline in human nutrition has not been established." According to the label on my bottle of inositol, "the need for inositol in human nutrition has not been established." I doubt that the manufacturer regards this as good advertising, especially since the labels contain no balancing statement about the evidence that choline and inositol may be useful to human nutrition. Uniform labeling is a federal requirement. It is apparently illegal for the producers to tell me why they think their product is worth buying.

Both federal regulation of labeling and state laws against raw milk are government interventions in an ongoing controversy between two groups of experts—nutritionists and doctors. The nutritionists argue that many apparently medical problems are at least partly caused by inadequate nutrition; the doctors argue that, with a few well-understood exceptions, a proper diet, without any special health foods or vitamin supplements, provides adequate nutrition. The argument is long and involved; to those who wish to examine the nutritionists' side, I recommend *Food Facts and Fallacies* by Carlton Fredericks and Herbert Bailey. My own opinion, based on a very limited examination of the literature, is that the nutritionists have a case. The accepted lists of 'minimum daily requirements' are overly conservative in both number of nutrients listed and amounts suggested. Some of the additional nutrients may turn out, in the long run, to be worthless, but taking them is worth the gamble.

Why do many doctors and their official representative, the AMA, take the opposite position? Partly, perhaps, from economic self-interest; the nutritionists, after all, are competing with them in the business of making people well. But more, I suspect, because the doctors, having been trained in one way of making people healthy, are suspicious of any others and regard the nutritionists as incompetent practitioners of medicine, quacks.

Some of them are. Any health food store with a bookrack will yield a colorful collection of tracts on how to live to one hundred on yogurt and bulgar wheat. The health food business is not exempt from Sturgeon's law. Neither is the doctor business nor the regulation business. No bureaucrat is eager to offend a powerful and respected interest group. Regulation is naturally biased in favor of the ins against the outs, the orthodox against the radical—in this case, the doctors and the AMA against the nutritionists. The orthodox side is able to give its position the force of law, to forbid manufacturers from stating arguments that the government, and the AMA, do not accept, or to forbid individual consumers from buying a product that in their judgment isn't good for them.

This is a bias, not for doctors and against manufacturers, or for experts and against the uninformed, but simply for old against new. The Food and Drug Administration (FDA) does not keep the food industry from labeling its breads and flours as 'enriched', even if, as many argue, more has been taken out than put back. The food industry is an established, respectable interest. It is only people with new and unpopular ideas who are likely to be labeled quacks or crackpots and treated accordingly.

The same problem occurs in government regulation of pharmaceuticals. Here the FDA does not limit itself to censoring labels; it has the power to give or withhold permission to market 'dangerous drugs'. Almost everyone approves of this power. The danger of an irresponsible producer releasing a new product prematurely, only to discover tragic side effects, is obvious. What is more natural than to have the government prevent such lethal gambles by keeping new drugs off the market until they are proven harmless? Why not play safe?

But there is no way to play safe. If a useful new drug is kept off the market, people who might be saved if the drug were available will die. Caution kills. Whom it kills may not be obvious; often the new drug is only an improvement on an old one, an improvement which might raise a cure rate from 80 percent to 85 percent. Which men and women and children make up the 5 percent killed by caution no one can ever know; their deaths are statistics, not headlines. A statistical corpse is just as real as a thalidomide baby on the front page; it is just less visible.

Visibility is an important element in politics and the FDA is a political institution. Given a choice between one tragedy on the front page and ten in the medical statistics, it inevitably prefers the latter. It thus has a strong bias in favor of overregulating, of stifling medical progress in the name of caution.

Drug companies have some of the same bias. Corpses on the front page are bad advertising. Damage suits can be expensive. But drug companies are also in the business of selling drugs to people who very much want to live; a new and improved product is a new source of income. The drug companies are, to some degree, in a position to balance the risk of tragedy against the value of a better chance at life—to people who want to live it.

My own conclusion—that drug companies should be free to sell, and their customers to buy, anything, subject to liability for damages caused by misrepresentation—must seem monstrous to many people. Certainly it means accepting the near certainty of a few people a year dying from unexpected side effects of new drugs.

I believe the cost of our present policy, although less visible, is even higher. How high I cannot tell. I know that at least one doctor associated with the development of cortisone believes it would not now be available if the FDA had at that time enforced as stringent safety standards as it does now. The same has been said—upon how much evidence I do not know—of penicillin. There will doubtless be people who gamble their lives on the use of new and unsafe drugs and lose. Against that we must set the lives of the millions who would be dead today if we had 'played safe' 50 years ago.

(The argument of this chapter received striking support in 1981, when the FDA published a press release confessing to mass murder. That was not, of course, the way in which the release was worded; it was simply an announcement that the FDA had approved the use of timolol, a ß-blocker, to prevent recurrences of heart attacks.

At the time timolol was approved, ß-blockers had been widely used outside the U.S. for over ten years. It was estimated that the use of timolol would save from seven thousand to ten thousand lives a year in the U.S. So the FDA, by forbidding the use of ß-blockers before 1981, was responsible for something close to a hundred thousand unnecessary deaths.)

22

THE RIGHTS OF YOUTH

A child, about ten years old, ran away from home. When found by the police several months later, he was well fed, had money in his pocket, had a place to stay, and was known and liked by his neighbors. Since his own home was unsuitable, he was put in an orphanage. He faked a suicide attempt in order to get out and was sent to a mental hospital. The doctors found him completely sane but were reluctant to return him to the orphanage, both because he obviously disliked it and because he was a good influence on the other patients. As far as I know, he is still in the hospital.

What rights should parents or, in their default, other adults, have over children? Philosophically, this involves the difficult problem of when a baby becomes, in some sense, a human being. Practically, I think that there is a simple solution. Any child above some very low age (say, nine years old) who is willing to arrange for his own support should be free from the authority of his parents. For the first year of his freedom, the child would retain the option of returning to his family; during this period he might be required to visit the family and reaffirm his decision several times. After he had supported himself for a year, his parents would no longer be obligated to take him back.

A child might support himself by his own efforts or by being adopted by another set of parents. In the latter case, the new parents would assume the obligations of support previously held by the natural parents. Persons wishing to help children and to protect them against unsuitable parents or other dangers could arrange suitable adoptions or set up free orphanages whose inmates would come by choice, not force.

Children often run away from home, and ten-year-olds who can support themselves are rare, but the normal young runaway is unlikely to stay away more than a few days. A child of that age whose situation is sufficiently desperate to make him run away from home and stay away may be better off doing so.

Teenagers present a more serious problem. Many run away and stay away for considerable periods. The decision to run away is doubtless a mistake in many cases. But do our present laws, which in theory make it possible for the parents to have the police haul the runaway home, achieve any useful purpose? Short of physical incarceration, there is no way to keep a child from running away again. The main effect of these laws, I believe, is to force runaways into hiding and thus to force them to associate with people who are themselves hostile to the laws and values of the society.

Some readers will object that what children need is not more freedom but more authority. This is a false dichotomy. Children in our society frequently suffer from a lack of parental authority, but it is not a kind of authority that can be provided by law.

Another story comes to mind, concerning a family whose adopted daughter was subject to almost no discipline and was, perhaps in consequence, very badly behaved. On one occasion the girl's aunt told her, at great length, what she thought of her behavior. Several days later the family had dinner at the aunt's house. The girl behaved with uncharacteristic politeness. After dinner she went up to the (adopted) aunt and asked if she could live with her.

It must be terrible to be brought up in a moral vacuum. It is no wonder that the girl preferred to live with someone who showed, by her very willingness to criticize, that she believed in some values that made criticism possible. It is this sort of authority that our generation needs. For those who lack it, the policeman's club is no substitute.

But reality has its own discipline. The alternative to parental authority is and should be freedom—in a world where those who do not work sometimes do not eat. That, too, is a sort of moral authority. Experiencing the real world directly—learning to survive in it—is not as pleasant a way of growing up as being taught about it by one's parents. But if the parents are unwilling or unable to do the job, it may be the best substitute available.

23

CREEPING CAPITALISM

One of the effective tactics of creeping socialism, especially in America, has been the annexation of words with favorable connotations. The best example is the word 'liberal'. In the nineteenth century, a liberal supported laissez-faire economic policy, free trade, broadly based democracy, and civil liberties. The word had strong positive connotations; even today, while 'conservative' is sometimes used favorably, 'illiberal' is always pejorative. The socialists opposed liberal economic policies. The more successful socialists, instead of saying that liberalism was bad and socialism good, called themselves liberals (or progressives, another 'good' word) and their opponents conservatives.

Nobody, except a few Brahmins in Delhi and two or three Trotskyites in New York, still believes that the earthly paradise can be achieved by nationalizing General Motors and turning the corner grocery store over to the Mayor's office. Socialism, as a coherent ideology, is dead and is not likely to be revived by student rebels in Paris or Soviet tanks in Prague. Yet many people, including the late reformers in Prague, call themselves socialists. 'Socialism' has become a word with positive connotations and no content.

Shortly after the Soviet invasion of Czechoslovakia, I spent an evening with two Czech economics students. They saw the aim of the Czech reforms as the creation of a society combining the best elements of socialism and capitalism. One of the elements of capitalism they especially liked was that bad workers did not get the same pay as good workers. Whatever socialism meant to them did not include 'from each according to his ability, to each according to his need'. They wished to preserve government health care and some other welfare measures, but these were not what they meant by socialism. To them, socialism meant a just society, a society where people were reasonably prosperous and reasonably free; it meant roughly what we mean by a liberal society.

This, I think, is what socialism means to much of the world. If so, socialism need not be opposed—merely improved. Any change that makes a socialist society better makes it, by definition, more socialist. If people are convinced that state ownership and control do not work, as the Eastern Europeans by bitter experience are, then the changes that will make their society 'more socialist' are changes such as the transfer of ownership and control from the state to workers' cooperatives and, at a later stage, from workers' cooperatives to the workers themselves.

The complete destruction of socialist institutions in the name of socialism is practical only if creeping capitalism tends to force itself to its logical conclusion. Otherwise socialists might move to some mixed economy, intermediate between capitalism and socialism, such as the present American economy, and stay there. As a libertarian, a liberal in the old sense, I would consider this unfortunate.

Evidence that capitalism creeps is seen in Yugoslavia. Yugoslavian workers' cooperatives, which, in effect, own factories as corporations own them here, must get capital for investment from either their own profits or the government. Some cooperatives that could get large returns from capital investments do not have enough profits to finance them, and others have large profits which they would be willing to invest for a reasonable return, but do not need additional capital in their own operations. The obvious solution, as many Yugoslav economists realize, is to allow cooperatives to make loans to each other and charge interest.

A worker cannot sell his share of his cooperative (which entitles him to a share of the profits), and he loses it on retirement. So the workers who control the cooperative have no incentive to make investments whose return will come after they retire. The solution is to make the share transferable, like a share of stock. Its market value would then depend on the expected future earnings of the cooperative. A long-term investment would lower the worker's dividends but raise the value of his share. This reform, when and if it is made, will constitute a further step in the effective conversion of Yugoslavia to a capitalist society.

In describing the objective of the Czechoslovakian reforms, my Czech friends said that in the system the reformers wanted most products would be controlled by the price system, but prices of necessities, such as milk and bread, would be fixed by the government. I argued that if the price system was better for other things, it was even more important to use it for necessities. Their English was not very good, so there may have been some confusion at this point. What I think one of them said was "Yes. That's what our teachers say too."

Your property is that which you control the use of. If most things are controlled by individuals, individually or in voluntary association, a society is capitalist. If such control is spread fairly evenly among a large number of people, the society approximates competitive free enterprise—better than ours does. If its members call it socialist, why should I object?

Socialism is dead. Long live socialism.

24

IF YOU WANT IT, BUY IT

As the previous chapter suggests, there could exist a society which some socialists would call socialist but which I would regard as both capitalist and free. Such a society would be produced by combining the 'socialist' principle of worker control with radical decentralization and the market structure that such decentralization necessitates. There would be no central authority able to impose its will on the individual economic units. Coordination would be by exchange, trade, by a market. Instead of firms, the normal form of organization would be workers' cooperatives controlled by their workers.

As long as individuals are free to own property, produce, buy, and sell as they wish, the fact that most people choose to organize themselves into workers' cooperatives is no more a limitation on the society's freedom than is the fact that people in this country presently organize themselves into firms. It would, doubtless, be inconvenient for those who wanted things arranged differently— aspiring capitalists, for instance, who could find no work force because all the workers preferred to work for themselves. In exactly the same way, our present society is inconvenient for a socialist who wants to set up a factory as a workers' cooperative but cannot find anyone to provide the factory. The right to trade only applies to a situation where the exchange is voluntary—on both sides.

I would have no objection to such a socialist society, beyond the opinion that its members were not acting in what I thought was their best interest. The socialists who advocate such institutions do object to our present society and would probably object even more to the completely capitalist society that I would like to see develop. They claim that the ownership of the means of production by capitalists instead of by workers is inherently unjust.

I think they are wrong. Even if they are right, there is no need for them to fight me or anyone else; there is a much easier way to achieve their objective. If a society in which firms are owned by their workers is far more attractive than one in which they are owned by stockholders, let the workers buy the firms. If the workers cannot be convinced to spend their money, it is unlikely that they will be willing to spend their blood.

How much would it cost workers to purchase their firms? The total value of the shares of all stocks listed on the New York Stock Exchange in 1965 was $537 billion. The total wages and salaries of all private employees that year was $288.5 billion. State and federal income taxes totalled $75.2 billion. If the workers had chosen to live at the consumption standard of hippies, saving half their after-tax incomes, they could have gotten a majority share in every firm in two and a half years and bought the capitalists out, lock, stock, and barrel, in five. That is a substantial cost, but surely it is cheaper than organizing a revolution. Also less of a gamble. And, unlike a revolution, it does not have to be done all at once. The employees of one firm can buy it this decade, then use their profits to help fellow workers buy theirs later.

When you buy stock, you pay not only for the capital assets of the firm—buildings, machines, inventory, and the like—but also for its experience, reputation, and organization. If workers really can run firms better, these are unnecessary; all they need are the physical assets. Those assets—the net working capital of all corporations in the United States in 1965—totalled $171.7 billion. The workers could buy that much and go into business for themselves with 14 months' worth of savings.

I do not expect any of this to happen. If workers wanted to be capitalists badly enough to pay that sort of price, many would have done so already. There are a few firms in which a large fraction of the stock is owned by the workers—Sears is the most prominent—but not many.

Nor is there any good reason why workers should want to be capitalists. Capitalism is a very productive system, but not very much of that product goes to the capitalists. In that same year of 1965 total compensation of all employees (public and private) was $391.9 billion, almost ten times the $44.5 billion that was the total profit after taxes of all corporations. ("After tax" is after corporate tax; the stockholders still have to pay income or capital gains taxes on those profits before they can spend them, just as the workers must pay income tax on their salaries.)

25

Scarce means finite

America: the land of the free.
Free means you don't pay, doesn't it?

ABBIE HOFFMAN, *REVOLUTION FOR THE HELL OF IT*

Hoffman and others like him argue that the institutions of property, public or private, are obsolete and should be abolished. They claim that an increasingly automated economy can make all goods plentiful, so that property is no longer necessary, and that it now prevents us from producing all we could—that people might starve in a society with unlimited food. There are several things wrong with this argument.

Many countries have access to modern technology and the resources needed to build automated factories of the sort imagined by believers in the cybernetic cornucopia. These countries have widely differing social, economic, and political systems. Yet we are the richest of the lot, and none of the others shows the sort of growth (say, 30 percent per year in per capita income) necessary to produce a revolutionary change (say, one-tenth of the workers producing 15 times the current GNP) by the year 2000.

Even if productivity does increase enormously, the argument assumes that total demand is limited; otherwise increases in productivity will be met by increases in demand, as in the past, and the conflict between different people who want the same resources will still exist.

Believers in such a saturation of demand argue that above some income (usually about twice their own) consumption ceases to be useful and becomes pure show, so that when production reaches this level, there need be no more scarce goods. This argument confuses amount of consumption with the physical quantity consumed. There is a limit to the amount of food I can eat or the number of cars I can conveniently use. There is no obvious limit to the resources that can be usefully employed in producing a better car or better food. For $10,000 a car can be made better than for $5,000; for $20,000, better than for $10,000. If the median income rises to $100,000 a year, we shall have no difficulty spending it.

The argument also confuses the technical economic meaning of 'scarce resources' with the conventional meaning of 'scarce'. Even if no one is hungry, food is still scarce, since some cost must be incurred in order for me to have more or better food. Either someone has to give up food or someone must pay the cost of producing more. The opposite of a scarce good is not a plentiful good but a free good, something available in sufficient supply for everyone at no cost. Air was a free good until demand, for breathing and for carrying off industrial wastes, exceeded supply.

A more relevant case might be book matches or sanitary drinking water, both of which must be produced, but whose cost is so low that it hardly seems worth the trouble of charging the individual user for them. They are therefore given away free, in loose conjunction with the sale of more expensive goods. No one has to pay to use a drinking fountain.

If Hoffman is right and automation produces a median income of $1 million a year, no one will bother to charge for food. Food machines will be provided as a free amenity for the convenience of potential customers at the stores where whatever goods are worth selling (art? entertainment? spaceships?) are sold, or they will be set up on street corners to commemorate dead spouses, just as water fountains are now. If medicine became automated and cheap, profit-grubbing capitalists would build free hospitals and make money renting out the interior walls as billboard space.

The problem of plenty is not a new one for capitalism. It has dealt with that problem by providing more and better ways to use larger and larger incomes—so successfully that Abbie Hoffman hardly realizes how rich we already are by the standards of previous centuries. Capitalism will continue to deal with the 'problem' of plenty in the same way. It's only fair: capitalism created the problem.

26

Pollution

The pollution problem exists because certain things, such as the air or the ocean, are not property. Anyone who wishes to use them as garbage dumps is free to do so. If the pollution were done to something that belonged to someone, the owner would permit it only if the pollutor were willing to pay him more than the damage done. If the pollutors themselves owned the property they were polluting, it would pay them to stop if the damage they did were greater than the cost of avoiding it; few of us want to dump our garbage on our own front lawns.

If all the things polluted were private property, pollution still would not stop entirely. Nor should it; the only way to completely stop producing pollution is for all of us to drop dead, and even that would create at least a short-run pollution problem. The proper objective in controlling pollution is to make sure that it occurs if, and only if, the damage it does is less than the cost of avoiding it.

The ideal solution is to convert unowned resources into property. One could, for instance, adopt the principle that people living along a river have a property right in the river itself and that anyone who lowers the value of the river to them by polluting it, without first getting their consent, is liable to suit. Similar rules already exist in water-poor areas to define the rights of landholders to use up, in irrigation, rivers that run through their land.

Some things, such as air, are extraordinarily difficult to deal with in this way. Consider the consequence of absolute property rights by each landholder to the air above his land. If I smoke a cigarette, some tiny amount of the smoke will eventually spread very far. Does that mean I cannot smoke without first getting permission from everyone on the continent?

The simplest solution to such a paradox is to permit parties injured by air pollution to sue for damages—presumably in class actions, by many victims against many pollutors. I would not be able to shut down your blast furnace merely by proving that a sufficiently sensitive instrument could occasionally detect sulfur dioxide in my air. But, if the concentration were high enough to be offensive, I could sue you for the damage done.

At present, pollution is 'controlled' by governments. The governments—federal, state, or local—decide who has enough pull to have his pollution considered necessary. This reduces control to a multitude of separate cases and makes it almost impossible for the victims of pollution to tell what is really going on or to impose effective political pressure.

If pollution control is to be handled by government, it should be done in a much simpler way. Let the government set a price, per cubic foot of each pollutant, for polluting. Such a price might vary according to where the pollution is created; air pollution in Manhattan presumably does more damage than in the Mojave desert. Every pollutor, from the United States Steel Corporation down to the individual motorist, would have to pay. If the cost of avoiding pollution is really high, the firm will continue to pollute—and pay for it. Otherwise, it will stop. If the voters think there is still too much pollution, they can vote to raise the price; it is a relatively simple issue.

Of course, the government claims that its present decisions are based on how 'avoidable' the pollution is. But every pollutor wants to keep polluting, as long as it does not cost him anything. Every pollutor will claim that his pollution is unavoidable. Who gets away with it depends not on real costs but on politics. If pollutors must pay for their pollution, however avoidable or unavoidable, we will rapidly find out which ones can or cannot stop polluting.

27

BUCKSHOT FOR A SOCIALIST FRIEND

A man that'd expict to thrain lobsters to fly in a year is called a
lunatic; but a man that thinks men can be tu-rrned into angels by
an iliction is called a rayformer and remains at large.

MR. DOOLEY

You object that even if private property institutions work perfectly,
they are still unfair. Each consumer, by spending a dollar on the
goods he wants, 'votes' for the production of those goods. Incomes
are unequal, reflecting (if nothing else) unequal abilities, so some
people have more votes than others. The ideal democratic socialist
society, on the other hand, allocates resources democratically, each
person having one vote. It is therefore superior to the ideal capitalist
society.

The analogy between spending and voting, although frequently used by defenders of capitalism, is imperfect. Equality
aside, spending is a much superior—paradoxically, a much more
egalitarian—way of allocating resources. This is because a dollar,
once spent, cannot be spent again, leaving you less to spend on
something else. Your vote can be used over and over.

Contrast the relationship between two men, one having an
income of $10,000 a year and one of $5,000, with the relationship
between two men, one part of a political faction with ten votes, one
part of a faction with five.

Bidding for necessities, the richer man outbids the poorer; if
there were only enough food on the market for one man, it would
be the poorer who would starve. But when the richer man is
bidding for luxuries and the poorer man for necessities, the poorer
man wins. Suppose the richer man, having bought enough flour to
make bread for himself, wishes to buy the rest of the flour on the
market to make papier-mâché for his children's Halloween masks.

The poorer man still does not have anything to eat; he is willing to use as much of his income as necessary to bid for the flour. He gets the flour, and at much less than $5,000. The richer man already has used half his income buying flour for bread (since there too, he was bidding against the poor). His remaining income is barely equal to that of the poorer man, and he certainly is not going to spend all of it, or even a substantial fraction, for Halloween masks.

Now consider the same situation with votes. The man with the larger faction votes to have the flour given to him (and his allies) for bread. Then he votes to have the remaining flour given to them for making papier-mâché. He wins both times, ten to five. Since voting is much more of an all-or-nothing thing than spending, such inequalities as do exist have much greater effects. This may explain why in our society, where the poor are also politically weak, they do far worse on things provided by the government, such as schooling and police protection, than on those sold privately, such as food and clothes.

Political institutions, such as congressional 'log rolling', have developed to mitigate the all-or-nothing features of voting. A congressman indicates how important his bill is to his constituents by how many votes on other bills he is willing to trade for support on his. This is an extremely crude and approximate substitute for the market—an attempt to represent, by bargaining among a few hundred men on a few thousand issues, the multitudinous diversity of two hundred million lives.

Could political institutions be created that would completely solve this problem? That question was investigated at considerable length by Ludwig von Mises in the 1920s; his arguments are in *Socialism: An Economic and Sociological Analysis* and, in a popularized form, in Henry Hazlitt's 'novel' *Time Will Run Back*. The answer is no. By the time a democratic socialist has modified socialism sufficiently to make its political control mechanisms as accurate and sensitive as the economic control mechanisms of capitalism, he has reinvented capitalism. As the Yugoslavs have discovered.

II

You concede everything I say about the corruption of regulatory agencies into servants of the special interests they regulate and about the redistribution by government from poor to rich. I regard that as evidence against the institution of public property. You regard it as evidence against the institution of private property. You argue that it is the inequality of income, power, and status in this private-property society that corrupts the elements of public property within it. It is only because some are richer than others that they have the power to make government steal from those others for their benefit.

But stealing from the poor to benefit the not poor is by no means the only stealing the government does. Consider the CAB. By fixing airline fares well above their market price, it benefits the airlines, which is to say their stockholders and employees, at the expense of airline passengers. By preventing the formation of new airlines, it benefits stockholders of existing firms at the cost of the potential stockholders, customers, and employees of the new airlines that might have been formed.

Airline passengers are not poor. Some are doubtless richer than the average stockholder of an airline, and many are richer than the average airline employee. How is it that they find themselves on the wrong end of a government transfer? The answer can best be understood in terms of what economists call externalities. An externality is an effect of my actions which benefits or harms someone whom I cannot charge for the benefit or need not recompense for the loss. If, for instance, I burn leaves on my lawn and the smoke bothers my neighbors, I am imposing a cost on them which they cannot force me to pay for. I may burn the leaves, even though the real cost of doing so, including my neighbors' watering eyes, is larger than the cost of having them hauled away. This, as the opponents of capitalism correctly argue, is an imperfection in the functioning of a capitalist economy.

Externalities play an enormously greater role in institutions controlled by voting. If I invest time and energy in discovering which candidate will make the best President, the benefit of that investment, if any, is spread evenly among 200 million people. That is an externality of 99.9999995 percent. Unless it is obvious how I should vote, it is not worth the time and trouble to vote 'intelligently', except on issues where I get a disproportionately large fraction of the benefit. Situations, in other words, where I am part of a special interest.

Consider the CAB again. In order for me, an occasional airline passenger, to do anything about it, I would have to keep track of how every member of the board voted, by whom he was appointed, and how my congressmen voted on every bill connected with airline regulation. Having done so, the chance that my vote or any pressure I might try to bring on my congressmen or the president would alter the situation is one in millions. And if I am successful, all I get is a savings of a hundred dollars or so a year in lower air fares. It isn't worth it. For the airline industry the same research, backed by enormously larger resources in votes and money, brings a return of many millions of dollars. For them it is worth it. It is not that they are richer than all airline passengers combined; they are not. But they are concentrated and we are dispersed.

Special interest politics is a simple game. A hundred people sit in a circle, each with his pocket full of pennies. A politician walks around the outside of the circle, taking a penny from each person. No one minds; who cares about a penny? When he has gotten all the way around the circle, the politician throws fifty cents down in front of one person, who is overjoyed at the unexpected windfall. The process is repeated, ending with a different person. After a hundred rounds everyone is a hundred cents poorer, fifty cents richer, and happy.

III

You object that capitalism works too well, that more efficient means of production drive out less efficient, leaving everyone with sterile and repetitive jobs in a soul-killing environment.

More efficient means of production do drive out less efficient means, but your definition of efficiency is too narrow. If under one arrangement a worker produces a dollar an hour more than under another, but the conditions are so much worse that he will gladly accept a wage of two dollars an hour less to work under the other, which is more efficient? For both the employer, who saves more on wages than he loses on production, and for the worker, the 'less productive' arrangement is the more efficient. The efficiency of capitalism takes account of nonmonetary as well as monetary costs and products.

IV

In the ideal socialist state power will not attract power freaks. People who make decisions will show no slightest bias toward their own interests. There will be no way for a clever man to bend the institutions to serve his own ends. And the rivers will run uphill.

PART III

ANARCHY IS NOT CHAOS

Anarchy, n. 4. a theory which regards the union of order with
the absence of all direct or coercive government as the political
ideal. 5. confusion in general; disorder.

THE AMERICAN COLLEGE DICTIONARY

Government produces all order.
Under anarchy there is no government.
Therefore anarchy is chaos.
Q.E.D.

In Washington there isn't any plan
With "feeding David" on page sixty-four;
It must be accidental that the milk man
Leaves a bottle at my door.

It must be accidental that the butcher
Has carcasses arriving at his shop
The very place where, when I need some
    meat,
I accidentally stop.

My life is chaos turned miraculous;
I speak a word and people understand
Although it must be gibberish since words
Are not produced by governmental plan.

Now law and order, on the other hand
The state provides us for the public good;
That's why there's instant justice on demand
And safety in every neighborhood.

28

WHAT IS ANARCHY? WHAT IS GOVERNMENT?

Is government, then, useful and necessary? So is a doctor. But suppose the dear fellow claimed the right, every time he was called in to prescribe for a bellyache or a ringing in the ears, to raid the family silver, use the family toothbrushes, and execute the *droit de seigneur* upon the housemaid?

H. L. MENCKEN

anarchism: 1. the theory that all forms of government are undesirable.
WEBSTER'S NEW WORLD DICTIONARY
OF THE AMERICAN LANGUAGE

In Part 1, I described myself as an anarchist and asserted that government has no legitimate functions. In this part I shall attempt to justify that statement. Conceivably I could do so by listing all the things the government does and explaining why each either should not be done or could be done better by private individuals cooperating voluntarily. Unfortunately, paper and ink are scarce resources; the list alone would fill this book. Instead, I will discuss in the next few chapters how private arrangements could take over the most fundamental government functions—police, courts, and national defense. When I finish, some readers will object that the institutions that provide these 'governmental' functions are by definition governments, that I am therefore not an anarchist at all. I merely want a different kind of government.

They will be wrong. An anarchist is not, except in the propaganda of his enemies, one who desires chaos. Anarchists, like other people, wish to be protected from thieves and murderers. They wish to have some peaceful way of settling disagreements.

They wish, perhaps even more than other people, to be able to protect themselves from foreign invasion. What, after all, is the point of abolishing your own government if it is immediately replaced by someone else's? What anarchists do not want is to have these useful services—the services now provided by police, courts, and national defense—provided by the kind of institution that now provides them: government.

Before I proceed with my argument, I must define what I mean by 'government'. *A government is an agency of legitimized coercion.* I define 'coercion', for the purposes of this definition, as the violation of what people in a particular society believe to be the rights of individuals with respect to other individuals.

For instance, people in this society believe that an individual has the right to turn down a job offer; the denial of that right is a form of coercion called enslavement. They believe that an individual has the right to turn down a request for money or an offered trade. The denial of that right is called robbery or extortion.

Government is an agency of legitimized coercion. The special characteristic that distinguishes governments from other agencies of coercion (such as ordinary criminal gangs) is that most people accept government coercion as normal and proper. The same act that is regarded as coercive when done by a private individual seems legitimate if done by an agent of the government.

If I yell 'Stop, thief!' at a stickup man escaping with my wallet, the bystanders may or may not help, but they will at least recognize the reasonableness of my act. If I yell 'Stop, thief!' at an employee of the Internal Revenue Service, leaving my house after informing me that he has just frozen my bank account, my neighbors will think I'm crazy. Objectively, the IRS is engaged in the same act as the thief. It seizes my resources without my permission. True, it claims to provide me with services in exchange for my taxes, but it insists on collecting the taxes whether or not I want the services. It is, perhaps, a fine point whether that is robbery or extortion. In either case, if it were the act of a private party, everyone would agree that it was a crime.

Suppose that a private employer, offering low wages for long hours of unpleasant work, failed to find enough workers and solved the problem by picking men at random and threatening to imprison them if they refused to work for him. He would be indicted on charges of kidnapping and extortion and acquitted on grounds of insanity. That is exactly how the government hires people to fight a war or sit on a jury.

It is often argued that government, or at least some particular government, is not merely legitimized but legitimate, that its actions only appear to be coercive. Such arguments often involve social contract theories—claims that the citizen is somehow contractually bound to obey the government. To those interested in that argument and its refutation I recommend *No Treason: The Constitution of No Authority* by Lysander Spooner.

Government is distinguished from other criminal gangs by being legitimized. It is distinguished from legitimate nongovernmental groups which may serve some of the same functions by the fact that it is coercive. Governments build roads. So, occasionally, do private individuals. But the private individuals must first buy the land at a price satisfactory to the seller. The government can and does set a price at which the owner is forced to sell.

Government is an agency of legitimized coercion. If the institutions which replace government perform their functions without coercion, they are not governments. If they occasionally act coercively but, when they do so, their actions are not regarded as legitimate, they are still not governments.

29

Police, courts, and laws—on the

market

How, without government, could we settle the disputes that are now settled in courts of law? How could we protect ourselves from criminals?

Consider first the easiest case, the resolution of disputes involving contracts between well-established firms. A large fraction of such disputes are now settled not by government courts but by private arbitration of the sort described in Chapter 18. The firms, when they draw up a contract, specify a procedure for arbitrating any dispute that may arise. Thus they avoid the expense and delay of the courts.

The arbitrator has no police force. His function is to render decisions, not to enforce them. Currently, arbitrated decisions are usually enforceable in the government courts, but that is a recent development; historically, enforcement came from a firm's desire to maintain its reputation. After refusing to accept an arbitrator's judgment, it is hard to persuade anyone else to sign a contract that specifies arbitration; no one wants to play a game of 'heads you win, tails I lose'.

Arbitration arrangements are already widespread. As the courts continue to deteriorate, arbitration will continue to grow. But it only provides for the resolution of disputes over pre-existing contracts. Arbitration, by itself, provides no solution for the man whose car is dented by a careless driver, still less for the victim of theft; in both cases the plaintiff and defendant, having different interests and no prior agreement, are unlikely to find a mutually satisfactory arbitrator. Indeed, the defendant has no reason to accept any arbitration at all; he can only lose—which brings us to the problem of preventing coercion.

Protection from coercion is an economic good. It is presently sold in a variety of forms—Brinks guards, locks, burglar alarms. As the effectiveness of government police declines, these market substitutes for the police, like market substitutes for the courts, become more popular.

Suppose, then, that at some future time there are no government police, but instead private protection agencies. These agencies sell the service of protecting their clients against crime. Perhaps they also guarantee performance by insuring their clients against losses resulting from criminal acts.

How might such protection agencies protect? That would be an economic decision, depending on the costs and effectiveness of different alternatives. On the one extreme, they might limit themselves to passive defenses, installing elaborate locks and alarms. Or they might take no preventive action at all, but make great efforts to hunt down criminals guilty of crimes against their clients. They might maintain foot patrols or squad cars, like our present government police, or they might rely on electronic substitutes. In any case, they would be selling a service to their customers and would have a strong incentive to provide as high a quality of service as possible, at the lowest possible cost. It is reasonable to suppose that the quality of service would be higher and the cost lower than with the present governmental protective system.

Inevitably, conflicts would arise between one protective agency and another. How might they be resolved?

I come home one night and find my television set missing. I immediately call my protection agency, Tannahelp Inc., to report the theft. They send an agent. He checks the automatic camera which Tannahelp, as part of their service, installed in my living room and discovers a picture of one Joe Bock lugging the television set out the door. The Tannahelp agent contacts Joe, informs him that Tannahelp has reason to believe he is in possession of my television set, and suggests he return it, along with an extra ten dollars to pay for Tannahelp's time and trouble in locating Joe. Joe replies that he has never seen my television set in his life and tells the Tannahelp agent to go to hell.

The agent points out that until Tannahelp is convinced there has been a mistake, he must proceed on the assumption that the television set is my property. Six Tannahelp employees, all large and energetic, will be at Joe's door next morning to collect the set. Joe, in response, informs the agent that he also has a protection agency, Dawn Defense, and that his contract with them undoubtedly requires them to protect him if six goons try to break into his house and steal his television set.

The stage seems set for a nice little war between Tannahelp and Dawn Defense. It is precisely such a possibility that has led some libertarians who are not anarchists, most notably Ayn Rand, to reject the possibility of competing free-market protection agencies.

But wars are very expensive, and Tannahelp and Dawn Defense are both profit-making corporations, more interested in saving money than face. I think the rest of the story would be less violent than Miss Rand supposed.

The Tannahelp agent calls up his opposite number at Dawn Defense. 'We've got a problem. . . .' After explaining the situation, he points out that if Tannahelp sends six men and Dawn eight, there will be a fight. Someone might even get hurt. Whoever wins, by the time the conflict is over it will be expensive for both sides. They might even have to start paying their employees higher wages to make up for the risk. Then both firms will be forced to raise their rates. If they do, Murbard Ltd., an aggressive new firm which has been trying to get established in the area, will undercut their prices and steal their customers. There must be a better solution.

The man from Tannahelp suggests that the better solution is arbitration. They will take the dispute over my television set to a reputable local arbitration firm. If the arbitrator decides that Joe is innocent, Tannahelp agrees to pay Joe and Dawn Defense an indemnity to make up for their time and trouble. If he is found guilty, Dawn Defense will accept the verdict; since the television set is not Joe's, they have no obligation to protect him when the men from Tannahelp come to seize it.

What I have described is a very makeshift arrangement. In practice, once anarcho-capitalist institutions were well established, protection agencies would anticipate such difficulties and arrange contracts in advance, before specific conflicts occurred, specifying the arbitrator who would settle them.

In such an anarchist society, who would make the laws? On what basis would the private arbitrator decide what acts were criminal and what their punishments should be? The answer is that systems of law would be produced for profit on the open market, just as books and bras are produced today. There could be competition among different brands of law, just as there is competition among different brands of cars.

In such a society there might be many courts and even many legal systems. Each pair of protection agencies agree in advance on which court they will use in case of conflict. Thus the laws under which a particular case is decided are determined implicitly by advance agreement between the protection agencies whose customers are involved. In principle, there could be a different court and a different set of laws for every pair of protection agencies. In practice, many agencies would probably find it convenient to patronize the same courts, and many courts might find it convenient to adopt identical, or nearly identical, systems of law in order to simplify matters for their customers.

Before labelling a society in which different people are under different laws chaotic and unjust, remember that in our society the law under which you are judged depends on the country, state, and even city in which you happen to be. Under the arrangements I am describing, it depends instead on your protective agency and the agency of the person you accuse of a crime or who accuses you of a crime.

In such a society law is produced on the market. A court supports itself by charging for the service of arbitrating disputes. Its success depends on its reputation for honesty, reliability, and promptness and on the desirability to potential customers of the particular set of laws it judges by. The immediate customers are protection agencies. But the protection agency is itself selling a product to its customers. Part of that product is the legal system, or systems, of the courts it patronizes and under which its customers will consequently be judged. Each protection agency will try to patronize those courts under whose legal system its customers would like to live.

Consider, as a particular example, the issue of capital punishment. Some people might feel that the risk to themselves of being convicted, correctly or incorrectly, and executed for a capital crime outweighed any possible advantages of capital punishment. They would prefer, where possible, to patronize protection agencies that patronized courts that did not give capital punishment. Other citizens might feel that they would be safer from potential murderers if it was known that anyone who murdered them would end up in the electric chair. They might consider that safety more important than the risk of ending up in the electric chair themselves or of being responsible for the death of an innocent accused of murder. They would, if possible, patronize agencies that patronized courts that did give capital punishment.

If one position or the other is almost universal, it may pay all protection agencies to use courts of the one sort or the other. If some people feel one way and some the other, and if their feelings are strong enough to affect their choice of protection agencies, it pays some agencies to adopt a policy of guaranteeing, whenever possible, to use courts that do not recognize capital punishment. They can then attract anti-capital-punishment customers. Other agencies do the opposite.

Disputes between two anti-capital-punishment agencies will, of course, go to an anti-capital-punishment court; disputes between two pro-capital-punishment agencies will go to a pro-capital-punishment court. What would happen in a dispute between an anti-capital-punishment agency and a pro-capital-punishment agency? Obviously there is no way that if I kill you the case goes to one court, but if you are killed by me it goes to another. We cannot each get exactly the law we want.

We can each have our preferences reflected in the bargaining demands of our respective agencies. If the opponents of capital punishment feel more strongly than the proponents, the agencies will agree to no capital punishment; in exchange, the agencies that want capital punishment will get something else. Perhaps it will be agreed that they will not pay court costs or that some other disputed question will go their way.

One can imagine an idealized bargaining process, for this or any other dispute, as follows: Two agencies are negotiating whether to recognize a pro- or anti-capital-punishment court. The pro agency calculates that getting a pro-capital-punishment court will be worth $20,000 a year to its customers; that is the additional amount it can get for its services if they include a guarantee of capital punishment in case of disputes with the other agency. The anti-capital-punishment agency calculates a corresponding figure of $40,000. It offers the pro agency $30,000 a year in exchange for accepting an anti-capital-punishment court. The pro agency accepts. Now the anti-capital-punishment agency can raise its rates enough to bring in an extra $35,000. Its customers are happy, since the guarantee of no capital punishment is worth more than that. The agency is happy; it is getting an extra $5,000 a year profit. The pro agency cuts its rates by an amount that costs it $25,000 a year. This lets it keep its customers and even get more, since the savings is more than enough to make up to them for not getting the court of their choice. It, too, is making a $5,000 a year profit on the transaction. As in any good trade, everyone gains.

If you find this confusing, it may be worth the trouble of going over it again; the basic principle of such negotiation will become important later when I discuss what sort of law an anarcho-capitalist society is likely to have.

If, by some chance, the customers of the two agencies feel equally strongly, perhaps two courts will be chosen, one of each kind, and cases allocated randomly between them. In any case, the customer's legal preference, his opinion as to what sort of law he wishes to live under, will have been a major factor in determining the kind of law he does live under. It cannot completely determine it, since accused and accuser must have the same law.

In the case of capital punishment, the two positions are directly opposed. Another possibility is that certain customers may want specialized law, suited to their special circumstances. People living in desert areas might want a system of law that very clearly defines property rights in water. People in other areas would find such detailed treatment of this problem superfluous at best. At worst, it might be the source of annoying nuisance suits. Thus the desert people might all patronize one protection agency, which had a policy of always going to a court with well-developed water law. Other agencies would agree to use that court in disputes with that agency but use other courts among themselves.

Most differences among courts would probably be more subtle. People would find that the decisions of one court were prompter or easier to predict than those of another or that the customers of one protection agency were better protected than those of another. The protection agencies, trying to build their own reputations, would search for the 'best' courts.

Several objections may be raised to such free-market courts. The first is that they would sell justice by deciding in favor of the highest bidder. That would be suicidal; unless they maintained a reputation for honesty, they would have no customers—unlike our present judges. Another objection is that it is the business of courts and legislatures to discover laws, not create them; there cannot be two competing laws of gravity, so why should there be two competing laws of property? But there can be two competing theories about the law of gravity or the proper definition of property rights. Discovery is as much a productive activity as creation. If it is obvious what the correct law is, what rules of human interaction follow from the nature of man, then all courts will agree, just as all architects agree about the laws of physics. If it is not obvious, the market will generate research intended to discover correct laws.

Another objection is that a society of many different legal systems would be confusing. If this is found to be a serious problem, courts will have an economic incentive to adopt uniform law, just as paper companies have an incentive to produce standardized sizes of paper. New law will be introduced only when the innovator believes that its advantages outweigh the advantages of uniformity.

The most serious objection to free-market law is that plaintiff and defendant may not be able to agree on a common court. Obviously, a murderer would prefer a lenient judge. If the court were actually chosen by the disputants after the crime occurred, this might be an insuperable difficulty. Under the arrangements I have described, the court is chosen in advance by the protection agencies. There would hardly be enough murderers at any one time to support their own protective agency, one with a policy of patronizing courts that did not regard murder as a crime. Even if there were, no other protective agency would accept such courts. The murderers' agency would either accept a reasonable court or fight a hopeless war against the rest of society.

Until he is actually accused of a crime, everyone wants laws that protect him from crime and let him interact peacefully and productively with others. Even criminals. Not many murderers would wish to live under laws that permitted them to kill—and be killed.

30

THE STABILITY PROBLEM

Anyone with a little imagination can dream up a radical new structure for society, anarcho-capitalist or otherwise. The question is, will it work? Most people, when they hear my description of anarcho-capitalism for the first time, immediately explain to me two or three reasons why it won't. Most of their arguments can be reduced to two: The system will be at the mercy of the mafia, which can establish its own 'protection agency' or take over existing ones and convert them into protection rackets. Or else the protection agencies will realize that theft is more profitable than business, get together, and become a government.

The main defensive weapon of organized crime is bribery. It works because policemen have no real stake in doing their job well and their 'customers' have no standard of comparison to tell them if they are getting their money's worth. What is the cost to the chief of a police department of letting his men accept bribes to permit crime? In most cases, nothing. The higher crime rate might even persuade the voters to vote more money and higher salaries to the police department.

If the employees of a private protection agency accept such bribes, the situation is rather different. The worse the job the protection agency does, the lower the fee it can charge. If the customers of one agency find they lose, on average, ten dollars a year more to thieves than the customers of another, they will continue to do business with the inferior agency only if it is at least ten dollars a year cheaper. So every dollar stolen from the customer comes, indirectly, out of the revenue of the protection agency. If the agency is one that guarantees performance by insuring its customers against losses, the connection is more direct. Either way, it is very much in the interest of the men running a protection agency to see that their employees do not take bribes. The only bribe it would pay the agency to take would be one for more than the value of the goods stolen—a poor deal for the thief.

This does not mean that employees of protection agencies will never take bribes. The interests of the employee and of the agency are not identical. It does mean that the men running the agencies will do their best to keep their men honest. That is more than you can say for a police force. Organized crime, if it continues to exist under anarcho-capitalism, should be in a much weaker position than it now is. In addition, as I shall argue later, most of the things that organized crime now makes money on would be legal in an anarcho-capitalist society. Thus both its size and its popularity would be greatly reduced.

What about the possibility of the mafia getting its own protection agency? In order for such a firm to provide its clients with the service they want—protection against the consequences of their crimes—it must either get the other protection agencies to agree to arbitration by a court that approves of crime or refuse to go to arbitration at all. In order to do the first, it must offer the other agencies terms so good that their customers are willing to be stolen from; as in the previous case, this reduces to the thief bribing the victim by more than the amount stolen, which is improbable. If it refuses to accept arbitration, then the mafia's protection agency finds itself constantly in conflict with the other protection agencies. The victims of theft will be willing to pay more to be protected than the thieves will pay to be able to steal (since stolen goods are worth less to the thief than to the victim). Therefore the noncriminal protection agencies will find it profitable to spend more to defeat the criminal agency than the criminal agency could spend to defeat them. In effect, the criminals fight a hopeless war with the rest of society and are destroyed.

Another and related argument against anarcho-capitalism is that the "strongest" protection agency will always win, the big fish will eat the little fish, and the justice you get will depend on the military strength of the agency you patronize.

This is a fine description of governments, but protection agencies are not territorial sovereigns. An agency which settles its disputes on the battlefield has already lost, however many battles it wins. Battles are expensive—also dangerous for clients whose front yards get turned into free-fire zones. The clients will find a less flamboyant protector. No clients means no money to pay the troops.

Perhaps the best way to see why anarcho-capitalism would be so much more peaceful than our present system is by analogy. Consider our world as it would be if the cost of moving from one country to another were zero. Everyone lives in a housetrailer and speaks the same language. One day, the president of France announces that because of troubles with neighboring countries, new military taxes are being levied and conscription will begin shortly. The next morning the president of France finds himself ruling a peaceful but empty landscape, the population having been reduced to himself, three generals, and twenty-seven war correspondents.

We do not all live in housetrailers. But if we buy our protection from a private firm instead of from a government, we can buy it from a different firm as soon as we think we can get a better deal. We can change protectors without changing countries.

The risk of private protection agencies throwing their weight—and lead—around is not great, provided there are lots of them. Which brings us to the second and far more serious argument against anarcho-capitalism.

The protection agencies will have a large fraction of the armed might of the society. What can prevent them from getting together and using that might to set themselves up as a government?

In some ultimate sense, nothing can prevent that save a populace possessing arms and willing, if necessary, to use them. That is one reason I am against gun-control legislation.

But there are safeguards less ultimate than armed resistance. After all, our present police departments, national guard, and armed forces already possess most of the armed might. Why have they not combined to run the country for their own benefit? Neither soldiers nor policemen are especially well paid; surely they could impose a better settlement at gunpoint.

The complete answer to that question comprises nearly the whole of political science. A brief answer is that people act according to what they perceive as right, proper, and practical. The restraints which prevent a military coup are essentially restraints interior to the men with guns.

We must ask, not whether an anarcho-capitalist society would be safe from a power grab by the men with the guns (safety is not an available option), but whether it would be safer than our society is from a comparable seizure of power by the men with the guns. I think the answer is yes. In our society, the men who must engineer such a coup are politicians, military officers, and policemen, men selected precisely for the characteristic of desiring power and being good at using it. They are men who already believe that they have a right to push other men around—that is their job. They are particularly well qualified for the job of seizing power. Under anarcho-capitalism the men in control of protection agencies are selected for their ability to run an efficient business and please their customers. It is always possible that some will turn out to be secret power freaks as well, but it is surely less likely than under our system where the corresponding jobs are labeled 'non-power freaks need not apply'.

In addition to the temperament of potential conspirators, there is another relevant factor: the number of protection agencies. If there are only two or three agencies in the entire area now covered by the United States, a conspiracy among them may be practical. If there are 10,000, then when any group of them start acting like a government, their customers will hire someone else to protect them against their protectors.

How many agencies there are depends on what size agency does the most efficient job of protecting its clients. My own guess is that the number will be nearer 10,000 than 3. If the performance of present-day police forces is any indication, a protection agency protecting as many as one million people is far above optimum size.

My conclusion is one of guarded optimism. Once anarcho-capitalist institutions are established with widespread acceptance over a large area, they should be reasonably stable against internal threats.

Are such institutions truly anarchist? Are the private protection agencies I have described actually governments in disguise? No. Under my definition of government—which comes closer than any other, I think, to describing why people call some things governments and not others—they are not governments. They have no rights which individuals do not have, and they therefore cannot engage in legitimized coercion.

Most people, myself included, believe that an individual has the right to use force to prevent another from violating his rights— stealing from him, say, or murdering him. Most agree that the victim has a right to take back what the thief has stolen and to use force to do so. Social contract theories start from the premise that individuals have these rights and delegate them to the government. In order for such a government to be legitimate, it must be established by unanimous consent, otherwise it has no special rights over those who refuse to sign the 'social contract'. Under a system of private protection agencies, the actual agencies, like the ideal government, are merely acting as agents for willing clients who have employed the agencies to enforce their own rights. They claim no rights over non-clients other than the right to defend their clients against coercion—the same right every individual has. They do nothing that a private individual cannot do.

This does not mean that they will never coerce anyone. A protection agency, like a government, can make a mistake and arrest the wrong man. In exactly the same way, a private citizen can shoot at what he thinks is a prowler and bag the postman instead. In each case, coercion occurs, but it occurs by accident and the coercer is liable for the consequences of his acts. The citizen can be indicted for postman-slaughter and the protection agency sued for false arrest. Once the facts that make an act coercive are known, it is no longer regarded as having been legitimate.

This is not true of government actions. In order to sue a policeman for false arrest I must prove not merely that I was innocent but that the policeman had no reason to suspect me. If I am locked up for twenty years and then proven innocent, I have no legal claim against the government for my lost time and mental anguish. It is recognized that the government made a mistake, but the government is allowed to make mistakes and need not pay for them like the rest of us. If, knowing that I am innocent, I try to escape arrest and a policeman shoots me down, he is entirely within his rights and I am the criminal. If, to keep him from shooting me, I shoot him in self-defense, I am guilty of murder, even after it is proved that I was innocent of the theft and so doing no more than defending myself against the government's (unintentional) coercion.

This difference between the rights claimed by a private protection agency and those claimed by a government affects more than the semantic question of what is or is not anarchy. It is one of the crucial reasons why a government, however limited, can more easily grow into a tyranny than can a system of private protection agencies. Even the most limited government has the sort of special rights I have described; everything I said in the previous paragraph was true of this country in its earliest and (for white males) freest days.

Such special rights allow a government to kill off its opponents and then apologize for the mistake. Unless the evidence of criminal intent is very clear, the murderers are immune from punishment. Even when the evidence is overwhelming, as in the case of the 1969 Chicago Black Panther raid, there is no question of trying those responsible for their actual crime. The Cook County state attorney responsible for the raid, in which two men were killed, and the police officers who executed it, were eventually charged not with conspiracy to commit murder but with obstruction of justice—not, in other words, with killing people but with lying about it afterwards.

This is not an isolated instance of the miscarriage of justice; it is the inevitable result of a system under which the government has certain special rights, above and beyond the rights of ordinary individuals—among them the right not to be held responsible for its mistakes. When these rights are taken away, when the agent of government is reduced to the status of a private citizen and has the same rights and responsibilities as his neighbors, what remains is no longer a government.

> . . . a policeman . . . is protected by the legislative and judicial arms in the peculiar rights and prerogatives that go with his high office, including especially the right to jug the laity at his will, to sweat and mug them, and to subdue their resistance by beating out their brains.
>
> H.L. MENCKEN, PREJUDICES

(State attorney Hanrahan and his codefendants were eventually acquitted, but in 1982, thirteen years after the raid, a civil case by the survivors and the mothers of the two men who were killed was settled for $1.85 million, paid by the city, county and federal governments.)

31

Is anarcho-capitalism libertarian?

A man who wants protection will fire patrolmen who waste their time harassing minorities. . . . No private policeman has ever spent many hours at a restroom peephole in hopes of apprehending deviates.

WILLIAM WOOLDRIDGE

I have described how a private system of courts and police might function, but not the laws it would produce and enforce; I have discussed institutions, not results. That is why I have used the term anarcho-capitalist, which describes the institutions, rather than libertarian. Whether these institutions will produce a libertarian society—a society in which each person is free to do as he likes with himself and his property as long as he does not use either to initiate force against others—remains to be proven.

Under some circumstances they will not. If almost everyone believes strongly that heroin addiction is so horrible that it should not be permitted anywhere under any circumstances, anarcho-capitalist institutions will produce laws against heroin. Laws are being produced for a market, and that is what the market wants.

But market demands are in dollars, not votes. The legality of heroin will be determined, not by how many are for or against but by how high a cost each side is willing to bear in order to get its way. People who want to control other people's lives are rarely eager to pay for the privilege; they usually expect to be paid for the 'services' they provide for their victims. And those on the receiving end—whether of laws against drugs, laws against pornography, or laws against sex—get a lot more pain out of the oppression than their oppressors get pleasure. They are willing to pay a much higher price to be left alone than anyone is willing to pay to push them around. For that reason the laws of an anarcho-capitalist society should be heavily biased toward freedom.

So compulsory puritanism—'crimes without victims'—should be much rarer under anarcho-capitalism than under political institutions. We can get some idea of how rare by considering the costs such laws now impose on their victims and the value of such laws to their supporters. If the value of a law to its supporters is less than its cost to its victims, that law, by the logic of the previous chapter, will not survive in an anarcho-capitalist society.

Heroin addicts pay over $2 billion a year for heroin. If heroin were legal, its cost would be very low. Almost all of the $2 billion now spent for heroin is the cost of the law, not the habit; addicts bear additional costs in prison sentences, overdoses caused by the poor quality control typical of illegal products, and other side effects of the laws against heroin. Heroin addicts would therefore be willing, if necessary, to bear a cost of $2 billion or more in order to have the drug legal. It would cost the nonaddicts about ten dollars per capita or forty dollars per family, per year, to match that.

If the choice had to be made on an all-or-nothing basis, public opinion is probably so strongly against heroin that people would be willing to bear that cost. But one of the advantages of a market system of laws is its ability to tailor its product to its customers— geographically, as well as in other ways. If the maximum return comes from having heroin illegal in some places and legal in others, that is what will happen.

Most of the population lives in areas where there are very few heroin addicts. For those people the cost of having heroin made illegal locally would be very small; there would be no one on the other side bidding to have it legal, except perhaps a few New York addicts who wanted to vacation away from the big city and bring their habit with them. In those areas protection agencies would accept arbitration agencies that viewed using or selling heroin as a crime. But people in those areas would have little to gain by paying a much higher price to have heroin illegal in New York as well.

That leaves 8 million New York nonaddicts bidding against 100,000 New York addicts, raising the cost to the nonaddicts of keeping heroin illegal in New York to over $100 a year per person. I predict that, if anarcho-capitalist institutions appeared in this country tomorrow, heroin would be legal in New York and illegal in most other places. Marijuana would be legal over most of the country.

By now the reader may be getting confused. This is natural enough; I am describing law making in economic terms, and you are used to thinking of it in political terms. When I talk of bidding for one law or another, I do not mean that we will have a legislature that literally auctions off laws. I mean that each person's desire for the kinds of laws he believes in will be reflected in the different rates he is willing to pay his protection agency according to how good a job it does of getting him the law he wants. This set of 'demands' for laws will be reconciled through the sort of bargaining described in the previous chapter. The process is analogous to the way you and I 'bid' to have a piece of private land used the way we want it used. Our demands—for the food that can be grown on it, the buildings that can be built on it, possible recreational uses, or whatever—determine how it eventually gets used.

What I have been saying is that, just as the market allocates resources to producing illegal drugs in response to the demands of those who want to use them, it would make use of those drugs legal in response to the same demand. The obvious question is why the same argument does not hold for making murder legal. The answer is that murder hurts someone, and it is worth much more to the victim not to be shot than to the murderer to shoot him. There is a market demand from me for a law saying that you cannot kill me. 'Crimes without victims' do not hurt anyone, except in the vague sense of arousing moral indignation in people upset over their neighbors' sins. There is little market demand for laws against them.

The same geographical effect that I described for drug laws would apply to other laws as well. Under present institutions the areas over which laws apply are determined by historical accident. If a majority of the population of a state supports one kind of law, everyone in the state gets it. Under anarcho-capitalism, insofar as it would be possible, everyone would have his own law. Diversity of law cannot be unlimited, since the same law must cover both parties to a dispute. But it is possible to have much more diversity than our present system allows. Where the majority and minority, or minorities, are geographically separate, the majority is mainly concerned with having the laws it wants for itself; it is only our political system that imposes those laws on the minority as well.

At this point in the argument, the question of poor people is often raised. Since dollars vote, won't the poor lose out?

Yes and no. The more money you are willing to spend for

protection, the better quality you can get and the better you will be able to get the details of law the way you want them. This is notoriously true now. Our political system of police and courts provides much better service to those with higher incomes. Here as elsewhere, although the market will not bring equality, it will greatly improve the position of the poor.

Why? Because the market allows people to concentrate their resources on what is most important to them. I discussed this point earlier, in the context of the poor man buying a necessity outbidding the rich man who wants the same good for a luxury. Protection from crime is not a luxury.

Currently, government expenditures on police and courts run about forty dollars a year per capita. According to Friedman's law, that means that private protection of the same average quality would cost about twenty dollars. There are many inhabitants of the ghetto who would be delighted to pay twenty dollars a year if in exchange they actually got protection; many of them have more than that stolen every year as a result of the lousy protection they get from our government-run protection system. They would be even happier if at the same time they were relieved of the taxes that pay for the protection that the government police do not give them.

In spite of popular myths about capitalism oppressing the poor, the poor are worst off in those things provided by government, such as schooling, police protection, and justice. There are more good cars in the ghetto than good schools. Putting protection on the market would mean better protection for the poor, not worse.

And, as a free bonus

A system of private courts and police has certain special advantages over our present government system, advantages associated with the political issues of freedom and stability discussed in the previous two chapters. Private courts and police have, in addition, the same advantages over the corresponding government institutions that market arrangements usually have over socialist arrangements.

When a consumer buys a product on the market, he can compare alternative brands. In the case of protection, he can compare how good a job different agencies do and their prices. His information is imperfect, as it is in making most decisions; he may make a mistake. But at least alternatives exist; they are there to be looked at. He can talk with neighbors who patronize different protection agencies, examine the contracts and rates they offer, study figures on the crime rates among their customers.

When you elect a politician, you buy nothing but promises. You may know how one politician ran the country for the past four years, but not how his competitor might have run it. You can compare 1968 Fords, Chryslers, and Volkswagens, but nobody will ever be able to compare the Nixon administration of 1968 with the Humphrey and Wallace administrations of the same year. It is as if we had only Fords from 1920 to 1928, Chryslers from 1928 to 1936, and then had to decide what firm would make a better car for the next four years. Perhaps an expert automotive engineer could make an educated guess as to whether Ford had used the technology of

1920 to satisfy the demands of 1920 better than Chrysler had used the technology of 1928 to satisfy the demands of 1928. The rest of us might just as well flip a coin. If you throw in Volkswagen or American Motors, which had not made any cars in America but wanted to, the situation becomes still worse. Each of us would have to know every firm intimately in order to have any reasonable basis for deciding which we preferred.

In the same way, in order to judge a politician who has held office, one must consider not only how his administration turned out but the influence of a multitude of relevant factors over which he had no control, ranging from the makeup of Congress to the weather at harvest time. Judging politicians who have not yet held office is still more difficult.

Not only does a consumer have better information than a voter, it is of more use to him. If I investigate alternative brands of cars or protection, decide which is best for me, and buy it, I get it. If I investigate alternative politicians and vote accordingly, I get what the majority votes for. The chance that my vote will be the deciding factor is negligible.

Imagine buying cars the way we buy governments. Ten thousand people would get together and agree to vote, each for the car he preferred. Whichever car won, each of the ten thousand would have to buy it. It would not pay any of us to make any serious effort to find out which car was best; whatever I decide, my car is being picked for me by the other members of the group. Under such institutions, the quality of cars would quickly decline.

That is how I must buy products on the political marketplace. I not only cannot compare the alternative products, it would not be worth my while to do so even if I could. This may have something to do with the quality of the goods sold on that market. *Caveat emptor*.

33

Socialism, limited government,

ANARCHY, AND BIKINIS

Most varieties of socialism implicitly assume unanimous agreement on goals. Everyone works for the glory of the nation, the common good, or whatever, and everyone agrees, at least in some general sense, on what that goal means. The economic problem, traditionally defined as the problem of allocating limited resources to diverse ends, does not exist; economics is reduced to the 'engineering' problem of how best to use the available resources to achieve the common end.

The organization of a capitalist society implicitly assumes that different people have different ends and that the institutions of the society must allow for that difference.

This is one of the things behind the socialist claim that capitalism emphasizes competition whereas socialism emphasizes cooperation; it is one of the reasons why socialism seems, in the abstract, to be such an attractive system. If we all have different ends, we are, in a certain sense, in conflict with each other; each of us wishes to have the limited resources available used for his ends. The institution of private property allows for cooperation within that competition; we trade with each other in order that each may best use his resources to his ends, but the fundamental conflict of ends remains. Does this mean that socialism is better? No more than the desirability of sunny weather means that women should always wear bikinis or that men should never carry umbrellas.

There is a difference between what institutions allow and what they require. If in a capitalist society everyone is convinced of the desirability of one common goal, there is nothing in the structure of capitalist institutions to prevent them from cooperating to attain it. Capitalism allows for a conflict of ends; it does not require it.

Socialism does not allow for it. This does not mean that if we set up socialist institutions everyone will instantly have the same ends.

The experiment has been tried; they do not. It means rather that a socialist society will work only if people do have the same ends. If they do not it will collapse or, worse, develop, as did the Soviet Union, into a monstrous parody of socialist ideals.

The experiment has been done many times on a more modest scale in this country. Communes that survive start with a common end, whether provided by a strong religion or a charismatic leader. Others do not.

I have encountered precisely the same error among libertarians who prefer limited government to anarcho-capitalism. Limited government, they say, can guarantee uniform justice based on objective principles. Under anarcho-capitalism, the law varies from place to place and person to person, according to the irrational desires and beliefs of the different customers that different protection and arbitration agencies must serve.

This argument assumes that the limited government is set up by a population most or all of whose members believe in the same just principles of law. Given such a population, anarcho-capitalism will produce that same uniform, just law; there will be no market for any other. But just as capitalism can accommodate to a diversity of individual ends, so anarcho-capitalism can accommodate to a diversity of individual judgments about justice.

An ideal objectivist society with a limited government is superior to an anarcho-capitalist society in precisely the same sense that an ideal socialist society is superior to a capitalist society. Socialism does better with perfect people than capitalism does with imperfect people; limited government does better with perfect people than anarcho-capitalism with imperfect. And it is better to wear a bikini with the sun shining than a raincoat when it is raining. That is no argument against carrying an umbrella.

34

National Defense: The Hard Problem

National defense has tradi-
tionally been regarded, even by believers in a severely limited state,
as a fundamental function of government. To understand why, one
must first understand the economic concept of a 'public good' and
the difficulties of financing a public good without coercion.

A public good is an economic good which, by its nature, cannot
be provided separately to each individual, but must be provided, or
not provided, to all the members of a pre-existing group. A simple
example is the control of a river whose flooding injures the land of
many farmers in the valley below. There is no way that an
entrepreneur who proposes to build a dam can protect only those
farmers who agree to pay part of the cost of the dam. An individual
farmer may refuse to pay, arguing that if the others all pay he will be
protected anyway and if they do not his contribution will not be
enough to build the dam. The small probability that his contribution will make the difference between the dam being built and not
being built, multiplied by the value to him of the dam, is not
enough to justify the expenditure.

This is the traditional problem of the public good. It is a problem
because if there are enough farmers like this, each acting rationally
on a correct calculation of his own self-interest, the dam will not be
built, even though the combined value to all the farmers is more
than the cost of building the dam.

In our society the usual solution is to use government force—
taxation—to make those benefited (and others) pay for the dam.
The trouble with this solution, aside from moral objections to the
use of force, is that the dam may be produced even when its total
value is less than its cost. The government has no market
mechanism for measuring the total value of the dam to the farmers.
And since government decisions are made on political grounds, the

government may choose to ignore cost and value entirely. In practice, public dams are often built even when the return on the capital spent building them, including a generous estimate of nonmonetary benefits, is far below the market interest rate.

There are several market solutions to the problem of providing a public good. For instance, the entrepreneur might estimate how much the dam is worth to each farmer, draw up a contract obligating each farmer to pay that amount on condition that every other farmer agrees to pay his share, and circulate it. Each farmer knows that, if he refuses to sign, the dam will not be built, since the contract has to be unanimous. It is therefore in his interest to sign.

In order for this to work, the entrepreneur must estimate correctly the value of the dam to each farmer. If he makes one mistake, the dam will not be built. His job is made more difficult by those farmers who realize that it is in their interest to pretend that they think the dam of little value in order to have only a small part of the cost assigned to them.

A farmer interested in raising rice, for instance, might find occasional floods a useful supplement to his irrigation and have no interest in paying for flood control. The entrepreneur would have to remove such a farmer's name from the contract in order to have any chance at all of getting it signed. That is fair enough; there is no reason for the farmer to pay for something that is worthless to him. But as soon as word spreads, other farmers realize that an interest in growing rice can save them a lot of money. *The Rice Growers' Gazette* acquires some new subscribers, all of whom are careful to leave their copies in prominent places around the house when the dam entrepreneur comes to call; talk at the general store shifts from mowing hay to the relative virtues of different strains of rice. The entrepreneur is faced with the problem of figuring out which farmers are really interested in growing rice and which are only interested in being interested in growing rice—with the objective of growing wheat and getting flood control without paying for it. If he guesses wrong and puts a real rice farmer on his unanimous contract, it does not get signed. If he plays safe and takes everyone who pretends to be interested in rice off the contract, he may not be able to raise enough money.

The larger the public for a given public good, the harder it is to arrange such a unanimous contract successfully. The larger the difference between the value of the good and its price, on the other hand, the easier the entrepreneur's job. He can leave a generous margin for error by only listing the farmers of whom he is sure and charging each of them less than the dam is probably worth to him, yet still raise enough money.

Another way to provide a public good without coercion is by temporarily converting it into a private good. The entrepreneur could do this by purchasing most of the land in the valley before telling anyone that he is thinking of building a dam. He then builds the dam and resells the land at a higher price, since the dam raises the land's value. The rise in value of the land measures the total benefit from the dam. If it is much larger than the cost of the dam, the entrepreneur makes a profit. There may be a few farmers who refuse to sell, but as long as the entrepreneur owns most of the land he receives most of the benefit.

Here again, the entrepreneur's job is harder the more people are involved. It becomes difficult to buy all the land before the owners realize what is happening and raise their prices. Here also, the job is easier the bigger the difference between cost and benefit. If the benefit is more than twice the cost of building the dam, the entrepreneur makes a profit even if he can only buy half the land.

In both cases the transactions themselves have a cost and thus increase the effective cost of building the dam. Gathering the information needed to draw up a successful unanimous contract may be expensive. Buying up all the land in the valley involves substantial brokerage fees. Farmers who were not planning to sell must be paid more than the market price to compensate for their inconvenience. A clever entrepreneur, buying not the land but merely an option to buy at a predetermined price, can reduce such costs but not eliminate them.

How does this apply to national defense? Is it a public good? Can it be financed without coercion?

Some contemporary anarchists argue that national defense can be provided or not provided for each individual or at least each small group. One form of this argument is the assertion that national defense is unnecessary in an anarchist society, since there is no nation to defend. Unfortunately, there will still be nations to defend against, unless we postpone the abolition of our government until anarchy is universal. Defense against nations, in the present state of military technology, is a public good. It is all very well to fantasize about fighting the invader village by village, commune by commune, or corporation by corporation, according to the dreamer's particular brand of anarchy. A serious invader would inform each unit that if it resisted or failed to pay tribute, it would be destroyed by a nuclear weapon. After the invader proved that he meant business, the citizens of the surviving communities would be eager to create the institutions, voluntary or otherwise, necessary to give the invader what he wanted.

Pending major technological change, defense against nations must be provided on a large enough scale to support retaliatory, and perhaps also defensive, nuclear forces. This makes it difficult to sell national defense on the free market. An ABM fired at a missile a thousand miles from its target cannot distinguish warheads aimed at those who have paid for defense from warheads aimed at those who have not. Even if defense is retaliatory and even if the retaliatory system is secure enough to hold its fire until it knows whether its customers have been hit, the problem remains. The citizens of New York, having paid their share of defense costs, can hardly look with equanimity on the H-bombing of Philadelphia, which has contributed not a penny. Not, at least, if the wind is blowing the wrong way.

So national defense—defense against nations—must defend areas of national size, whether or not they contain nations. It is thus a public good, and one with a very large public.

Can this public good be financed by some variant of one of the noncoercive methods I have discussed? It is not obvious how. The size of the public is so enormous that a unanimous contract is virtually impossible, especially since one secret supporter of a foreign power could prevent the whole deal. Buying up most of the land affected by national defense might be less difficult than negotiating a unanimous contract among 200 million people, but hardly easy. The land must be purchased before sellers realize what is going on and increase their price. Raising enough money to buy the United States would be a hard project to keep secret. In addition, the transaction costs would be substantial—about $100 billion in realtor commissions for all the fixed property in the United States.

There is one favorable factor to help offset these difficulties. The cost of a minimal national defense is only about $20 billion to $40 billion a year. The value to those protected is several hundred billion dollars a year. National defense is thus a public good worth about ten times what it costs; this may make it easier, although not easy, to devise some noncoercive way of financing it.

The problem would be simpler if it could be subdivided. Groups much smaller than our present population might be able to create defense organizations and finance them voluntarily. It would be in their interest to do so if such groups could defend themselves. Once such organizations existed, hundreds of them could combine, via unanimous contracts, to defend areas of national or even continental size. One could imagine an alternate history in which, as military technology developed, such voluntary arrangements evolved, just as coercive governments evolved in our history.

But in the present world small groups cannot defend themselves. They therefore have no incentive to develop voluntary arrangements to finance defense.

A solution to this problem of developing institutions that provide defense without the state, paradoxically enough, might be provided by the state itself. Suppose that over the next fifty or a hundred years private institutions gradually take over all governmental functions except defense. The state, without control of local institutions, might find the cost of collecting taxes substantial and be tempted to raise money in the manner of the French monarchy, by selling tax exemptions. It could offer to exempt any community from taxation in exchange for either a capital sum or an annual payment. Such a tax exemption would itself be a public good (defense, via bribery, from one's own state) for the community. Since the collection costs of taxation are high, the value of a tax exemption is greater than its cost. The members of the community might therefore find it in their interest to set up an organization designed to pay off the state. It could be financed voluntarily by one of the ways of financing public goods that I have described. It would probably pay an annual fee instead of a lump sum in order to make sure the state stayed bought.

Over a period of time, many or most communities develop such institutions. There then exists a group of organizations, voluntarily funded (either by the interest on a capital endowment or by contractual agreements to pay on the part of members of the community) and charged with the task of "defending" their communities. These organizations could then contract with each other to take over from the existing state the job of financing and providing national defense.

So one solution to the problem of national defense might be the development, for some related purpose, of local defense organizations. These must be organizations permanently endowed for the purpose of providing defense; they cannot be simply local firms with an interest in the protection of their territory, since such firms, having agreed to pay part of the cost of national defense, would be driven out of business by new competitors who had not. This is the problem with Morris and Linda Tannahill's idea of financing national defense through an insurance company or companies which would insure customers against injury by foreign states and finance national defense out of the money saved by defending the customers. Such an insurance company, in order to pay the cost of defense, would have to charge rates substantially higher than the real risk justified, given the existence of its defense system. Since people living in the geographical area defended would be protected whether or not they were insured by that particular company, it would be in their interest either not to be insured or to be insured by a company that did not have to bear the burden of paying for defense and could therefore charge lower rates. The national defense insurance company would lose all its customers and go bankrupt, just as it would if it were simply selling national defense directly to individual customers who would be defended whether or not they paid.

The same difficulty occurs with Ayn Rand's suggestion of financing national defense by having the government charge for the use of its courts. In order to raise money for defense, such a government must either charge more than competing private court systems or provide a worse product. Such private courts, if permitted, would therefore drive the government out of the court business, depriving it of its source of income.

Miss Rand apparently expects her government to have a monopoly of the court (and protection) business. But if the government does not use coercion to keep out competitors there is no obvious reason why the sorts of institutions described earlier in this section should not arise. If the government does claim special rights that it does not give to private courts and protection agencies—for instance, the right of policemen to make mistakes and not be responsible for the damage done or the right of government courts to subpoena witnesses—then it becomes a government in my sense of the term (Miss Rand uses a different definition)—an agency of legitimized coercion. Either the things the government does but forbids its competitors from doing are coercion, in which case it is coercing private citizens, or they are not coercion, in which case it coerces the private protective agencies by forbidding them to do the same (noncoercive) things. Either way, Rand's government must be coercive in order to work, so it is not a solution to the libertarian's problem of providing national defense without coercion.

Although local defense organizations must be endowed, they might evolve in ways other than those I have described. For instance, existing insurance companies would receive a capital windfall at the time an adequate national protection system was first constructed, since outstanding policies that had been sold at high rates under high risk conditions could be paid off under low risk conditions. They could use this windfall (which comes only from policies already written and thus represents only that small part of the benefit of defense which accrues in the near future to those already insured) to endow national defense. Such an endowment would not be sufficient to pay all the costs of national defense, unless it becomes far cheaper than it now is, but it might cover some of them.

There are other ways that part of the cost might be paid. Charities exist for the purpose of financing public goods. They currently collect billions of dollars a year. There is no reason why national defense should not be partly financed by charitable contributions. Historically it has been; in time of war people often donate money, labor, and weapons and purchase war bonds for more than their market value.

There is another common way of financing public goods that is intermediate between normal economic methods and charity. The best example is the institution of tipping. Customers at a restaurant leave a tip even if they have no intention of eating there again and therefore no personal interest in rewarding good service. In effect, the rewarding of good service is a public good; if everyone does it, everyone will benefit by the improved service, but if I do it at a restaurant where I rarely eat most of the benefit goes to the other members of a pre-existing group—the other people who use the restaurant. I tip partly because I realize this and view good restaurant service as a desirable goal—in effect, a worthy object of charity. A more important reason is that I feel I *ought* to tip; an internal feeling of obligation or external social pressure make me act according to a sort of implicit contract, an obligation to reward the waiter if he does a good job, even though I know that there is nothing forcing me to do so and that I will suffer no material loss if I do not. Similarly, if national defense were financed voluntarily, people would give money not as a matter of charity but because they felt that they were receiving something and *ought* to pay for it. As with tipping, the amount received might have some connection with how good a job they thought was being done. And, like tipping, people might feel obligated to give something even if the job were only barely satisfactory; however bad the service, few of us have the temerity to leave no tip at all.

How much are people willing to pay on such a basis? I do not know, but one way of getting a rough idea is by seeing how much they pay in tips under circumstances where they receive no direct benefit by tipping well. This is the normal case with taxis, since few of us expect to get the same driver twice; with restaurants it only sometimes holds, since many customers go to the same restaurant regularly. Taxi tips total about $150 million a year; all sorts of tips combined total about $2 billion. Such figures suggest that individual feelings of obligation, reinforced by social pressure, might provide a substantial fraction of the cost of defending against foreign enemies—a service most of us regard as somewhat more important than keeping up the quality of restaurant service.

Although national defense is primarily a public good, there are parts of it which can be sold separately to individuals or groups. Foreign states would probably treat a national defense agency as a government with respect to such matters as passports and extradition treaties. It could get some income by selling passports, arranging to extradite criminals from foreign countries at the request of local protection agencies, and similar enterprises.

In addition, there would be some areas which a national defense agency would have the option of defending or not defending. Hawaii, to take an extreme example, could be excluded from the nuclear umbrella covering the mainland. Communities on the edges of the defended area, although necessarily protected from nuclear attack by any national defense system, could be defended or not defended against conventional attack. A national defense agency could go into these areas and inform those individuals and corporations who had the most to gain by being defended (large landholders, insurance agencies, and the like) that they would have to pay a price for defense.

In all of these ways a national defense agency might raise enough money to finance national defense without taxation. Obviously, a system that depends on local agencies evolved for a different purpose or a ramshackle system financed by charity, passport sales, and threats to Hawaiian insurance companies is economically very imperfect. So is a system financed by coercion and run by government.

These arguments suggest that it may be possible to defend against foreign nations by voluntary means. They do not prove that it will be; I am only balancing one imperfect system against another and trying to guess which will work better. What if the balance goes the other way? What will I do if, when all other functions of our government have been abolished, I conclude that there is no effective way to defend against aggressive foreign governments save by national defense financed by taxes—financed, in other words, by money taken by force from the taxpayers?

In such a situation I would not try to abolish that last vestige of government. I do not like paying taxes, but I would rather pay them to Washington than to Moscow—the rates are lower. I would still regard the government as a criminal organization, but one which was, by a freak of fate, temporarily useful. It would be like a gang of bandits who, while occasionally robbing the villages in their territory, served to keep off other and more rapacious gangs. I do not approve of any government, but I will tolerate one so long as the only other choice is another, worse government. Meanwhile, I would do my best to develop voluntary institutions that might eventually take over the business of defense. That is precisely what I meant when I said, near the beginning of this book, that I thought all government functions were divided into two classes—those we could do away with today and those we hope to be able to do away with tomorrow.

The numbers in this chapter are for about 1970; current dollar figures would be about three times as high.

35

IN WHICH PREDICTION IS REDUCED TO

SPECULATION

In the preceding chapters I have described a particular kind of anarcho-capitalist society, complete with private protection agencies, private arbitration agencies, and perhaps private defense against Russia. That is certainly not the only kind of anarchist, or even anarcho-capitalist, society that could exist. In the first section of this book I discussed the history of existing capitalist societies. But those are by no means the only kinds of societies that could exist under institutions of private property; indeed, many of their institutions would have been impossible without the active support of government.

Libertarian anarchy is only a very sketchy framework, a framework based on the idea of individual property rights—the right to one's own body, to what one produces oneself, and to what others voluntarily give one. Within that framework there are many possible ways for people to associate. Goods might be produced by giant, hierarchical corporations, like those that now exist. I hope not; it does not strike me as either an attractive way for people to live or an efficient way of producing goods. But other people might disagree; if so, in a free society they would be free to organize themselves into such corporations.

Goods might be produced by communes, group families, inside which property was held in common. That also does not seem to me to be a very attractive form of life. I would not join one, but I would have no right to prevent others from doing so.

My own preference is for the sort of economic institutions which have been named, I think by Robert LeFevre, agoric. Under agoric institutions almost everyone is self-employed. Instead of corporations there are large groups of entrepreneurs related by trade, not by authority. Each sells, not his time, but what his time produces. As a free-lance writer (one of my professions), I am part of an agoric economic order.

I have described one particular set of anarcho-capitalist institutions, not because I am certain that they are the ones that will evolve if our government is slowly reduced to nothing, but in order to show that it is at least possible for voluntary institutions to replace government in its most essential functions. The actual arrangements by which the market provides an economic good, be it food or police protection, are the product of the ingenuity of all the entrepreneurs producing that good. It would be foolish for me to predict with any confidence what will turn out to be the cheapest and most satisfactory ways of producing the services now produced by government. Even so, I am at least one step ahead of the Marxists—who predict the eventual withering away of the state but offer no real description, tentative or otherwise, of what a stateless society might be like.

36

WHY ANARCHY?

No man's life, liberty or property are safe while the legislature is in session.

QUOTED BY JUDGE GIDEON J. TUCKER
OF NEW YORK, C. 1866

Many libertarians advocate not anarchy but limited constitutional government. In my discussion of the public good problem in national defense, I accepted their arguments to the extent of conceding that there might be circumstances in which voluntary institutions could not defend themselves against a foreign state. Under such circumstances a limited government might perform a useful function. The same public good argument applies, in varying degrees, to things other than defense. Why, then, do I take as my objective a society of completely voluntary institutions, of total private property? Would it not be better to have a severely limited government doing those few things which it could do better?

Perhaps it would be—if the government stayed that way. Here we run into the problem discussed in Chapter 4. One cannot simply build any imaginable characteristics into a government; governments have their own internal dynamic. And the internal dynamic of limited governments is something with which we, to our sorrow, have a good deal of practical experience. It took about 150 years, starting with a Bill of Rights that reserved to the states and the people all powers not explicitly delegated to the federal government, to produce a Supreme Court willing to rule that growing corn to feed to your own hogs is interstate commerce and can therefore be regulated by Congress.

Suppose that a government is given the job of doing only those things that cannot be done well privately because of the public good problem. Someone, almost certainly the government, must decide what things those are. Practically every economic activity has some element of public good. Writing this book will not only benefit those who are entertained by reading it; it will also, I hope, increase at least infinitesimally the chance that I, and you, will live in an increasingly free society. That is a public good; I cannot make America free for me without making it free for you and even free for people so benighted as not to have bought this book. Does that mean that our ideal limited government should control the publishing industry? My judgment is no; the element of public good is small and the costs of public control enormous. The judgment of a government official, with his eye on power and patronage, might be different.

The logic of limited governments is to grow. There are obvious reasons for that in the nature of government, and plenty of evidence. Constitutions provide, at the most, a modest and temporary restraint. As Murray Rothbard is supposed to have said, the idea of a limited government that stays limited is truly utopian. Anarchy at least might work; limited government has been tried.

Of course, one should ask the same questions about anarchist institutions. What is their internal dynamic? Will private protection agencies, once established, continue as private profit-making concerns, or will they conclude that theft is more profitable and become governments? Will the laws of private arbitration agencies be just laws, allowing individuals to pursue their own affairs without interference, or will they allow self-righteous majorities to impose their will on the rest of us, as do many present laws? There is, after all, no absolute guarantee that the laws of an anarchist society will themselves be libertarian laws.

These are questions I attempted to answer in Chapters 30 and 31. My conclusion was one of guarded optimism. Anarchist institutions cannot prevent the members of a sufficiently large and impassioned majority from forcing their prejudices into private law codes and so imposing them on the rest of us. But they make it far more difficult and expensive, and therefore more unlikely, than under governmental institutions. Anarchist institutions cannot guarantee that protectors will never become rulers, but they decrease the power that protectors have separately or together, and they put at the head of protection agencies men who are less likely than politicians to regard theft as a congenial profession.

For all these reasons I believe that anarchist institutions, if they can be established and maintained, will be better than any government, even one initially limited and constitutional. I am willing to accept a slightly less than optimal production of a few public goods in exchange for the security of there being no government to expand into the 95 percent of human affairs where it can do nothing but damage. The ultimate objective of my political actions is not limited government: it is anarchy.

At this point another question is sometimes raised. We are a long way from the objective of a severely limited government and a longer way still from anarchy. Even if anarcho-capitalism is ideally a better system, is it not wise to focus on the more immediate goal of reducing the government and put off to the future any discussion of abolishing it?

I think not. It is important to know what road we must take, but it is also important to know where we want to go. In order to understand our position ourselves and explain it to others we must know what we ultimately want, not just what compromises we may be forced to accept.

I suspect that one reason for the enormous success of the socialist ideas of fifty and a hundred years ago—ideas which in many cases are the orthodoxy of today—was the willingness of socialists to be utopian. Their politics were Fabian, but their polemic was not. Their vision of an ultimate perfection was one of the most effective weapons in the practical struggle.

There are utopias and utopias. A utopia that will work only if populated by saints is a perilous vision; there are not enough saints. Such a vision—liberalism, socialism, call it what you will—we have followed; it has led us to where we now are.

I have not tried to construct a utopia in that sense. I have tried, to the best of my ability, to describe plausible institutions under which human beings not very different from ourselves could live. Those institutions must evolve over a period of time, as did the institutions under which we presently live; they cannot be instantly conjured up from the dreams of an enthusiastic writer. The objective is distant but not necessarily unreachable; it is well to know where one is going before taking even the first step.

37

Revolution *IS* THE HELL OF IT

After a revolution, of course, the successful revolutionists always try to convince doubters that they have achieved great things, and usually they hang any man who denies it.

H. L. MENCKEN

The case against violent revolution, for an anarchist, is simple. Government exists, ultimately, because most people believe that it performs necessary functions. The most fundamental of all these functions is protection against violence and disorder. When people view anarchy as the ultimate evil, it is not because they are concerned about mail not being delivered or streets not being cleaned. They are afraid of theft, murder, and rape, riot and arson.

The greater these fears, the greater the degree of government tyranny which people will tolerate, even support. Civil disorder leads to more government, not less. It may topple one government, but it creates a situation in which people desire another and stronger. Hitler's regime followed the chaos of the Weimar years. Russian communism is a second example, a lesson for which the anarchists of Kronstadt paid dear. Napoleon is a third. Yet many radicals, and some anarchists, talk and act as though civil disruption were the road to freedom.

For those radicals whose vision of freedom is a new government run by themselves, revolution is not a totally unreasonable strategy, although they may be overly optimistic in thinking that they are the ones who will end up on top. For those of us whose enemy is not *the* government but government itself, it is a strategy of suicide. Yet it is a strategy some anarchists advocate. What are their arguments?

One is that civil disorder is educational. A government threatened by insurrection becomes more and more tyrannical, revealing itself to the populace in its true colors. The populace, thus radicalized, rises and abolishes the government. Experimentally, the truth of this argument—that revolution leads to repression and repression to freedom—is demonstrated by the thriving anarchist communities now occupying the territories once ruled by the oppressive governments of Russia, China, and the German Reich.

Another, more unworthy, argument for revolution is simple opportunism. There is going to be a revolution whether we like it or not; one must be on one side of the barricades or the other. If a libertarian does not support the revolution, he has only himself to blame if he witnesses its triumph from an exalted position— intermediate between a lamp post and the street. Even if he escapes such a fate, he can hardly expect to influence the policy of the revolutionaries if he has not helped to make the revolution.

Even on its own terms this argument is unconvincing. Successful revolutionaries do occasionally end up in positions of power, but they seem more likely, on the historical record, to end up dead, courtesy of their comrades. In any case, revolution has its own logic, and it is, like that of politics, a logic of power. So revolution, like politics, selects out for success those with the desire and ability to wield power. A libertarian is defeated before the game starts. And by the time the revolution is successful, the population will want nothing so much as order and security. If those who began the revolution have scruples about providing what they want, someone else will be found to end it.

The case seems better, on purely opportunistic grounds, for supporting counterrevolution. There are more old falangists in Spain than old bolsheviks in Russia. But the best policy of all, if there must be a revolution, is, on moral as well as opportunistic grounds, neutrality. Climb into a hole, pull the hole in after you, and come out when people stop shooting each other.

A third argument for revolution, one which may have had more influence than either of the others, is the argument from desperation. It holds that there are reasons intrinsic to our present situation which make it impossible to weaken or destroy government by any actions 'within the system'. The only possible strategy, however bleak its chances, is to destroy the system from the 'outside', whether by nonviolent resistance or violent revolution. The crucial concept in this argument is the 'ruling class', the set of people who control the current institutions and benefit by that control. In the next chapter I will try to deal with that concept. In the chapter after that I will discuss strategies to achieve libertarian anarchy that seem more productive than revolution.

> Hurrah for revolution and more cannon-shot!
> A beggar upon horseback lashes a beggar on foot.
> Hurray for revolution and cannon come again!
> The beggars have changed places, but the lash goes
> on.
>
> W. B. YEATS

THE ECONOMICS OF THEFT OR THE NONEXISTENCE OF THE RULING CLASS

It could probably be shown by facts and figures that there is no distinctly American criminal class except Congress.

MARK TWAIN

Consider a free-market society in which theft does not exist. Suppose that some change, social, technological, or whatever, suddenly makes theft possible. What is the overall effect? One might suppose that it would be simply a transfer of the amount stolen from one group of people to another; the victims become poorer and the thieves richer by the same amount. This is not true.

People enter the profession of theft, like any other profession, until their numbers are sufficient to drive down the return from theft to the point where it is no more attractive than other professions available to them. Thieves end up working a normal eight-hour night and receive the same salary as other workers with the same talents employed elsewhere (allowing, of course, for such special business expenses as legal fees and time lost while imprisoned). The 'marginal' thief—the man who finds it just barely in his interest to be a thief and would go straight if the returns of theft were just a little lower—is better off only to the extent that the added demand for his particular talents caused by the opening of opportunities in theft has slightly raised the salary those talents can command. The nonmarginal thief—the man who happens to be better suited to theft or less suited to honest employment than most other thieves or potential thieves—benefits somewhat more, but even for him the benefit is only a part of his income, since he could be spending the same effort earning somewhat less in a different profession.

Meanwhile, the victims are worse off by the entire amount

stolen, which is at least as great as the total wages of the thieves. In addition, they pay the cost of burglar alarms, police, and other expensive concomitants of theft. The net effect of theft has been not the transfer of income but the diversion of labor from productive to unproductive uses, which reduces the total income of the members of the society by about the amount stolen.

If there is a plentiful supply of qualified thieves, or if the qualities required for theft are roughly the same as those required in other professions, the benefit to the thieves from the existence of theft will be small. If, in addition, the number of thieves is a sizable part of the population, the thieves themselves may be worse off because of the existence of theft. There is, after all, no honor among thieves; a man may return from a night of labor only to find that a fellow worker has paid him a call. In addition, the price of the goods thieves buy is increased by the cost of insurance, guards, and the like, which are necessitated by theft. Thieves themselves may lose more by theft than they make; if moderately rational, they might themselves prefer that theft be impossible.

Exactly the same argument can be made for the fences, the ultimate purchasers of stolen property, and everyone else who at first appears to be benefited by theft. In each case competition drives earnings down to the market rate, while some of the costs of theft are borne by those who appear to benefit by it.

This analysis of private theft is useful for understanding the nature of government. Government consists largely of various forms of legalized theft. The same economic principles apply to it as to illegal theft. There is competition both for employment (as politician, bureaucrat, and so on) and for purchasing stolen goods (lobbying for subsidies and other government favors). This competition drives down the income of both politicians and their customers until it reaches its market level. Just as with private theft, individuals are benefited only to the extent that their particular talents are peculiarly suitable for governmental professions. As with private theft, the wealth taken is mostly a net loss, not a transfer. If a million dollars of the taxpayers' money is being handed out, the people competing for it are willing to—and will—spend most of a million dollars to get it, just as a private thief will put in twenty dollars worth of labor to steal twenty-five dollars worth of loot. In addition, as with private theft, more resources are consumed by the cost of protection against government—the cost of tax lawyers, the cost of inefficient allocation of labor and capital in planning enterprises to minimize tax costs instead of to maximize real production, and so on. In the long run, society is probably poorer by more than the total amount stolen.

Just as private thieves may be injured by theft, it is possible that those who work in or through government may be injured, on net, by the existence of government. Indeed, it is probable, for the number of 'thieves' is enormous (virtually the entire population, to one degree or another, is using the government to steal something from someone), and the total amount stolen is a sizable fraction of the national income.

It might be argued that the chief beneficiaries of government, in particular politicians, have no talent except for theft and that the increase in their income resulting from the government's demand for that talent is therefore considerable. This argument is or-atorically satisfying, but it is probably false. There is stiff competi-tion for high office, and the men who win usually have considerable ability. Human ability is, I believe, quite generalizable; a man who is good at one thing usually can be good at others. If government were drastically reduced or eliminated, politicians could go into legitimate activities, perhaps as entertainers, perhaps as execu-tives. Most politicians, if they had stayed out of politics, would probably be earning nearly as much as they are now. But if there were no politics, everyone's income would be much higher. The abolition of government, although it might lower the relative income of those who now are, or would have become, politicians, would substantially raise their absolute income.

This entire analysis, as the title of the chapter suggests, is intended to answer the argument that the government cannot possibly be abolished legally, since the people who control it profit by it and, since they control it, they will not allow it to be destroyed 'within the system'. Such a 'ruling class' analysis fails to explain government activities, such as airline regulation, which consist mostly of destroying wealth, and the wealth of the rich at that. By imposing high airline fares, the CAB imposed a cost of about $2 billion a year on airline passengers. Many of them were surely members of the 'ruling class', if there was one. The airlines benefited by a small fraction of that amount; their total net income was only about half a billion dollars. If we assume that 40 percent of that income was a result of the CAB's activities, that all of that goes to members of the 'ruling class', and that fully half the money spent on airline fares is spent by students, low-income couples on honeymoons, and similar nonmembers of the 'ruling class', we still have the curious spectacle of a ruling class that steals a billion dollars from itself and pays eight hundred million for the privilege. It seems more reasonable to suppose that there is no ruling class, that we are ruled, rather, by a myriad of quarreling gangs, constantly engaged in stealing from each other to the great impoverishment of their own members as well as the rest of us.

Even if this is correct, there are still people who have sunk money into the existing system, have spent time and energy working their way into a profitable job, and thus have a short-run interest in maintaining that system. This is only a transitional problem. Those people will fight fiercely against any attempt to abolish their jobs while they are in them, but they have no interest in preserving them for their successors. The abolition of government will take longer than the career of one generation of bureaucrats and politicians.

This does not mean that we can achieve anarchy by merely posting a few Xerox copies of this chapter around Capitol Hill and waiting for the congressmen to recognize their long-run interests. In the next two chapters I suggest more practical—and longer—roads to freedom than that. But at least we can remove from our map one roadblock—the satanic ruling class, raking in the shekels with its right hand and stuffing the ballot box with its left.

39

THE RIGHT SIDE OF THE PUBLIC

GOOD TRAP

The analysis of public goods in Chapter 34 and the discussion of government viewed as a market in several other chapters make it possible to analyze the merits of government and anarchy in a new, or at least a more explicit, fashion. Under a government, good law is a public good. That is why it is not produced.

The concept of a public good originates in economics, but it can apply to politics as well. Under our current institutions, people do, in a sense, buy laws. They bear various costs—going to the polls and voting, investigating the implications of different proposals on the ballot and the voting patterns of different politicians, supporting campaigns with time or money—in order to influence legislation. Many discussions of democracy assume that these costs are essentially zero, that if 60 percent of the people want something it will get done. But that is true only for very simple issues. More often, the cost of finding out what is really going on and influencing it is substantial. One cannot simply go to the polls and vote for the good guys; no candidate takes 'I am a bad guy' as his campaign slogan. The political process can be viewed as a peculiar sort of economic process, intermediate between a grocery store and a horse race. Each voter decides what cost he is willing to bear in trying to get the laws he wants according to how likely his efforts are to succeed and how valuable such success may be. He 'buys' law. And, by the nature of the peculiar marketplace on which we buy law, we are likely to buy more bad law than good. For good law, like national defense, is a public good.

A public good, you will remember, is something which, if produced at all, must be produced for all the members of a pre-existing group. It is difficult for the person who produces it to charge those who benefit, since he has no way of refusing the good to those who refuse to pay. For this reason a public good may fail to be produced even when the cost of producing it is much less than its value. Since laws apply to everyone in their jurisdiction, whether or not he has worked or voted for them, good laws under governmental institutions are a public good and are consequently underproduced. Worse still, bad law is often a less public 'good' than good law. The result is that the laws of a government are worse, not better, than its citizens, in terms of their individual values and beliefs, 'deserve'.

Consider a specific example. I have a choice of two ways of making $1,000; both are political. The first way is to work for the repeal of an enormous number of different special interest laws—CAB and ICC price-fixing, agricultural subsidies, oil quotas, and so on ad nauseam—each of which costs me from a few cents to a few hundred dollars a year. The second way is by working to pass one more special interest law which will benefit a small special interest of which I am a member and which will cost everyone else a few dollars. Suppose that I have no moral preference for one method over the other. Obviously, I will choose the second; it is enormously easier to pass one law than to repeal a hundred. Of course, the first method not only benefits me, it benefits everyone else—but I get nothing from that. The second method benefits me and a few others and harms everyone else—but that costs me nothing. Even if I am just as willing to make money in a way that benefits others as in a way that harms them, the existence of governmental institutions makes it enormously easier for me to do the latter. The result is that in a society such as ours, in which most people would rather produce than steal, we all spend a large part of our time using the laws to steal from each other. The theory of democracy may be, as Mencken said, that the common people know what they want and deserve to get it—good and hard. The practice of democracy is that people get something a good deal worse than they either want or deserve.

Any attempt to improve the society as a whole is caught in the same public good trap. Anything I do to make America freer will benefit everyone; the small part of that benefit going to me is rarely sufficient to justify my doing very much. This is an especially bitter dilemma for those libertarians who are objectivists. Improving the world mainly for the benefit of other people would be altruism, which they view on philosophical grounds as the ultimate evil.

How we may succeed in working our way through that trap is the subject of the next chapter. The point I wish to make here is that once an anarchist society has been established, good law ceases to be a public good. Instead it is bad law—more precisely, the reintroduction of government—which becomes a public good. Or, rather, a public bad.

Since under the anarcho-capitalist institutions I have described each individual 'buys' his own law and gets the law he buys, law itself ceases to be a public good. Good law is still expensive—I must spend time and money determining which protection agency will best serve me—but having decided what I want, I get what I pay for. The benefit of my wise purchase goes to me, so I have an incentive to purchase wisely. It is now the person who wishes to reintroduce government who is caught in the public good problem. He cannot abolish anarchy and reintroduce government for himself alone; he must do it for everyone or for no one. If he does it for everyone, he himself gets but a tiny fraction of the 'benefit' he expects the reintroduction of government to provide. He may be sufficiently altruistic to think it desirable that everyone receive the benefit of government, but he will hardly value every other person's receiving it as much as he values receiving it himself. Nobody is altruistic enough to be as happy about everyone in the country getting a penny as about himself getting two million dollars.

Meanwhile, the people who defend the anarchist institutions— individual consumers insisting on laws that leave them free to run their own lives, members of protection agencies protecting their clients from coercers (such as thieves, hoodlums, and altruists who want to set up governments)—are all producing private goods and getting the benefit of what they produce.

Let me repeat the argument once more. The producer of a public good can get only a part of the value of producing that good; therefore a public good is produced only if it is worth much more than it costs. The producer of a private good gets virtually all the value (by selling it for what it is worth, usually) and so produces it whenever it is worth more than it costs. Thus public goods are underproduced relative to private goods. Under the institutions of government, bad laws—laws that benefit special interests at the expense of the rest of us—are private goods (more precisely, they are more nearly private goods than are good laws), and good laws, laws that benefit everyone—such as laws that leave people alone—

are public goods. Under an anarchy good laws are private goods and bad laws are public goods. Public goods are underproduced. The citizens of a government get worse laws than they deserve. The inhabitants of an anarchy get better. It is no more than a slightly exuberant exaggeration to say that a government functions properly only if it is made up exclusively of saints, and an anarchy fails only if it is inhabited exclusively by devils.

This argument should not be confused with the argument popularized by John Kenneth Gailbraith—that public goods (meaning goods produced by the government) are underproduced and that we should therefore have higher taxes and more government spending. In the technical sense in which I use the term, the benefits of increased government spending are usually *less* of a 'public good' than the costs, since the taxes that pay for a given program are usually more evenly distributed than the benefits of the program. The amount of government spending is determined by the balance of costs and benefits in the political marketplace. Since the costs are more of a public good and thus have less weight in that marketplace than the benefits, there will be too much spending not, as Gailbraith argues, too little.

40

How to get there from here

You can't get there from here.

OLD JOKE (I HOPE)

Why don't we have libertarian anarchy? Why does government exist? The answer implicit in previous chapters is that government as a whole exists because most people believe it is necessary. Most particular government activities, beyond the most fundamental, exist because they benefit some special interest at the cost of the rest of us. Each special interest will fight, in most cases successfully, to protect its private racket. Yet the individuals who make up the special interest are on the receiving end of everyone else's racket. Most of them lose, on net, by the whole transaction. To the extent that they realize this, they will support general reductions in government power. So the fundamental task is one of education.

The obvious way to educate is to write books, give speeches, argue with friends, use all available means of communication to spread libertarian ideas. That is the strategy on which I concentrate my efforts—hence this book.

It is not the only strategy. Showing is an effective way of teaching; people believe what they see. If it is the government that protects them from crime, delivers the mail, builds the streets, they will naturally conclude that without government these things will not get done. The most effective way to demonstrate that these things can be done privately is to do them. So a second strategy is the development of 'alternative institutions'—the skeleton of anarcho-capitalism within the structure of contemporary society. UPS is doing it for postal service. Similarly, private arbitrators have to some degree replaced government courts; in Chapter 18 I suggested ways of hastening that process.

Private protection is already a big business; more than one-third of all expenditure for protection against crime goes to private firms, and a majority of all security personnel are private. Some housing developments are now being built complete with their own security systems. At some point, if this trend continues, voters will find themselves protected almost entirely by private services paid for out of their own pockets. They will be understandably reluctant to pay a second time, in taxes, for a superfluous police force, just as parents whose children go to parochial schools are reluctant to vote for school taxes.

Even if these strategies are highly successful, government will continue for some decades to wield enormous powers and spend huge sums. Fortunately politicians, although usually in favor of expanding their own power, are not motivated by any altruistic desire to guarantee the oppression of our grandchildren. It may often be possible to propose a step that benefits an incumbent politician in the short run but reduces the total power of government in the long run. An example is the voucher plan described in Chapter 10. It has been supported, in a limited form, by a number of powerful politicians, including at least one governor. I do not credit the governor with a passionate dedication to reducing the power of his office, merely with the desire to use Catholic votes to keep such power as he already had.

Another example is the minicity proposal discussed in Chapter 17. For reasons given there, it might be in the interest of the governors of several large states.

So a third strategy is to create and support proposals which are in the short-run interest of some present politicians and in the long-run interest of the rest of us.

I have said nothing about direct political action—running libertarian candidates or pressuring candidates to take libertarian stands. I believe that such action, although it may be useful as a publicity device, a way of getting attention for libertarian ideas, serves no other purpose. People get more or less the politicians they want. Some would say the politicians they deserve. If the voters become so libertarian that they will only elect candidates who abolish each office as they leave it, such candidates will be found. If the voters want a powerful government, a few libertarians in Congress will not stop them.

I have described what should be done, but not who should

organize and control it. I have not said who should command the libertarian legions.

The answer, of course, is no one. One of the central libertarian ideas is that command, hierarchy, is not the only way of getting things done; it usually is not even the best way. Having abandoned politics as a way of running the country, there is no reason for us to accept politics as a way of running the conspiracy to abolish politics.

If this society is made freer, it will be done by a large number of people working individually or in small groups. I see no reason why we should all be part of some hierarchical group, some political party or libertarian conspiracy, modeled on the political institutions we are fighting against. Better, surely, for us to cooperate through the sorts of institutions we are fighting for, the institutions of the market.

A market has room for firms of varying sizes. The Society for Individual Liberty, one of the older libertarian organizations, is a firm in the business of selling libertarian literature, publishing a magazine, arranging speeches and conferences, and coordinating libertarian activities. It has things called chapters, but their members are in no way the constituents of a political organization. SIL is the personal property of (I think) four people, who started it and run it. That should, I hope, keep its internal politics down to manageable size.

An example of libertarian organization on a larger scale is the Libertarian Party. Like other political parties, it runs candidates for local, state, and national office. Its greatest successes so far are the election of two representatives to the Alaska state legislature; its most successful presidential candidate got about a million votes. Some libertarians regard it as a serious political party designed eventually to win national elections; others, myself included, regard it as a way of getting publicity for libertarian ideas.

The market for liberty has room for small firms as well. I am not an active member of any libertarian organization. I write articles and give speeches and get paid for it. I don't have to worry about whether a majority of libertarians approve of me; I do not hold any office they can vote me out of. I only have to please my customers.

When I used to give speeches in favor of abolishing the draft, there was a dirty word that kept cropping up—'mercenary'. A mercenary, as far as I could figure it out, was someone who did something because he wanted to. A soldier who fought for money.

Or glory. Or patriotism. Or fun. The opposite of a mercenary was a draftee. Someone who fought because if he did not, he would be put in jail.

According to that definition, there are only two kinds of people. Mercenaries and slaves. I'm a mercenary.

If this country is worth saving, it's worth saving at a profit.

H. L. HUNT

Postscript for perfectionists

Whenever I give a speech or write an article, I am always annoyed by how much I must leave out, and I always think that if only I were writing a book, I could say everything. I have now written a book and am forced to conclude that if only I were writing an encyclopedia. . . .

I therefore close by commenting on what I have not said. I have said almost nothing about rights, ethics, good and bad, right and wrong, although these are matters central to the ideas of most libertarians, myself included. Instead, I have couched my argument throughout in terms of practicality. I have asked, not what people should want, but how we can accomplish those things which most of us do want.

I have done this for two reasons. I am very much surer where I stand—where my arguments come from and where they will lead me—with regard to practical questions than with regard to ethical ones. And I have found that it is much easier to persuade people with practical arguments than with ethical arguments. This leads me to suspect that most political disagreement is rooted in questions of what is, not what should be. I have never met a socialist who wanted the kind of society that I think socialism would produce.

PART IV

FOR LIBERTARIANS: AN EXPANDED

POSTSCRIPT

Don't write a book; my friends on either hand
Know more than I about my deepest views.
Van den Haag believes it's simply grand
I'm a utilitarian. That's news;
I didn't know I was. Some libertairs
Can spot sheep's clothing at a thousand yards.
I do not use right arguments (read 'theirs')
Nor cheer them loudly as they stack the cards.

Assuming your conclusions is a game
That two can play at. So's a bomb or gun.
Preaching to the converted leads to fame
In narrow circles. I've found better fun
In search of something that might change a mind;
The stake's my own—and yours if so inclined.

41

Problems

Many libertarians appear to believe that libertarianism can be stated as a simple and convincing moral principle from which everything else follows. Popular candidates are 'It is always wrong to initiate coercion' and 'Everyone has the absolute right to control his own property, provided that he does not use it to violate the corresponding rights of others.' If they are right, then the obvious way to defend libertarian proposals is by showing that they follow from the initial principle. One might even argue that to defend libertarian proposals on the grounds that they have desirable consequences, as I have done throughout this book, is not only a waste of time but a dangerous waste of time, since it suggests that one must abandon the libertarian position if it turns out that some coercive alternative works better.

One problem with deducing libertarian conclusions from simple libertarian principles is that simple statements of libertarian principles are not all that compelling. Lots of people are in favor of initiating coercion, or at least doing things that libertarians regard as initiating coercion. Despite occasional claims to the contrary, libertarians have not yet produced any proof that our moral position is correct.

A second problem is that simple statements of libertarian principle taken literally can be used to prove conclusions that nobody, libertarian or otherwise, is willing to accept. If the principle is softened enough to avoid such conclusions, its implications become far less clear. It is only by being careful to restrict the application of our principles to easy cases that we can make them seem at the same time simple and true.

The easiest way to demonstrate this point is with a few examples. In order to define coercion, we need a concept of property, as I pointed out at the beginning of this book—some way of saying what is mine and what is yours. The usual libertarian solution includes property rights in land. I have the absolute right to do what I want on my land, provided that I refrain from interfering with your similar right on your land.

But what counts as interfering? If I fire a thousand megawatt laser beam at your front door I am surely violating your property rights, just as much as if I used a machine gun. But what if I reduce the intensity of the beam—say to the brightness of a flashlight? If you have an absolute right to control your land, then the intensity of the laser beam should not matter. Nobody has a right to use your property without your permission, so it is up to you to decide whether you will or will not put up with any particular invasion.

So far many will find the argument convincing. The next step is to observe that whenever I turn on a light in my house, or even strike a match, the result is to violate the property rights of my neighbors. Anyone who can see the light from his own property, whether with the naked eye or a powerful telescope, demonstrates by doing so that at least some of the photons I produced have trespassed onto his property. If everyone has an absolute right to the protection of his own property then anyone within line of sight of me can enjoin me from doing anything at all which produces light. Under those circumstances, my 'ownership' of my property is not worth very much.

A similar problem arises with pollution. Libertarians sometimes claim that since polluting the air over anyone else's property is a violation of his property rights, pollution can be forbidden in a libertarian society except when the pollutor has the consent of the owners of all affected land. This argument is used to attack schemes such as effluent fees (discussed in Chapter 26), which are designed to limit pollution to its economically efficient level—the point at which further reductions cost more than they are worth—but not to eliminate it.

Here again, the problem is that an absolute right to control one's property proves too much. Carbon dioxide is a pollutant. It is also an end product of human metabolism. If I have no right to impose a single molecule of pollution on anyone else's property, then I must get the permission of all my neighbors to breathe. Unless I promise not to exhale.

The obvious response is that only significant violations of my property rights count. But who decides what is significant? If I have an absolute property right, then I am the one who decides what violations of my property matter. If someone is allowed to violate my property with impunity as long as he does no significant damage, we are back to judging legal rules by their consequences.

A similar problem arises if we consider effects that are small not in size but in probability. Suppose I decide to play Russian roulette, with one small innovation; after putting one cartridge in my revolver and spinning the cylinder, I point it at your head instead of at mine before pulling the trigger. Most people, libertarian or otherwise, would agree that you have every right to knock the gun out of my hand before I pull the trigger. If doing something to someone (in this case shooting him) is coercive, then so is an action that has some probability of doing that something to him.

But what if the revolver has not six chambers but a thousand or a million? The right not to be coerced, stated as an absolute moral principle, should still apply. If libertarianism simply consists of working out the implications of that right, then it seems to imply that I may never do anything which results in some probability of injuring another person without his consent.

I take off from an airport in a private plane with a cruising radius of a thousand miles. There is some (small) probability that my instruments will fail, or I will fall asleep, or for some other reason I will go wildly off course. There is some probability that the plane, having gone off course, will crash. There are things I can do which will reduce these probabilities, but not to zero. It follows that by taking off I impose some (small) probability of death and destruction on everyone through whose roof I might crash. It seems to follow from libertarian principles that before taking off I must get permission from everyone living within a thousand miles of my starting point.

I am not claiming that libertarians who argue from rights rather than from consequences believe that you cannot light a match on your own property, or fly an airplane, or breathe out; obviously they do not. My point is that simple statements of libertarian rights taken literally lead to problems of this sort.

One can avoid such results by qualifying the statements: saying that they apply only to 'significant' violations of my rights, or violations that 'really injure' me, or that by breathing and turning on lights and doing other things that impose tiny costs on others I am implicitly giving them permission to do the same to me. But once one starts playing this game one can no longer use rights arguments to draw clear conclusions about what should or should not happen. People who believe in taxes can argue just as plausibly that taxes do not really injure you, since the benefits they produce more than make up for the cost, or that everyone implicitly consents to taxes by using government services.

The longer I have thought about these issues, the more convinced I have become that arguments about fundamental moral principles do not provide answers to enough important questions. In particular, they provide no answer, and no way of getting an answer, to a whole range of questions about where to draw lines. It seems obvious that we want property rules that prohibit trespass by thousand megawatt laser beams and machine-gun bullets but not by flashlights and individual carbon dioxide molecules. But how, in principle, do you decide where along that continuum the rights of the property owner stop? We want rules that prohibit me from demonstrating my marksmanship by shooting a rifle at flies hovering around your head but do not prohibit all airplane flights. We want rules that prohibit trespass by elephants but not by satellites orbiting three thousand miles over my roof.

One tempting approach to such issues is to try to go back to the origin of property in land. If we knew how I acquired ownership of land, we might also know what that ownership consists of. Unfortunately, we do not know how I acquired ownership to land. John Locke, several centuries ago, suggested that we acquire land by mixing our labor with it, but he did not explain how, when I clear a piece of forest, I acquire not only the increased value due to my efforts but complete ownership over the land. How, in particular, do I acquire the right to forbid you from walking across the land— something you could have done even if I had never cleared it? Later libertarian theorists have suggested other grounds for establishing ownership in land, such as claiming it or marking its boundaries. But no one, so far as I know, has presented any convincing reason why, if land starts out belonging equally to everyone, I somehow lose my right to walk on it as a result of your loudly announcing that it is yours.

It is easy enough to show reasons why the conversion of common property into private property is a good thing—why it makes us better off—but it is very much harder to derive property in land from some *a priori* theory of natural rights. That is why, at the beginning of this book, I conceded that the basis of property in unproduced resources such as land is shaky, and argued that it does not matter very much, since only a small fraction of the income of a modern society is derived from such resources.

The problems I have discussed so far are all associated with the definition of property rights to land. A host of similar problems arise in specifying the rules of a legal system designed to enforce libertarian rights in a libertarian way. A criminal trial rarely if ever produces a certainty of guilt. If you jail (or fine) someone after concluding that there is a 98 percent chance that he has committed a crime, there remains a two percent chance that you are violating the rights of someone who is innocent. Does that mean that you can never punish anyone unless you are a hundred percent certain he is guilty? If not, how in principle do libertarian moral principles tell you what degree of proof should be necessary for conviction and punishment?

Once someone is convicted, the next question is what you can legitimately do to him. Suppose I have stolen a hundred dollars from you. If all you are allowed to do is take your money back, then theft is an attractive profession. Sometimes I am caught and give the money back, sometimes I am not caught and keep it. Heads I win, tails I break even.

In order to prevent theft, you must be able to take back more than was stolen. But how much more? When I raised that question once in a talk to a libertarian audience, I was told that it had already been answered by a prominent libertarian—you are entitled to take back exactly twice what is stolen. That was many years ago, but nobody yet has given me a reason why it should be twice. Two is a nice number, but so is three, and there may be much to be said for four, or ten, or a hundred. The problem is not to invent answers but to find some way of deriving them.

I could continue with a wide range of other problems for which the natural rights approach to libertarianism offers, so far as I can tell, no solution. I would prefer instead to suggest a different criticism of that approach. Even if we ignore situations that involve vanishingly small rights violations, the usual statements of libertarian principle imply conclusions that almost nobody, libertarian or otherwise, believes in.

Consider the following example. A madman is about to open

fire on a crowd; if he does so numerous innocent people will die. The only way to prevent him is to shoot him with a rifle that is within reach of several members of the crowd. The rifle is on the private property of its legitimate owner. He is a well known misanthrope who has publicly stated on numerous occasions that he is opposed to letting anyone use his rifle without his permission, even if it would save hundreds of lives.

Two questions now arise. The first is whether members of the crowd have a right to take the rifle and use it to shoot the madman. The answer of libertarian rights theory, as I understand it, is no. The owner of the rifle is not responsible for the existence of the madman, and the fact that his rifle is, temporarily, of enormous value to other people does not give them a right to take it.

The second question is whether it is desirable that someone take the rifle and use it to shoot the madman—whether, to put it more personally, I wish that someone do so, or whether I would rather see the members of the crowd stand there and be shot down. The answer to this question seems equally unambiguous. If someone takes the rifle, there is a relatively minor violation of the legitimate rights of its owner; if no one does, there is a major violation of the legitimate rights (not to be killed) of a large number of victims— plus a substantial cost in human life and human pain. If asked which of these outcomes I would prefer to see, the answer is obviously the first.

This result is not, in any strict sense, paradoxical. An outcome may be desirable even though there is no morally legitimate way of achieving it. Indeed, this possibility is implied by the idea (due to Nozick) of viewing libertarian rights as 'side constraints' within which we seek to achieve some objective; the constraints would be irrelevant unless there were some circumstances in which we could better achieve the objective by ignoring them.

While not in any strict sense paradoxical, the result is, at least to me, an uncomfortable one. It puts me in the position of saying that I very much hope someone grabs the gun, but that I disapprove of whoever does so.

One solution to this problem is to reject the idea that natural rights are absolute; potential victims have the right to commit a minor rights violation, compensating the owner of the gun after- wards to the best of their ability, in order to prevent a major one. Another is to claim that natural rights are convenient rules of thumb which correctly describe how one should act under most circumstances, but that in sufficiently unusual situations one must abandon the general rules and make decisions in terms of the ultimate objectives which the rules were intended to achieve. A third response is to assert that the situation I have described cannot occur, that there is some natural law guaranteeing that rights violations will always have bad consequences and that committing one rights violation can never decrease the total of rights violations.

All of these positions lead to the same conclusion. Under some circumstances rights violations must be evaluated on their merits, rather than rejected *a priori* on conventional libertarian natural rights grounds. Those who believe that rights violations are always undesirable will be sure that the result of the evaluation will be to reject the violation, but that does not mean that they can reject arguments to the contrary without first answering them. Any such argument claims to provide a counterexample to their general theorem, and if one such counterexample is true the general theorem must be false.

I have made my point so far in terms of an issue created for the purpose; whether or not to steal rifles in order to shoot madmen is not a burning issue in libertarian (or other) circles. I will now carry the argument a step further by defending one of the particular heresies which, it is widely believed, no libertarian can support— that under some conceivable circumstances a draft would be desirable.

Suppose we are threatened with military conquest by a particularly vicious totalitarian government; if the conquest is successful we shall all lose most of our freedom and many of us will lose our lives. It is claimed that only a draft can protect us. Two replies are possible. The first is that since coercion is always wrong we should reject the draft whatever the consequences. I have tried to show that that answer is not satisfactory—at the most it should lead us to refuse to enforce a draft ourselves while hoping that someone with fewer principles imposes one for us. Temporary slavery is, after all, better than permanent slavery.

The other possible reply is to deny that the draft is necessary. This can be done in many ways. The economist is inclined to argue that collecting taxes in cash and using them to hire soldiers is always more efficient than collecting taxes in labor; the moralist may claim that a society whose members will not voluntarily defend it is not worth defending. I have myself used the first argument many times; I believe that in the circumstances presently facing the U.S. it is correct. But the question I am currently concerned with is not whether under present circumstances, or even under likely circumstances, a draft is desirable. The question is whether under any conceivable circumstances it could be.

The answer is yes. Imagine a situation in which the chance of a soldier being killed is so high that a rational individual who is concerned chiefly with his own welfare will refuse to volunteer even at a very high wage. Imagine further that the percentage of the population required to defeat the enemy is so large that there are simply not enough patriotic, or altruistic, or adventure-loving, or unreasonably optimistic recruits available; in order to win the war the army must also include selfish individuals with a realistic view of the costs and benefits to themselves of joining the army. Recruiters and preachers will of course point out to such individuals that 'if everyone refuses to fight we will be conquered and you will be worse off than if everyone volunteers to fight.' The individual will reply, correctly, that what he does does not determine what everyone else does. If everyone else volunteers, he can stay safely at home; if nobody else volunteers and he does, he will almost certainly be killed and if not killed will be enslaved.

Under such circumstances, an army could be recruited without a draft by paying very high salaries and financing them with taxes so high that anyone who does not volunteer starves to death. The coercion of a tax is then indistinguishable from the coercion of a draft. While a libertarian may still argue that to impose either a draft or a tax is immoral and that he himself would refuse to do so, I find it hard to see how he can deny that, under the circumstances I have hypothesized, he would rather see himself and everyone else temporarily enslaved by his own government than permanently enslaved by someone else's.

The point of this argument is not that we should have a draft. As it happens, I not only believe that under present circumstances a draft is a bad thing, I also believe that if the government has the power to impose a draft it is very much more likely that it will use it when it should not than that the rather unlikely circumstances I have described will occur. That is, however, a practical argument, and one that might depend on the particular circumstances of a particular time and place; it is not an argument of principle that would apply everywhere and everywhen.

Perhaps what these examples show is not that we cannot accept a simple statement of libertarian principle but only that I picked the wrong one. Perhaps we should replace a statement about what one should do ('never initiate coercion') with a statement about what objective one should seek ('do whatever minimizes the total amount of coercion'). Both seizing the rifle and imposing a draft are then, in the particular circumstances I have described, not only consistent with libertarian principle but required by it.

While I cannot speak for other libertarians, I find that this version of libertarianism does not always fit my moral intuition. Suppose the only way I can stop someone from stealing two hundred dollars from me is by stealing your hundred-dollar rifle (which you are unwilling to lend or sell me) and using it to defend myself. The result is to reduce the total amount of coercion, at least if we measure amount by value of what is stolen. Yet it seems, at least to me, that stealing the rifle is still wrong.

A second problem with this approach is that it is of no help when we must choose between a small cost in coercion and an enormous cost in something else. Suppose you happen to know that everyone in the world is going to die tomorrow (by some natural catastrophe, say the earth colliding with a large asteroid), unless you prevent it. Further suppose that the only way to prevent it involves stealing a piece of equipment worth a hundred dollars from someone who, in your opinion, rightfully owns it. Your choice is simple: violate libertarian principles by stealing something or let everyone die.

What do you do? You cannot justify stealing as a way of minimizing total coercion. Being killed by an asteroid is not coercion, since it is not done by a person. After the asteroid strikes there will be no more coercion ever again, since there will be no one left to either coerce or be coerced.

Speaking for myself, the answer is that I steal. When I put such questions to other libertarians, one common response is a frantic attempt to reinterpret the problem out of existence. One example might be the reply that, since the person you are stealing from will himself be killed if you do not take the device, he would be in favor of your taking it, so you are not really stealing—you are using the device in the way he would want you to if he knew what you know. Another response might be that you should not steal the equipment because your belief that doing so will save the world may be wrong.

All such evasions are futile. I can always alter the assumptions to force the issue back to its original form. Perhaps the owner of the device agrees that using it is necessary if the world is to be saved, but he is old, tired of living, and not very fond of his fellow humans. Perhaps the situation is so clear that everyone agrees that without your act of theft we shall all die.

Our response to such questions demonstrates that we do not really believe in simple single values. Most libertarians, myself among them, believe that a libertarian society is both just and attractive. It is easy enough to claim that we are in favor of following libertarian principle whatever the consequences—given that we believe the consequences would be the most attractive society the world has ever known. But the claim that we put individual rights above everything else is, for most of us, false. Although we give some value, perhaps very great value, to individual rights, we do not give them an infinite value. We can pretend the contrary only by resolutely refusing to consider situations in which we might have to choose between individual rights and other things that are also of great value.

My purpose is not to argue that we should stop being libertarians. My purpose is to argue that libertarianism is not a collection of straightforward and unambiguous arguments establishing with certainty a set of unquestionable propositions. It is rather the attempt to apply certain economic and ethical insights to a very complicated world. The more carefully one does so, the more complications one is likely to discover and the more qualifications one must put on one's results.

42

Wʜᴇʀᴇ ɪ Sᴛᴀɴᴅ

In the previous chapter, I argued that simple statements of libertarian principle lead to unacceptable conclusions and must therefore be rejected. There is no obvious logical inconsistency in a moral principle that implies that nobody should be permitted to breathe, but it is not a principle that many people are likely to accept.

One possible response is that libertarianism is an absolute principle, an ultimate value which cannot be overridden, but that it is not adequately expressed by the simple statements I have been attacking. If those statements are only approximations to a much more complicated and subtle description of libertarian principle, it is hardly surprising that the approximation sometimes breaks down in difficult situations.

This is a view with which I have a good deal of sympathy, but it is not very useful for answering real-world questions, at least until someone manages to produce an adequate statement of what libertarian principles really are. Moral philosophy is a very old enterprise and its rate of progress has not been rapid in recent centuries, so I do not plan to hold my breath while I wait.

A second response, and one with which I also have a good deal of sympathy, is that there are a number of important values in the world. They cannot be arranged in any simple hierarchy, or at least are not going to be any time soon. Individual liberty is an important value in and of itself, not merely as a means to happiness, so we should not be willing to sacrifice large amounts of it in exchange for small amounts of happiness. But liberty is not the only value, nor is it infinitely important compared to other values, so we should not be willing to sacrifice unlimited amounts of happiness for small gains in liberty.

A third possibility is that the conflict between libertarian and utilitarian values is only apparent. Perhaps there is some deep connection between the two, so that libertarian ethics, properly understood, is the set of rules that leads to the maximum of human happiness. The counterexamples given in the previous chapter must then be interpreted as some combination of mistakes about what is possible—for some reason those situations could not arise in the real world—and mistakes about what is implied by a correct statement of libertarian principle. Something along these lines seems to be suggested by the arguments of those libertarian philosophers who claim to get their principles not by generalizing from what seems right or wrong to them but by deducing what set of rules is appropriate to the nature of man.

One argument in favor of this approach is that it fits the observation that libertarianism and utilitarianism, while quite different in principle, frequently lead to the same conclusion. Through most of this book I have used utilitarian arguments to justify libertarian conclusions. By doing so, I provided evidence that the potential conflicts between the two approaches which I discussed in the previous chapter are the exception rather than the rule. In Chapter 31 I tried to show that the institutions of anarcho-capitalism would tend to generate libertarian laws. A key step in that argument was my claim that the value to individuals of being able to run their own lives is typically greater than the value to anyone else of being able to control them—or in other words, that increases in liberty tend to increase total utility.

A fourth possibility, and the last which I will consider, is that libertarianism is wrong and we should accept utilitarianism instead. According to the strict utilitarian position, rules, actions, ethics, must be judged solely by their effect on the sum (some utilitarians would say the average) of human happiness. Whatever increases happiness is good; whatever decreases it is bad. Libertarian principles are then valued only as a means, a set of rules that frequently lead to increases in total utility and should be rejected when they do not. This again is a possible interpretation of arguments that claim to derive libertarian principles from the nature of man, although not, in my experience, an interpretation that those who make such arguments are willing to accept.

One argument against utilitarianism is that it cannot be a correct moral rule because there is no way we can tell whether we are following it. We cannot observe other people's utility and are therefore unable to judge what will increase it. Even if we could observe individual utilities, we do not know how to compare the utility of different people and so have no way of judging whether a gain in happiness to one person does or does not balance a loss to another.

I find this argument unconvincing. Consider the act of buying a present. If you really have no knowledge at all about what makes other people happy, then buying a present is pure guesswork; you might just as well open a page of the Sears catalog at random, throw a dart at it, and buy whatever you hit. Nobody believes that; if we did, we would not buy presents.

Consider a court awarding damages. If we really know nothing at all about other people's utility, how can a court decide how much someone owes me for breaking my arm? For all the judge knows, I enjoyed having my arm broken. Assuming that I disliked it, he has no way of knowing whether my disutility for a broken arm is measured by a penny or a billion dollars.

We give presents and award damages, and we do not believe that other people's utility is entirely unobservable. What we do believe, or at least what many of us believe, is that each of us knows more about his own values than most other people do, and that people are therefore usually better off deciding what they want for themselves. That is one of the main arguments in favor of a free society. It is a long step from that to the claim that we know nothing at all about other people's values.

Even if we were entirely unable to observe other people's values, that would not necessarily prevent us from constructing a society designed to maximize total utility. Each person knows his own values, so all of us put together know everybody's values. In order to maximize the total utility of the society, we would construct rules and institutions that utilized all of that information via some sort of decentralized decisionmaking system, with each person making the decisions that require the particular knowledge he has.

This is not, of course, merely an abstract possibility. One of the strongest arguments in favor of letting people interact freely in a market under property rights institutions is that it is the best known way to utilize the decentralized knowledge of the society— including the knowledge that each individual has about his own values. The field of welfare economics largely consists of the analysis of the rules that lead to optimal outcomes under specified circumstances, where the outcomes are evaluated in terms of the preferences of the individuals concerned. One originator of modern economics, including much of welfare economics, was Alfred Marshall, an economist and utilitarian who viewed economic theory in part as a way of figuring out how to maximize total utility.

Even if individual preferences can be observed, either directly or as reflected in actions, we are still left with the problem of comparing them. How can we say whether something which makes one person worse off and another better off produces a net increase in human happiness?

The answer, I believe, is that we may not be able to make such comparisons very well or describe clearly how we make them, but we still do it. When you decide to give ten dollars' worth of food and clothing to someone whose house has just burned down instead of sending a ten-dollar check as an unsolicited gift to a random millionaire, you are expressing an opinion about which of them values the money more. When you decide where to take your children for vacation, you are making a complicated judgment about whether their total happiness will be greater camping in a forest or wading on the seashore. We cannot reduce the decision to a matter of precise calculation, but few of us doubt that the unhappiness A gets from the prick of a pin is less than the unhappiness B gets from being tortured to death.

Utilitarianism is a possible moral rule. The difficulties of applying it to real world problems are substantial, but so are the difficulties of applying an alternative rule such as minimizing coercion. One would face very similar problems in defining and measuring the amount of coercion and in judging the tradeoff between increased coercion for one person and decreased coercion for another.

Utilitarianism is a possible moral rule, but it is not one that I am willing to accept. Why? For the same reason that I reject all simple statements of libertarianism—because I can construct hypothetical situations in which it seems clear to me that the rule gives the wrong answer.

You are the sheriff of a small town plagued by a series of particularly brutal murders. Fortunately, the murderer has left town. Unfortunately, the townspeople do not believe that the murderer has left, and will regard your assertion that he has as an attempt to justify your own incompetence in failing to catch him.

Feeling is running high. If no murderer is produced, three or four innocent suspects will get lynched. There is an alternative. You can manufacture evidence to frame someone. Once he has been convicted and hung, the problem will be gone. Should you do it?

On utilitarian grounds, it seems clear that the answer is yes. You are killing one innocent person but saving several—and you have no reason to believe that the one you kill values life any more than the ones you save. You yourself may receive disutility from knowing that you have framed an innocent man—but if it gets bad enough you can always kill yourself, leaving a profit of at least one life's worth of utility.

I am not willing to accept the conclusion. In an earlier hypothetical, I said that I would steal; in this one, I would not frame. To save a million lives, perhaps, but for a net profit of one or two, no. It follows that I am not a utilitarian.

Although I reject utilitarianism as the ultimate standard for what should or should not happen, I believe that utilitarian arguments are usually the best way to defend libertarian views. While most people do not believe that maximizing human happiness is the only thing that matters, most do believe that human happiness is important. Libertarians are not the only ones who avoid conflicts by believing that the system they favor works both morally and practically. To the extent that I can show that a particular libertarian proposal—abolition of heroin laws, or minimum wage laws, or all government—produces attractive results, I have an argument which will have some weight in convincing almost anyone to support it.

So one reason to base my arguments on consequences rather than justice is that people have widely varying ideas about what is just but generally agree that making people happy and prosperous is a good thing. If I argue against heroin laws on the grounds that they violate the addicts' rights, I will convince only other libertarians. If I argue that drug laws, by making drugs enormously more expensive, are the chief cause of drug-related crime, and that the poor quality control typical of an illegal market is the main source of drug-related deaths, I may convince even people who do not believe that drug addicts have rights.

A second reason to use practical rather than ethical arguments is that I know a great deal more about what works than about what is just. This is in part a matter of specialization; I have spent more time studying economics than moral philosophy. But I do not think that is all it is. One reason I have spent more time studying economics is that I think more is known about the consequences of institutions than about what is or is not just—that economics is a much better developed science than moral philosophy.

If so, the implications are not limited to the best choice of arguments with which to convince others. In the previous chapter I gave a long list of questions which I saw no way of using libertarian principles to answer. In the next chapter I will argue that they are all questions that can, at least in principle, be answered by using economic theory to discover what rules maximize human happiness. If so, then economics is not only a better way of persuading others. It is also a better way of figuring out what I myself am in favor of.

43

ANSWERS: THE ECONOMIC ANALYSIS

OF LAW

W e wish to know what the laws of a society—statist or anarchist—ought to be. The obvious way to find out is to start with general principles of justice and see what laws are necessary to implement them. In an earlier chapter, I argued that that cannot be done; libertarian principles of justice cannot, at least as they now exist, answer the relevant questions. They provide no way of deciding what ought to be included in property rights, how they may legitimately be defended, or how violations ought to be punished.

When I say that libertarian principles cannot answer the questions, I do not merely mean that answering them is hard. That would be true wherever we started; these are hard questions. I mean that I cannot see how to even start answering these questions—what facts I need, what calculations I should do. It is as if I were faced with an engineering problem and had no way of finding out how to start setting up the relevant equations.

Perhaps someone else does know how to do it—but someone else is not writing this book. My solution is to find a different starting point from which to solve the problem. That starting point is utilitarianism. As a moral philosopher I am a libertarian, insofar as I am anything. As an economist I am a utilitarian.

One could describe most of this book as a utilitarian approach to libertarianism, but only by using 'utilitarian' in a very general sense. I have tried to show that libertarian institutions produce attractive results, but I have not defined 'attractive' as anything so specific as 'tending to maximize the sum total of human happiness'. In this chapter, however, I am trying to answer much more specific questions—not merely 'should we have property rights?' but 'exactly what sort of property rights should we have?' To do so I require a more specific definition of the objective I am trying to achieve. When I am finished, your conclusion, if you agree with everything I say, should not be 'we should have property rights X, Y, and Z' but rather 'If we wanted to maximize total utility we would want property rights X, Y, and Z'.

Even if I can demonstrate that, why should I bother? By adopting a philosophical position that I believe is false, merely because it makes it easier to answer a particular set of questions, am I not making the same error as the drunk who, having lost his wallet in the middle of the block, looked for it under the streetlamp at the corner because the light was better there?

I think not. Even if utilitarianism is not true it may still be useful. There seems to be a close correlation between rules that make people free and rules that make them happy; that is why it is the East Germans and not the West Germans who erect barbed wire fences and guard towers on their common border. Perhaps that correlation comes from some deep connection between freedom and happiness; perhaps it is merely an accident. In any case, it is there. I conclude that, by figuring out what legal rules would best make people happy, I may learn something about what legal rules are suitable for a free society.

A second reason utilitarian arguments may be useful is that even if they cannot tell us what the legal rules should be they may, under some circumstances, tell us what they will be. In Chapter 31 I tried to show that the institutions of anarcho-capitalism tend to produce economically efficient law. By figuring out what legal rules would be economically efficient we can learn something about what rules would be generated by such a society. Richard Posner, one of the leading writers on the economic analysis of law, has made the same claim for the existing body of common law. If he is right, then economic efficiency is useful for understanding what the law is as well as what it ought to be. Economic efficiency and total happiness are, as you will shortly see, closely related; the former is best understood as an approximate measure of the latter.

A third reason was suggested at the end of the previous chapter. Most people, myself included, are at least partly utilitarians. While a demonstration that a particular legal rule tends to increase the total of human happiness does not prove that the rule is a good one, it is a strong argument for it. Since I have no very good way to settle disagreements about values, it makes sense to base my argument on values that most people share.

The final reason is that, whether or not people care about the sum total of human happiness, most of us care a good deal about our own happiness. If a particular legal rule increases the average level of happiness there is at least a presumption that it will, on average and in the long run, make me better off. That is a reason, although not necessarily a compelling reason, why I should favor it.

For all of these reason, it makes sense to ask what legal rules tend to maximize human happiness. The rest of this chapter is devoted to trying to answer that question. My tool for doing so is the economic analysis of law. The first steps are to explain what economic efficiency means, how it can be used to choose legal rules, and why it may be a useful measure of total happiness.

Consider some change that affects only two people. For each, one may ask how much the change is worth to him—how many dollars he would if necessary pay in order to get it (positive value) or prevent it (negative value). One could then sum the answers to get a dollar value for the effect of the change. If one person was willing to pay four dollars to get the change and the other two dollars to prevent it, one might say that the change increased total value by two dollars. One could make the same calculation with any number of people, summing the positive values of those who favor the change and the negative values of those opposed to it. If the net is positive we describe the change as an economic improvement or an increase in efficiency, if negative as an economic worsening or decrease in efficiency.

Although we are measuring values in dollars, no money need actually be involved. The change might be the transfer of an apple from you to me. The apple is worth two dollars to you and four to me. You would pay up to two dollars to keep the apple (prevent the transfer), so the change has a value to you of minus two dollars. I would pay up to four to get the apple, so the change has a value to me of plus four dollars. The change produces an economic gain of two dollars.

How would we find out whether a particular change produced a net gain or a net loss? The best way would be to observe people's values as reflected in their actions. Suppose I offer you three dollars for the apple and you accept. The fact that I make the offer implies that the apple is worth more than three dollars to me; the fact that you accept implies it is worth less than three dollars to you. Assuming that we are the only people affected, the transfer must result in a net gain. Generalizing the argument, we conclude that any voluntary transaction that has no effect on third parties must result in an economic improvement.

Voluntary transactions are improvements, but improvements are not necessarily voluntary transactions. Suppose I am lost in the woods and starving. I stumble upon your locked cabin, break in, and use the telephone to summon help. Being both grateful and responsible, I leave you an envelope containing enough money to pay for the damage several times over. The exchange is not voluntary; you did not give me permission to break into your cabin. But, just as with a voluntary transaction, we have both ended up better off (assuming my calculation of how much to leave was correct), so there was a net improvement.

In both cases—selling the apple and breaking into the cabin—the cash payment provided evidence that there was a net gain, but the gain was produced by the transfer not by the payment. The same two-dollar gain would have occurred if you had accidentally lost the apple and I had found it, although in that case it would have been the sum of a four-dollar gain and a two-dollar loss instead of the sum of two one-dollar gains (lose an apple valued at two dollars, get three dollars for you; gain an apple valued at four dollars, lose three dollars for me).

So far, we have been talking about changes, not about rules. The next step is to ask what legal rule will result in only efficient changes—changes that produce a net economic benefit. In the case of the apple, we want a rule that will result in the apple being transferred to me if and only if it is worth more to me than to you, since only then is the transfer an economic improvement. The obvious solution is to allow the transfer if and only if both of us agree to it. If the apple is worth more to me than to you I will make you an offer for it that you will accept; if it is not I will not. In this case, the solution is simply property rights, enforced by a punishment for anyone who steals an apple.

What about the case of the cabin? Property rights will not solve that problem, since the owner of the cabin is not available to rent out the use of his phone. This time the solution is a damage rule. If I break into the cabin (and turn myself in for doing so), I owe the owner a payment equal to the amount of damage I have done to his property. If the use of his phone is not worth that price, I will keep wandering; if it is, I will break in. That is, in each case, the economically efficient outcome.

I have now gotten far enough so that you can see how, in principle, economic analysis can be used to figure out what laws ought to be. Before I go on to discuss these two examples in more detail and to apply the analysis to some of the problems mentioned in Chapter 41, I should first fill in a missing step in the argument. I have talked about maximizing total happiness and about economic improvement, but have not shown that the two have anything to do with each other. I have not shown when or why the fact that some change is an economic improvement implies that it increases total utility.

There are two important differences between the economist's criterion and the philosopher's. The first involves the measurement of utility for an individual, the second the comparison of the utility of different people.

In defining value, the economist accepts the individual's own evaluation of whether something does or does not make him better off. If I prefer gaining an apple and losing four dollars to doing neither, that shows that the apple is worth at least four dollars to me. That definition of value is what economists call 'the principle of revealed preference'. The possibility that I am wrong in judging my own interest, that I am willing to pay for apples even though they are bad for me, is assumed away.

One implication of that assumption is that the value of heroin to a heroin addict is just as real as the value of insulin to a diabetic. If you are unwilling to accept such implications you will conclude that an economic improvement is not inevitably an increase in total human happiness; some of the values gained may represent mistakes by individuals about what is in their own interest. You may still agree that, for most people most of the time, revealed preference is the best available way of measuring value, and that economic efficiency is therefore a good, although not a perfect, measure of total happiness.

The second divergence between economic improvement and increased utility involves comparisons between people. In summing individual values in order to decide whether some change is an improvement or a worsening, we count a one-dollar gain to one person as just cancelling a one-dollar loss to another. We act as if a dollar (or what a dollar can buy) were worth the same amount of happiness to everyone.

If the rule that the economist uses for making interpersonal comparisons is wrong, why should we use it and how can it tell us anything about what legal rules maximize total happiness? The answer to the first question is that we use the rule because my value for an apple is much easier to observe than my utility for an apple. We can observe my value for an apple by how much I am willing to pay for one, and we can, as I have just demonstrated, set up legal rules (property rights) that give me the apple if and only if its value to me is greater than its value to anyone else.

A system of rules that gave me the apple only if I got more utility from it than anyone else would be very much harder to construct. My actions show my utility for an apple relative to my utility for some other good that I am offering to exchange for it (dollars in this case), not relative to someone else's utility for the same apple. In order to give the apple to the person who got the highest utility for it, someone would have to judge how much happier an apple made each of us. Observing other people's utility may not be impossible, but it is much harder than observing our own. It follows that it is much easier to design institutions that maximize value—that produce changes if and only if they are economic improvements— than to design institutions that maximize total utility.

It is easier to figure out what increases value than what increases utility, but is the answer of any use? Am I not again searching where the light is best instead of where I dropped my wallet? I think not. In many situations, although not in all, the fact that a change is an economic improvement—increases total value— is strong evidence that it also increases total utility. Since changes in economic value are much easier to measure than changes in utility, we may use the former as a proxy for the latter.

Consider, for example, the abolition of a tariff on U.S. imports. Suppose we could show (as in many cases we can) that, in addition to benefitting our trading partners abroad, it is an economic improvement from the standpoint of residents of the U.S.—the gain to Americans who are better off as a result of abolishing the tariff (workers and stockholders in U.S. export industries and American consumers of imported goods), measured in dollars, is greater than the loss to those who are worse off (workers and stockholders in industries that compete with imports). Individual gainers and losers may have greatly varying values for a dollar; a change that benefits one of them by six dollars and hurts another by five is not necessarily an improvement in total utility. But both gainers and losers are large and diverse groups, and there is no obvious reason to expect the one group, on average, to value dollars more or less than the other. If the average is about the same for both groups, then a change that produces a gain in value probably produces a gain in utility as well. That was the argument used by Alfred Marshall, who invented the idea of economic improvement, to justify using it as an approximate way of identifying changes that increase total utility.

The approximation should be a good one as long as we are considering situations where there is no reason to expect gainers and losers to have, on average, different utilities for a dollar— different relations between value measured in dollars and utility measured in some absolute units of happiness. In many cases that is a reasonable assumption. Buyers and sellers of apples, lost hunters and owners of locked cabins in the woods, are likely to be similar people—even the same people at different times.

There is one obvious exception. We expect, as a general rule, that the more money you have the less an additional dollar is worth to you, and therefore that, on average, a dollar represents more happiness for someone with very little money than for someone with a lot of money. That is why we rarely give charity to millionaires. We therefore expect that, if gainers and losers have very different incomes, the net change in value will be a poor measure of the net change in happiness.

A change that makes a rich man ten dollars worse off and a poor man nine dollars better off is an economic worsening, but it may well increase the amount of happiness in the world. The same is true for a change that harms a large group of rich people by a total of ten million dollars and benefits a large group of poor people by a total of nine million. The obvious conclusion, and one that many utilitarians have drawn, is that income redistribution is a good thing. Taxing the rich and giving the money to the poor may be an economic worsening, due to collection costs and disincentives, and yet a utilitarian improvement.

My reasons for disagreeing with that conclusion are two. The first is that since the poor are, as a rule, politically weak, they are at least as likely to be the victims of governmental income transfers as they are to be the beneficiaries. That is the point that I made in Chapter 4. The second is that the struggle among groups trying to make themselves beneficiaries rather than victims is likely to be an expensive one, making practically all of us, rich and poor, worse off in a society that permits such redistribution than in one that does not. That is the point that I made in Chapter 38. Those two chapters were a utilitarian attack on one of the chief doctrines that divides utilitarians from libertarians.

Some pages back, I abandoned the subject of specific rules in order to show the connection between economic improvement and increases in total happiness—to show why designing rules to maximize economic efficiency makes sense as a way of increasing human happiness. I have now done so. I have not shown that economic improvement and increases in total utility are the same; they are not. I have shown why the former is an approximate measure of the latter, and may, for practical purposes, be the best measure available. Readers who are not convinced may want to look at Marshall's original argument or at the much more detailed discussion of economic efficiency in another book of mine; both books are listed in Appendix 2. Readers who are economics students should be warned that those are almost the only places to look. Modern economics texts other than mine use a different, although for most purposes equivalent, definition of improvement.

It is now time to go back to discussing specific rules. The question I shall be investigating is how one would design legal rules to maximize economic efficiency—to permit changes that are economic improvements and prevent changes that are economic worsenings.

Consider again the solution to the apple problem. If we do not enforce property rights in apples at least two kinds of inefficient change may occur. First, apples may be transferred from owners who value them more to thieves who value them less. Second, thieves may spend time and money stealing apples instead of buying them.

Suppose the apple is worth two dollars to you and four dollars to me. Instead of buying it for three dollars I sneak into your orchard at night and steal it, at a cost of a dollar's worth of time and effort. You are worse off by two dollars (the value of the apple to you) and I am better off by three dollars (the value of the apple to me minus the cost to me of getting it), so there is a net gain of one dollar; my stealing the apple is an economic improvement over my not getting it at all. But not getting the apple is not the only alternative; I could have bought it instead. Stealing the apple is worse than buying the apple, since that would have produced a net gain of two dollars. An efficient legal system will include some way of making it in the interest of people who want apples to buy them instead of stealing them. That is why we punish thieves.

How much should we punish them? If all thieves were caught, a fine equal to the value of what is stolen would be sufficient; since stealing things is more trouble than buying them, theft would be the less attractive of the two alternatives. If only a fraction of thieves are caught, say one in ten, the same argument suggests that the punishment should be scaled up accordingly. If the fine for stealing an apple is ten times the price of buying one, then stealing costs the thief, on average, as much money as buying and more trouble.

We now have the same rule for apples and for cabins. The rule I suggested for someone who broke into a cabin was that he should pay a fine equal to the damage done—provided he turned himself in. I included that condition in order to make it a case where the probability of being caught was one.

In order to eliminate inefficient transactions, the amount of the fine (or the probability times the amount, if only a fraction of thieves are caught) must be at least the value of what is taken. The case of the cabin in the woods is an argument against making the fine any higher than that. While we could have one legal rule for apples and a different one for cabins, it may be easier to have a single set of rules defining what property rights are and what happens if you violate them. Such a set of rules should take account of the possibility that some violations of property rights, such as the lost hunter breaking into the cabin, are desirable changes that for some reason cannot be arranged via a voluntary exchange. A punishment lower than the damage done permits some inefficient changes; a punishment higher than the damage done prevents some efficient ones. So the ideal punishment equals the damage done, appropriately adjusted for the probability of catching and convicting the criminal.

If I were devoting a book instead of a chapter to the economic analysis of law, I would qualify this conclusion in many ways, to take account of complications such as the cost of enforcing law (preventing inefficient crimes may sometimes cost more than it is worth) and the possibility of error in determining guilt. Readers who are interested in a more detailed analysis should look at the books and articles on economic analysis of law cited in Appendix 2.

So far, I have treated the probability of catching a thief as if it were simply a fact of nature. It is not. By hiring more policemen or offering higher rewards we can increase the probability that thieves will be caught. In setting up a system of legal rules, one of the decisions to be made is whether to catch half the thieves and fine each of them twice what he stole, catch a tenth of the thieves and fine each ten times what he stole, or catch one thief in a thousand and shoot him.

In choosing the proper combination of punishment and probability, we are trading off two kinds of costs. Enforcement cost is the cost of catching criminals—paying policemen, distributing pictures of wanted criminals, or whatever. Punishment cost is the cost of punishing criminals once we have caught them. As we move from a combination of high probability and small punishment to a combination of low probability and large punishment, enforcement costs decline, since we only have to catch one criminal in a hundred instead of one in two. Punishment costs, however, tend to rise with the size of the punishment. So we maximize total value by choosing the combination of probability and punishment that produces the appropriate level of deterrence—probability times punishment equal to damage done by the crime—at the lowest cost.

What is punishment cost and why does it increase with the size of the punishment? Consider first a fine. The cost to the criminal is the amount of money he has to pay; having to pay a ten-dollar fine makes me worse off by exactly ten dollars. That cost is balanced, however, by the benefit to whoever receives the fine—the victim under a system of civil law, where the fine is called a damage payment, or the state under a system of criminal law. The net cost of the fine is only the administrative expense of collecting it.

As the size of the punishment becomes larger it becomes less likely that the criminal can pay it as a fine and more likely that it must take some other form, such as imprisonment or execution. Imprisonment and execution serve at least as well as fines to discourage people from violating other people's property rights, but the cost to the criminal is no longer a benefit to someone else. When the criminal loses his life, nobody else gets an extra life in exchange; when you are imprisoned, nobody gets the freedom you lose and someone must pay the additional cost of maintaining the prison.

The recognition that punishment is costly provides part of the answer to another problem mentioned in Chapter 41—how sure we have to be that someone is guilty before convicting him. Punishing the innocent results in the same sorts of costs as punishing the guilty without providing the benefit of deterrence. In designing the optimal system of legal rules, we must balance the punishment cost of convicting innocent defendants against the costs of a higher standard of proof—hiring more policemen and acquitting more guilty defendants.

One conclusion is that we will want a higher standard of proof for an offense that results in a costly punishment, such as execution, than for an offense that results in an inexpensive punishment, such as a fine. That is, in fact, the way our present legal system works. A higher standard of proof is required in criminal cases ("beyond a reasonable doubt") than in civil cases ("the preponderance of the evidence"). This is not simply a matter of taking more care in more important cases; a million dollar damage payment is a bigger punishment than a two-week jail sentence, but the standard of proof required to impose it is lower.

We have now seen, at least in a general way, how and why property rights should be enforced. There is one feature of the analysis that I find interesting and some readers may find shocking. In calculating the costs and benefits whose sum we try to maximize, costs and benefits to the thief have the same weight as costs and benefits to the victim. In judging whether a change was inefficient and should therefore be prevented, gains to the criminal were balanced against costs to the victim. In choosing a combination of probability and punishment we included the cost of the punishment to the criminal along with costs of enforcement and costs paid (or benefits received) by the court system in the total to be minimized.

What is interesting about this is that we are deriving libertarian results rather than assuming them. We start with an assumption, utilitarianism, that says nothing at all about the relative virtue of thieves and victims. We end with a legal system in which thieves are punished.

Before leaving the question of enforcing property rights and going on to discuss how those rights should be defined, there are a few more things worth noting. As I pointed out in the previous chapter, there are two ways of measuring utility. One is from the outside, by trying to estimate how much someone else values something; I argued that doing so is not impossible but that it is difficult to do it very well. The other is from the inside; each of us knows quite a lot about what he values, and his actions reflect that knowledge.

The legal rules I have suggested use both methods. Apples are allocated by revealed preference; if I think the apple is worth more to me than you think it is worth to you, I buy it from you. Locked cabins in the woods are allocated by a combination of revealed preference and outside observation. The hunter decides whether to break in according to how much he values access to a telephone, but the court decides the damages he must pay according to how much it thinks that the owner values not having his door broken down. This is a point I made earlier, when I suggested that the existence of courts making damage awards is evidence that we believe it is possible to know something about other people's values.

If revealed preference is a better way of measuring values, why not construct a legal system that depends entirely on revealed preference and never tries to measure someone else's value for something? The answer is suggested by the example of the cabin in the woods. Since the owner is not present when the lost hunter shows up, there is no way to negotiate a price for the use of the owner's telephone.

Are there ways to solve this problem without having a court measure value? Perhaps. The owner might decide for himself how much he objected to people breaking into his cabin and post a price list on the door—50 dollars for breaking the lock and another ten for using the phone. The problem with this is that there are many different situations in which one person might very much want to use someone else's property and not have an opportunity to get his permission first; the price list would have to be a long one and it might be necessary to post it not only on the door but on every tree. It would have to cover not only breaking down the door to use the telephone but also trespassing onto the property while running away from a bear, cutting dead wood to make a fire to keep from freezing, and perhaps even bulldozing down the cabin to stop the spread of a forest fire. All things considered, using a court to estimate damages seems a more practical solution.

Another alternative would be to arrange a contract in advance between the hunter and the property owner, defining the circumstances and conditions under which the former could use the latter's property. Here again, there are practical difficulties, due to the variety of possible problems and the large number of people involved. Each individual hunter has a very low probability of being lost and having to break into a cabin, and an even lower probability of having to break into any particular cabin. Negotiating terms in advance for an event that has only one chance in ten million of happening is unlikely to be worth the trouble. If we try to draw up advance contracts covering every possible contingency we shall have no time to do anything else.

What these examples suggest is that it is not practical to set up a legal system in which outcomes are entirely determined by revealed preference and voluntary transactions. At the same time, because the market provides a less expensive and more accurate way of measuring values, we would like a system that uses courts only when markets are not a viable alternative. If, for example, there is some class of cases where we are sure that market transactions are always practical and the efficient level of crime is therefore zero, we might make the punishment much more than the court's estimate of damage done ('punitive damages') in order to make it less likely that mistakes by the court system will encourage inefficient crimes. A full discussion of such issues would again carry us beyond what can be done in a chapter.

I have now finished sketching the answer to one of the problems raised in an earlier chapter—the appropriate punishment for a thief. In doing so, I have laid the groundwork for answering two other questions raised in that chapter: the proper restrictions on risky activity and the proper definition of property rights.

The case of risky activity, as exemplified by the pilot with a small chance of crashing anywhere within a thousand miles of his starting point, is similar to the case of the starving hunter. The pilot, unlike the hunter, does not actually decide to break into someone's house. He does decide how often to fly, how often to have his plane checked, and what kind of safety equipment to buy. By making those decisions he controls the probability that he will end up entering someone's house through the roof. Similarly, someone who drives a car or uses dynamite to remove stumps from his land does not choose to have an accident that results in injury to someone else's person or property. He does, however, choose how much to drive or blast and how carefully. In each case, the proper legal rule is one that forces him to pay for any damage produced by his actions. Under such a rule, he will take an action if and only if its value to him is great enough to make up for the probabilistic damage he causes.

A full discussion of the complications associated with problems of risk would again take us far beyond the constraints of even a very long chapter. One of the points we would have to deal with is the possibility that someone whose airplane destroys my house may not have enough money to pay for the damage—even assuming he is alive to worry about it. If so, we might want legal rules that allow potential victims to forbid my taking off unless I can show that I have suitable insurance. A second point is that accidents are frequently a product of decisions made by both parties concerned. Your car would not have collided with my bicycle if I had not been riding in dark clothes at night—but my carelessness would have produced only a close call if your brakes had been functioning correctly. This makes it harder to design efficient rules to control accidents. If I know that you will be liable for all the costs of the accident, I have no incentive to take precautions; if you know I will be liable, you have no incentive; if the liability is divided between us, both of us have an inefficiently low incentive.

The final question to be dealt with is how property rights should be defined—the question implicit in my discussion of trespass by single photons and single molecules of carbon dioxide. We start by noting that what we call a property right—the ownership of a piece of land, for instance—is actually a complicated bundle of such rights. Under current American law it includes the right to forbid trespass but not, under most circumstances, the right to shoot trespassers, or even to plant land mines where you expect them to step. It does not include the right to forbid overflights by airplanes nor trespass by (small numbers of) carbon dioxide molecules or photons. The questions I raised in Chapter 41 are questions about what belongs in the bundle.

It seems at first that the answer is obvious; when I acquire land I acquire all of the rights associated with it. The problem is that some rights are associated with more than one piece of land. The right to decide whether a light beam crosses the border from your land to mine is associated with both my property and yours. It is useful to me because if I control the right I can keep you from firing laser beams at my front door; I can even keep you from shining a flashlight at my darkroom window. It is useful to you because if you do not own that right you cannot do anything on your property that can be seen from mine.

In this particular case, there is an obvious commonsense

solution; you have the right to make any light whose intensity can be seen but not felt. The line is drawn somewhere between the brightest light likely to be produced by your normal activities and the weakest likely to do damage to my property. Unless your normal activities include outdoor testing of high powered lasers or nuclear weapons, there should be no problem finding a suitable dividing line.

The problem arises, however, in a great variety of different forms, for many of which there is no easy answer. One can get some idea of the ambiguity about what right belongs in what bundle by reading a good casebook on tort law. Real-world law cases have included questions such as whether my building can block your sunlight, whether I am allowed to make an addition to my house that prevents your chimney from drawing properly, and whether a candy factory is allowed to produce vibrations in the ground that only become a problem when a neighboring physician builds a consulting room on his own property adjacent to the factory.

The first step in dealing with such problems is to realize that the problem is not simply one person injuring another; if it were, we could prohibit the injury or charge damages. It is rather a case of two people engaged in inconsistent activities. My candy factory would be no problem if you had built your consulting room somewhere else on your lot; your building your consulting room where you did would be no problem if I were not running a candy factory. This is a different way of saying that the relevant right—in this case, the right to decide whether I can run machinery that produces vibrations on your land—seems to be an appropriate part of two different bundles of rights, my ownership of my land and your ownership of yours.

The second step is to realize that in many cases it does not much matter how the initial bundles of rights are defined, at least from the standpoint of economic efficiency. If a right is valuable to two people and belongs to the one who values it less, his neighbor can always offer to buy it from him. If you have the right to order me to shut down my candy factory, I can offer instead to pay the cost of tearing down your consulting room and rebuilding it on the other side of the lot. If the right is more valuable to me than to you, I should be able to make some offer that you will accept.

This insight leads us to the Coase Theorem, named after Ronald Coase, the economist whose ideas are largely responsible for this part of the chapter. The Coase Theorem states that any initial definition of property rights will lead to an efficient outcome, provided that transaction costs are zero.

The condition—zero transaction costs—is as important as the theorem. Suppose we start with a definition of property rights that forbids trespassing photons; anyone may forbid me from making a light that he can see. The right to decide whether or not I turn on the lights in my house is worth more to me than to my neighbors, so in principle I should be able to buy their permission. The problem is that there are a lot of people living within sight of my house. Buying permission from most of them does no good, since I need permission from all. The result is likely to be a difficult bargaining game, with at least some of my neighbors trying to extort from me a sizable fraction of the value of my land in exchange for their permission to use it.

This suggests that, in deciding how property rights ought to be bundled, there are two important considerations. The first is that, so far as possible, rights should go in the bundle where they are most valuable. The right to control the air a foot over a piece of land is worth more to the owner than to anyone else, so ownership of land usually includes ownership of the space immediately above it. The second is that, since the proper composition of bundles of rights will often be uncertain and may change over time, they should be defined in a way that makes it as easy as possible to trade rights. Property rights should be defined in a way that minimizes the transaction costs of likely transactions.

One of the questions to be decided is how to bundle the rights; another and closely related question is what the rights are that we are bundling. Does my right to forbid intense lights and sounds from my property mean that I can forbid my neighbor from testing lasers and nuclear weapons—and holding loud parties—or only that I can collect damages afterwards?

The answer has been suggested in an earlier discussion. Where transactions between the two parties are easily arranged, as in the case where only two neighbors are involved, there is much to be said for an absolute right to forbid, backed up by punitive damages. That way the court does not have to engage in the difficult task of measuring the value to me of not being blown up—or kept awake. If what my neighbor wants to do is sufficiently important to him he can offer to buy my permission—or my land.

But where transactions are impractical, a damage rule may be the best solution. It is not practical to buy the right to emit unpleasant fumes from all of the three thousand people who can occasionally smell what comes out of my smokestack. Even if it is worth much more to me to be able to run my factory than it is to them not to smell it, I will not be able to buy the permission of all of them. I face the same sort of bargaining problem as in the previous case of trespassing photons; one holdout can prevent the entire deal. Efficient legal rules might allocate the relevant right to my neighbors instead of to me but make it a right to collect damages rather than a right to close down the factory.

I believe I have now justified the title of this chapter. I have shown that economic analysis can answer questions about what the law ought to be that I cannot answer—that I believe cannot be answered—on the basis of libertarian principles.

That claim must be qualified in several ways. I have shown what the law should be only in the sense in which an engineering textbook shows how a bridge should be built. The engineering textbook shows how general physical principles can be applied to specific information, such as the strength of available materials and the width of the river to be bridged, to figure out how to build a specific bridge. I have shown how economic principles can be applied to specific information, such as the value of one right to the owner of another or the costs associated with arranging different sorts of transactions, to figure out what legal rules maximize human happiness in a particular society. Economics is a newer field than engineering, and more is known about the strength of materials than about the cost of transactions, so the engineering textbook does its job better than I can do mine.

A second qualification is to point out that what I have given in this chapter is a very sketchy description of one part of a large field. A full analysis of what legal rules are implied by economic efficiency requires several volumes, not all of which have yet been written. Furthermore, the question of what rules are economically efficient is not the only question that the economic analysis of law deals with. It is merely the question that seems to me most relevant to this book. Much of the existing economics and law literature is devoted to the very different objectives of understanding why particular legal rules exist and what their consequences are.

Most of the ideas I have been explaining were invented within the past thirty years; they are part of a field that is still being developed and much of which is still controversial. Readers who are interested in my own work in the field, and in particular in the question of whether law should be enforced privately, as our civil law in part is, or publicly, as our criminal law is, will find the relevant articles cited in Appendix 2. They may also find the next chapter of interest. It is based on one of my published articles and describes a society in which all laws, including the law against murder, were privately enforced.

Before ending the chapter, there is one final qualification to be made. Economic efficiency is only an approximate measure of total utility and total utility is only a very partial description of what I and, I think, other people value. Even if we can prove that certain legal rules are economically efficient, it does not necessarily follow that we should be in favor of them.

What I find interesting and useful about the economic analysis of law is not that it tells me for certain what the law should be but that it starts with objectives based on what most of us want and apparently unrelated to questions of right and wrong and ends with answers—conclusions about what the law should be—not all of which are obvious.

44

PRIVATE LAW ENFORCEMENT, MEDIEVAL
ICELAND, AND LIBERTARIANISM

Iceland is known to men as a land of volcanoes, geysers and glaciers. But it ought to be no less interesting to the student of history as the birthplace of a brilliant literature in poetry and prose, and as the home of a people who have maintained for many centuries a high level of intellectual cultivation. It is an almost unique example of a community whose culture and creative power flourished independently of any favouring material conditions, and indeed under conditions in the highest degree unfavourable. Nor ought it to be less interesting to the student of politics and laws as having produced a Constitution unlike any other whereof records remain, and a body of law so elaborate and complex, that it is hard to believe that it existed among men whose chief occupation was to kill one another.

JAMES BRYCE, *STUDIES IN HISTORY AND JURISPRUDENCE*
(1901), P. 263.

The traditional history of many nations starts with a strong ruler who put the country together—Arthur, Charlemagne, George Washington. The history of Iceland also starts with a strong ruler. His name was Harald, and he ruled over one of the small kingdoms making up what is now Norway. After being rejected by the woman he wanted to marry on the grounds that he was too small a king, Harald swore that he would neither wash nor comb his hair until he had made himself king over all of Norway; for some years they called him Shaggy Harald. When he had completed his career of conquest he washed his hair; everyone was impressed at how much better he looked. He went down in Norwegian history as Haraldr inn hárfagri—Harald Fairhair.

What Harald established was not merely a single monarchy over all of Norway, it was also a monarchy with considerably more power over the Norwegian populace than its predecessors. The change was not uniformly popular. Norwegians of the ninth century had two major professions—farming and piracy. Many of those who disapproved of the change voted with their feet—or rather, their oars. They loaded their longships with their families, their retainers, and as much of their stock as would fit and sailed west; by some estimates as much as ten percent of the population left. Many of them went to Iceland, which had recently been discovered. That is the beginning of the history of Iceland, as the Icelanders tell it.

The settlement began, according to the Icelandic sources, about 870 AD. In 930 AD, the Icelanders held an assembly at which they agreed on a common legal system for the whole island. It was based on Norwegian legal traditions, with one major exception. The Icelanders decided they could do very well without a king.

The central figure in the Icelandic system was the chieftain. The Icelandic term was Goði, originally meaning a pagan priest; the first chieftains were apparently entrepreneurs among the settlers who built temples for the use of themselves and their neighbors and so became local leaders. The bundle of rights that made up being a chieftain was called a goðorð. A goðorð was private property; it could be sold, lent, inherited. If you wanted to be a chieftain, you found one who was willing to sell his goðorð, and bought it from him. The term goðorð was also used for the group of men who followed a particular chieftain.

What were the rights that made up the position of being a chieftain? One, perhaps the most important, was the right to be the link by which ordinary people were attached to the legal system. If you wanted to sue someone, one of the first questions you had to ask was who his chieftain was. That would determine what court you ended up suing him in—just as, in the U.S. at present, the court you are sued in may be determined by what state you are a citizen of. Everyone had to be connected with a chieftain in order to be part of the legal system. But the link between the chieftain and his thingmen was a voluntary one—the chieftain, unlike a feudal lord, had no claim over his thingman's land. The thingman was free to switch his allegiance to any chieftain willing to have him.

Other rights included in the goðorð were a vote in the legislature and a hand in picking the judges (by our standards jurymen—there were 36 on a court) who decided legal cases. The court system had several levels, starting at the thing court and going up through the quarter courts to the fifth court.

Under the legal system set up in 930, the 'government' of Iceland had one part-time employee. He was called the lawspeaker and was elected (by the inhabitants of one quarter, chosen by lot) for a three-year term. His job was to preside over the legislature, memorize the law, give legal advice, and, during the course of his three years, recite the entire law code aloud once. The recitation took place at the Allthing—an annual assembly, lasting two weeks, of people from all over Iceland. The Allthing was also where the legislature met and where cases in the four quarter courts and the fifth court were tried. At each Allthing the lawspeaker recited a third of the law. If he omitted something and nobody objected, that part of the law was out. Think of it as an early form of sunset legislation.

I have described the legislative and judicial branch of the government established by the Icelandic settlers but have omitted the executive. So did they. Aside from the lawspeaker there were no government employees.

You and I are Icelanders; the year is 1050 AD. You cut wood in my forest. I sue you. The court decides in my favor, and instructs you to pay ten ounces of silver as damages. You ignore the verdict. I go back to the court and present evidence that you have refused to abide by the verdict. The court declares you an outlaw. You have a few weeks to get out of Iceland. When that time is over, I can kill you with no legal consequences. If your friends try to defend you, they are violating the law and can in turn be sued.

One obvious objection to such a system is that someone sufficiently powerful—where power is measured by how many friends and relatives you have, how loyal they are, and how good they are at fighting—can defy the law with impunity, at least when dealing with less powerful individuals. The Icelandic system had a simple and elegant solution to that problem. A claim for damages was a piece of transferable property. If you had injured me and I was too weak to enforce my claim, I could sell or give it to someone stronger. It was then in his interest to enforce the claim in order both to collect the damages and to establish his own reputation for use in future conflicts.

The victim, in such a situation, gives up part or all of the damages, but he gets something more important in exchange—a demonstration that anyone who injures him will pay for it. The point is made in a more permanent sense if it is clear that the same person who enforced this claim would do so under similar circumstances again. The powerful individual who took over such claims and enforced them might be a chieftain acting for one of his thingmen or he might be merely a local farmer with a lot of friends; both patterns appear in the Icelandic sagas.

It may help to understand the legal institutions of medieval Iceland if we look at them as an extreme case of something familiar. Our own legal system has two kinds of law—civil and criminal. There is a sense in which civil law is enforced privately and criminal law publicly. If someone breaks your arm, you call a policeman; if someone breaks a window—or a contract—you call a lawyer. The lawyer in a civil case does, as an employee of the plaintiff, the same things that the district attorney would do as an employee of the state.

In medieval Iceland all law was civil. The victim was responsible for enforcing his claim, individually or with the assistance of others. The victim who transferred his claim to some more powerful individual in exchange for half what he was owed was like a plaintiff who agrees to split the damages with his lawyer instead of paying him a fee.

It could be argued that even if this provides a workable way of enforcing the law, it is unfair. Why should the victim of an aggressor have to give up part or all of the damages owed him in order to win his case? Perhaps it is unfair—but less so than the system under which we now live. Under our system, the victim of a civil offense, like the injured Icelander, must pay the cost of proving his case, while the victim of a criminal offense gets no damages at all unless he files, and pays for, a parallel civil suit.

Because the Icelandic system relied entirely on private enforcement, it can be seen as a system of civil law expanded to include what we think of as criminal offenses. It is similar to our civil law in another sense as well. Under our system, the loser of a civil case typically, although not inevitably, ends up paying money damages to the winner; the loser of a criminal case typically ends up with a non-monetary payment, such as a jail term or, in extreme cases, execution. Under the Icelandic system the typical settlement was a cash payment to the victim or his heirs. The alternative, if you lost your case, was outlawry. The payment for killing someone was called wergeld—man gold.

Before assuming that such a punishment is obviously insuffi-
cient to deter crime, it is worth asking how large the payment was.
My estimate is that the payment for killing an ordinary man was the
equivalent of something between 12.5 and 50 years of an ordinary
man's wages; the analysis leading to that number is in an article of
mine listed in Appendix 2. That is a considerably higher punishment than the average killer receives today, allowing for uncertain
conviction and probable parole.

The comparison is even more favorable to the Icelandic system if
one allows for the distinction made under that system between
killing and murder. If you were a law-abiding Icelander and
happened to kill someone, the first thing you did after putting
down your sword or your axe was to go to the nearest neighbor,
stick your head in the door and announce 'I am Gunnar. I have just
killed Helgi. His body is lying out by the road. I name you as
witness.' One of the early Norwegian law codes specifies that "The
slayer shall not ride past any three houses, on the day he committed
the deed, without avowing the deed, unless the kinsmen of the
slain man, or enemies of the slayer lived there, who would put his
life in danger." By reporting the killing you established yourself as a
killer, not a murderer. A murderer was a secret killer, someone who
killed and tried to conceal the deed. The wergeld paid for a killing
corresponds to the punishment imposed on a murderer in our
system who turns himself in immediately after the deed.

The distinction between killing and murder was important in
two ways. Murder was regarded as shameful; killing, in a society
where many people were armed and where going viking was a
common activity for young men out to see the world, was not. The
two acts also had different legal consequences; by committing
murder you forfeited all justifications, such as self-defense, that
might make your action legal.

One question which naturally arises in reading a description of
the Icelandic system—or anything else very different from our own
society—is how well it worked in practice. Did powerful chieftains
routinely succeed in defying the law with impunity? Did the
system result in widespread violence? How long did it last? What
was the society which developed under that legal system like?

A powerful chieftain who wished to defy the law, as some
certainly did, faced two problems. The first has already been
discussed; his victim could transfer his claim to someone who was
also a powerful chieftain. The second was that, under the Icelandic

system, the party who lost a court case and ignored the verdict was in an inherently weak position. Many of his friends might refuse to support him. Even if he had supporters, every fight would create a new set of law cases—which his side would lose. If someone on the other side was killed, his kinsmen would expect to collect wergeld; if it was not paid, they would join the coalition against the outlaw. Thus the coalition against someone who defied the law would tend to expand. As long as power was reasonably well distributed, so that no single faction had anything approaching half the fighters in Iceland on its side, the system was, in essence, self-enforcing.

There is a scene in *Njal's Saga* that provides striking evidence of this stability. Conflict between two groups has become so intense that open fighting threatens to break out in the middle of the court. A leader of one faction asks a benevolent neutral what he will do for them in case of a fight. He replies that if they start losing he will help them, and if they are winning he will break up the fight before they kill more men than they can afford. Even when the system appears to be breaking down, it is still assumed that every enemy killed must eventually be paid for. The reason is obvious enough; each man killed will have friends and relations who are still neutral— and will remain neutral if and only if the killing is made up for by an appropriate wergeld.

Our main sources of information on the Icelandic system are the sagas, a group of histories and historical novels written in Iceland, mostly in the late thirteenth and early fourteenth centuries. On first reading, they seem to describe quite a violent society. That is hardly surprising. At least since Homer, the spectacle of people killing each other has been one of the principal ways in which writers entertain their audience. The chief innovation of the saga writers was to spend as much time on law suits as on the violent conflicts that generated them. The one error in the quotation from Bryce with which I started this chapter is the claim that the chief occupation of Icelanders was killing each other. The chief occupation of the characters of the sagas appears to be suing each other; the killings merely provide something to litigate about.

A more careful reading of the sagas tells a different story. The violence, unlike that in contemporary accounts elsewhere in Europe, is on a very small scale. The typical encounter in a saga feud involves only a handful of people on each side; everyone killed or injured is named. When two such encounters occur in consecutive chapters of a saga it seems as though the feuding is continual—

until you notice that a character not yet born at the time of the first encounter is participating in the second as an adult. The saga writers telescope the action, skipping over the years that separate the interesting parts.

The Icelandic system finally collapsed in the thirteenth century, more than three hundred years after it was established. The collapse was preceded by a period of about fifty years characterized by a relatively high level of violence. According to an estimate by one scholar, deaths from violence during the final period of collapse (calculated by going through the relevant historical sagas and adding up the bodies) totalled about 350. That comes to 7 deaths a year in a population of about 70,000, or about one death per ten thousand per year.

That is comparable to our highway death rate, or to our combined rates for murder and non-negligent manslaughter. If the calculation is correct, it suggests that even during what the Icelanders regarded as the final period of catastrophic breakdown their society was not substantially more violent than ours. To put the comparison in terms of contemporary societies, one may note that in three weeks of the year 1066 Norway, Normandy, and England probably lost as large a fraction of their combined population to violence (in the battles of Fulford, Stamford Bridge, and Hastings) as Iceland did in fifty years of feuds.

It is not clear what the reason for the breakdown was. One possibility is that increasing concentration of wealth and power made the system less stable. Another is that Iceland was subverted by an alien ideology—monarchy. Traditionally, conflicts involved limited objectives; each party was trying to enforce what he viewed as his legal rights. Once the conflict was settled, today's enemy might well become tomorrow's ally. During the final period of breakdown, it begins to look more and more as though the fighting is no longer over who owes what to whom but over who is going to rule Iceland.

A third possible cause is external pressure. From Harald Fairhair on, the kings of Norway took a special interest in Iceland. In the thirteenth century, after the end of a long period of civil war, Norway had a strong and wealthy monarchy. The Norwegian king involved himself in Icelandic politics, supporting one side and then another with money and prestige. Presumably, his objective was to get one or another of the chieftains to take over Iceland on his behalf. That never happened. But in the year 1262, after more than fifty years of conflict, the Icelanders gave up; three of the four quarters voted to ask the king of Norway to take over the country. In 1263, the north quarter agreed as well. That was the end of the Icelandic commonwealth.

This is not a book on history, even history as interesting as that of Iceland. The reason for including this chapter is that the medieval Icelandic legal system comes closer than any other well-recorded historical society that I know of to being a real-world example of the sort of anarcho-capitalist system described in Part III. One might almost describe anarcho-capitalism as the Icelandic legal system applied to a much larger and more complicated society.

In both systems, enforcement of law is entirely private; neither depends on enforcement by an organization with special rights beyond those possessed by all individuals. Private enforcement agencies are a more formalized version of the arrangements by which individuals and coalitions in Iceland used force to protect their rights. The major difference between the two systems is that in Iceland there was a single system of courts and legislature, whereas under the institutions I described in Part III of this book there could be many independent courts, each using whatever set of laws it thought would sell.

One more thing should be said about the Icelandic Common-wealth. If we judge societies by how much they produced that is still of interest to us, Iceland must rank, along with such better-known societies as Periclean Athens and Elizabethan England, as one of the great successes. It had a population of about 70,000—a large suburb by current standards. Of the sagas that it produced, there are probably half a dozen or more currently in print in English paperback translations, some seven hundred years after they were written. The best of them—I would recommend *Egil's Saga* and *Njal's Saga* to start with—are better stories better written than the great bulk of what is published today.

I once tried to construct a crude measure of the importance of Iceland to our civilization, in part as a response to friends who wondered how I could be interested in such an obscure place and time. I did it by counting trays in the card catalogs of two major university libraries, in order to estimate what fraction of the cards were for books filed under Iceland or the Icelandic language. It came to about a tenth of a percent—one book in a thousand. That is a very small fraction of a library, but it is a very large influence for seventy thousand people seven hundred years ago.

45

Is THERE A LIBERTARIAN FOREIGN POLICY?

One can describe a foreign policy as libertarian in either of two senses. In the first and stronger sense a foreign policy is libertarian if it is implied by libertarian principles—if libertarians must follow it because it can, and alternative policies cannot, be carried out without violating anyone's rights. One thesis of this chapter is that there is, in that sense, no libertarian foreign policy, or at least none whose consequences many libertarians are willing to accept. The second thesis of this chapter is that there is a libertarian foreign policy in a second and weaker sense—a policy that libertarians would expect to work better than alternative policies for some of the same reasons that they expect a libertarian society to work better than alternative societies.

In discussing foreign policy I will, for the most part, ignore the question of who conducts it and how it is paid for. Those libertarians who believe in limited government may think of it as the foreign policy of such a government. Those who believe, as I do, in some form of society without government may think of it as the foreign policy of whatever institutions within that society are responsible for defending it from foreign governments, or as the foreign policy that we should urge our government to follow until we succeed in abolishing it.

I find it is useful to start by considering two broad classes of foreign policy: interventionist and non-interventionist. Under an interventionist foreign policy a nation defends itself by a network of alliances. It supports those powers, and those political forces, that it believes will be useful allies in the future; it opposes those it regards as likely enemies. Under a non-interventionist policy a nation makes few or no alliances and takes little or no interest in what the governments of other nations are doing. It defends itself by shooting enemy soldiers who try to cross its border or firing nuclear missiles at any country that fires nuclear missiles at it.

Some might argue that an interventionist policy is non-libertarian because, by intervening in the internal affairs of other nations, we are violating their freedom to rule themselves. This argument confuses the independence of nations with the freedom of individuals. Whether my nation is independent and whether I am free are two quite different questions. That my nation is independent merely means that I am ruled by people who happen to live near me. I know of nothing in libertarian theory that makes coercion morally legitimate merely because the coercers and their victims live in the same part of the world, speak the same language, or have the same color skin.

A better argument against an interventionist policy is that such a policy almost inevitably involves allying with oppressive governments. There are, after all, not many libertarian governments available to ally with. Even if we allow alliances with governments similar to our own, we are still locking ourselves out of most of the world, and so gravely handicapping any serious attempt at an interventionist policy. In practice, an interventionist policy almost inevitably involves alliances with the Shah of Iran, or the present government of China, or Joseph Stalin, or Ferdinand Marcos, or, in the case of the actual policy of the U.S. over the past 45 years, all of the above.

Allying with unattractive governments does not merely mean offering to help them against our common external enemies. Oppressive governments have internal enemies as well. If we are not willing to provide such governments with the assistance they need to stay in power, they will find other allies with fewer scruples. So, in practice, an alliance with the Shah cannot be limited to defense against a Russian invasion—it also includes arming and training the secret police.

If we are supporting, training, arming, subsidizing the forces which a government uses to coerce its people, we are in part responsible for that coercion. If, as libertarians, we believe that we cannot initiate coercion, it would seem to follow that we cannot help other people initiate coercion. It follows from that that we cannot have an interventionist foreign policy, or at least not much of one. Even if the best way of defending ourselves against coercion by the Soviet Union is by allying with the Shah of Iran or the Chinese

Communist Party, we are not entitled to buy our defense at the cost of the Iranians and the Chinese.

I find this a persuasive argument. Unfortunately, it can be carried one step further. The obvious alternative to an intervention-ist policy is a non-interventionist policy. Under such a policy we defend ourselves not by a network of foreign alliances but by a large number of missiles equipped with thermonuclear warheads. The missiles are pointed at the Soviet Union; if the Soviet Union attacks the U.S., we fire them. The result is to kill something between fifty million and two hundred million inhabitants of the Soviet Union. While a few may be high ranking party officials, most will be innocent victims of the Soviet system, no more guilty for the sins of their government than are the Iranians or Chinese.

Both interventionist and non-interventionist foreign policies involve, for libertarians, the same moral dilemma. Under an interventionist policy we defend ourselves, when it seems neces-sary, by helping the governments we ally with to oppress their citizens. Under a non-interventionist policy we defend ourselves, when it seems necessary, by killing innocent citizens of the governments we are fighting against.

In both cases, it is tempting to justify our actions by treating countries as if they were people. We would like to say that if the Russians attack us we are justified in killing them in return, just as, if John Smith tries to kill me, I am entitled to kill him in self-defense. But 'the Russians', unlike John Smith, are not a person. Speaking the same language or living in the same country as someone does not make me responsible for his crimes. Similarly, we would like to say that, whatever sort of aid we give to the Iranian government, we cannot be guilty of coercion, since the Iranians asked for the aid. But the Iranians who asked for the aid and the Iranians against whom it is used are different people.

If libertarian principles rule out both interventionist and non-interventionist foreign policies, are there any alternatives left? The answer, I think, is yes, but not very attractive ones.

One strategy supported by a few libertarians is to defend ourselves with guerrilla warfare and propaganda instead of either alliances or missiles. I doubt it would work. So far as I know, guerrilla movements without external support have been uniformly unsuccessful against regular armies. Further, guerrillas generally pay no more regard to the rights of innocent parties than do the government armies they are fighting against. If we choose guerrilla warfare in order not to violate any individual rights, our guerrillas will fight under severe restraints. They may never explode a bomb where it would damage private property. They may never use automatic weapons if there are civilians in the background who are likely to get hit. They are, in effect, fighting with one hand behind their backs.

It is sometimes argued that one advantage to defending a libertarian society in a libertarian fashion is that the Soviets cannot conquer us if there is nobody to surrender to them. Perhaps, if we have no state, the Soviets will find that constructing a puppet government starting with nothing is simply more work than it is worth. Where, after all, will they find enough Communist bureaucrats who speak English?

Unfortunately, as I pointed out in Chapter 34, there is a simple solution to this dilemma, and it is likely to occur to the Soviets or any other conqueror. All they need do is pick out a medium-sized city of no great importance and announce how much tribute they expect and when it is due. They also announce that if the tribute is not forthcoming by the deadline, the city will be used as a test site for a nuclear weapon. The organization of the government that will provide the tribute can safely be left to local initiative. If the tribute is not paid the Soviets drop the bomb, film the result, and send the film on tour. The next city pays.

If my arguments so far are correct, it appears that we have only two choices. Either we follow a policy which makes it easy—and profitable—for any powerful nation to conquer us, or we defend ourselves by means that are at least questionable in terms of libertarian principles. If we make the latter choice, we are taking the position that, if the only way to defend ourselves involves injuring innocent people, we are entitled to do so. Our moral position is then similar to that of an armed man who is attacked in the middle of a crowd and shoots back at his attacker, knowing that he may well hit one of the bystanders. It seems unfair to the bystanders to make them bear the cost of his defense, but it also seems unfair to say that his only moral alternative is to stand there and be killed.

If we are not willing to impose costs on others in defending ourselves, then there is a libertarian foreign policy—surrender. That is not a policy that very many libertarians of my acquaintance are willing to accept. If we are willing to impose such costs, then libertarian principles do not tell us whether we should adopt an interventionist policy and impose the costs on the citizens of oppressive governments with whom we ally or adopt a non-interventionist policy and impose the costs on the citizens of our enemies. In that sense, there is no libertarian foreign policy. On one interpretation of libertarian principles neither alternative is acceptable, on the other interpretation both are.

I believe, however, that there is a libertarian foreign policy in another sense, a foreign policy that libertarians would expect to work better than its alternatives for some of the same reasons we expect a free society to work better than its alternatives. To show why, it is convenient to start with the argument for an interventionist policy and the problems with that argument.

The case for an interventionist policy can be summed up in one phrase: the lesson of Munich. It has been widely argued that if only the British and French had been willing to stop Hitler at the time of the Munich agreements, he would have backed down and World War II would never have happened. Many people conclude that the appropriate way to deal with potential enemies, especially enemies aiming at world conquest, is to fight them before they get strong enough to fight you, to prevent their expansion by allying with the nations they want to annex, to ally with any government willing to join you in opposing them.

If the Nazis attack Czechoslovakia, the Czechs will fight in their own defense as long as they see any chance of winning. If we help them, we fight the Nazis, in large part, with Czechoslovakian blood and treasure. If we let Czechoslovakia go, five years later we find ourselves fighting against the products of the Skoda arms works in the hands of the German army. It is a persuasive argument. It seems to have persuaded U.S. policy makers and much of the U.S. public, with the result that we have tried to follow such a policy in dealing with the Soviet Union.

The weak point in the argument is its assumption that the interventionist foreign policy will be done well—that your foreign minister is Machiavelli or Metternich. In order for the policy to work, you must correctly figure out which countries are going to be your enemies and which your allies ten years down the road. If you get it wrong, you find yourself unnecessarily blundering into other people's wars, spending your blood and treasure in their fights instead of theirs in yours. You may, to take an example not entirely at random, get into one war as a result of trying to defend China from Japan, spend the next thirty years trying to defend Japan (and Korea, and Vietnam, . . .) from China, then finally discover that the Chinese are your natural allies against the Soviet Union.

One problem with an interventionist foreign policy is that you may intervene unnecessarily or on the wrong side; that, arguably, is the history of much of our China policy. A second problem is that, even if you are on the right side, you are frequently involved in conflicts which are much more important to the other players, with the result that you end up paying the cost of intervention but not achieving very much.

One of the striking things about the Vietnamese war is that the Vietnamese on both sides continued to fight after taking casualties which, considered as a fraction of their population, were immensely larger than the casualties which drove the U.S. out of the war. That is not, if you think about it, very surprising. Vietnam is worth a great deal more to the Vietnamese, North or South, communist or anticommunist, than it is to the Americans. Even though we were much larger and more powerful than the other forces involved in the war, we found that the price of winning was more than we were willing to pay. The Soviets seem to have learned a similar lesson in Afghanistan; we may yet be taught it again in Nicaragua.

The problem with an interventionist foreign policy is that doing it badly is much worse than not doing it at all. Something which must be done well to be worth doing is being done by the same people who run the post office—and about as well.

To say that our foreign policy is badly run is in a sense misleading. Perhaps when we support dictators who contribute very little to the defense of the U.S., the reason is that they contribute instead to the profits of American firms who do business in their countries, and the American firms in turn contribute to the politicians who make our foreign policy. If so, what we are observing is not the incompetence of the people making our foreign policy but their competence at achieving objectives other than the defense of the U.S.—most notably their own wealth and power.

But exactly the same thing can be said of the Post Office. One of the reasons it appears badly run is that postal jobs are political plums used to reward faithful supporters of the party in power. When one describes government as incompetent to achieve its objectives, one is speaking metaphorically; the government is not a person. It does not have objectives any more than it has hands or feet or ideas. What I mean by saying that government does a bad job of running the Post Office is that one consequence of many individuals using the government to achieve their own objectives is that the mail gets delivered infrequently and late. What I mean by saying that government does a bad job of running our foreign policy is that another outcome of individuals using the government to achieve their own objectives is a foreign policy poorly designed to defend the U.S. Whether the reason is incompetence or corruption is irrelevant.

There is a lesson to be drawn from Munich, but it is a different lesson than is usually drawn. At the time of the Munich agreement, England and France had interventionist foreign policies; that is why Hitler made sure he had their permission before he invaded the Sudetenland. If they made the wrong decision and missed their opportunity to prevent World War II, that is evidence of what is wrong with the usual argument for such a policy. One should not base decisions about what kinds of things a government should do on the assumption that it will always do them well.

This argument suggests that libertarians ought to be skeptical of an interventionist foreign policy. It is difficult to run a successful interventionist policy, and as libertarians we do not expect the government to do difficult things well. Even if foreign policy were conducted by some private organization, funded along the lines suggested in Chapter 34, many of the same problems would exist. Such an organization, although private, would be more like the Red Cross than like an ordinary private firm, since it would have neither competitors nor an easy way of measuring performance.

If an interventionist policy can be expected to work badly, the obvious next question is whether a non-interventionist policy can adequately defend us. If the answer is no, then, however skeptical we are of the government's ability to conduct an interventionist policy well, we may have no alternative.

The case against a non-interventionist policy starts with the observation that Western Europe and Japan possess a large part of the world's resources. By resources I do not mean natural resources. In the modern world, natural resources have very little to do with world power; that is why Australia, Canada, Kuwait, Zaire, and Zimbabwe are not world powers and Japan is. When I say that Japan and Western Europe have a large part of the world's resources I mean that they have skilled workers, machines for those workers to use, and political and social institutions which result in those workers and machines producing lots of useful things. It seems likely that if those areas were conquered by the Soviet Union, the Soviet Union would become a more dangerous enemy than it now is. It would seem to follow that the U.S., in its own interest, must defend Japan and Western Europe.

But the same things which make those countries worth conquering also make them capable of defending themselves. West Germany, France, and Japan have each about half the GNP of the Soviet Union—Japan somewhat more, West Germany and France somewhat less. The combined GNP of the Western European countries, their ability to build tanks and fighters and missiles, is greater than the GNP of the Soviet Union and its satellites.

Of course, the Europeans may not be able to get together to defend themselves—but they do not have to. If West Germany had half the army of the Soviet Union and half the missiles and half the airplanes, the Soviets would be very unlikely to invade West Germany. The Soviets have a long border with China to worry about. They have a collection of fraternal allies whose friendship is causally related to the availability of Soviet troops. And besides, it would not be much of a victory if they annihilated West Germany and lost fifty percent of their own population.

If this argument is right, then the parts of the world worth defending are the same parts that can defend themselves. We are left only with a problem of transition. Given that the Germans and the Japanese do not currently have the military forces to defend themselves, how do we persuade them to acquire those forces and make sure that they do not get conquered before they do so?

The first step is to make it clear that the U.S. is moving towards a non-interventionist policy, that at some point in the near future we will stop defending the countries that have been our allies. A possible second step, to shorten the transition period, is to sell our allies some of the weapons—including the warheads—with which we are presently defending them.

One advantage to having West Germany and Japan defended primarily by Germans and Japanese is that it should substantially reduce the possibility of war by miscalculation. Suppose that, under the present system, the Soviets are considering an invasion of Western Europe. They will ask themselves whether the U.S. is willing to risk its own nuclear destruction in order to save its allies. They may decide the answer is no, and invade. Whether they are right or wrong, the result, from the standpoint of both Americans and Europeans, is an unfortunate one.

The Soviets may reasonably doubt whether the U.S. is willing to start World War III in order to defend Germany or France. There is much less doubt that Germany or France would be willing to. So a world in which major countries are responsible for their own defense is likely to be a good deal safer than one in which they depend on us.

There is a second reason why the world produced by a non-interventionist foreign policy might be safer than the world we now live in. Since World War II we have had a two-power world—historically an unusual situation. It seems likely that a two-power world is inherently less stable than a many-power world. If there are only two great powers and one of them manages to defeat the other without being totally wiped out in the process, it has won the whole game. If one of the two powers has a temporary lead, it may be tempted to attack—if it does not, the situation might reverse next decade. If, on the other hand, there are five or six great powers, then a successful war by A against B simply means that C through F pick up the pieces. That is a good reason for A not to attack B.

My conclusion is that the U.S. should move towards a non-interventionist policy. This is not, in any sense, a principled conclusion; it is the result of balancing what I judge to be the relative advantages of the two alternatives. In order to simplify the discussion, I have put it in terms of polar alternatives—interventionist and non-interventionist. While my arguments suggest that we should prefer a policy near the non-interventionist end of the spectrum, they do not imply that the U.S. government, or some libertarian successor, should have nothing at all to do with foreign governments. One can easily imagine particular cases—a treaty to permit U.S. radar stations in Canada to give early warning of an attack over the pole, for instance—where the advantages would outweigh the disadvantages.

I started this chapter by asking whether there was a libertarian foreign policy. In one sense my answer is no. Any foreign policy that is likely to be successful in defending us involves serious moral problems for libertarians. That is one example of a point I made in an earlier chapter—the difficulty of defining individual rights in a way that does not at least occasionally lead to conclusions we are unwilling to accept.

In another sense, I believe that there is a libertarian foreign policy—a foreign policy which libertarians can expect to work better than alternative policies. That policy is to defend ourselves by fighting those who actually attack us rather than by maintaining a global network of alliances. The argument is a simple one. An interventionist policy done badly is very much worse than one not done at all, and we can be sure that an interventionist foreign policy run by the U.S. government will be done badly.

> The great rule of conduct for us, in regard to foreign nations is, in extending our commercial relations to have with them as little *political* connection as possible. . . . 'Tis our true policy to steer clear of permanent alliances, with any part of the foreign world.
>
> GEORGE WASHINGTON, FAREWELL ADDRESS TO THE PEOPLE OF THE UNITED STATES, SEPTEMBER 1796.

46

THE MARKET FOR MONEY

Discussions of alternative monetary systems usually focus on what kind of money we are to have—gold coins, pieces of green paper redeemable for gold coins, or pieces of green paper redeemable for other pieces of green paper. This is, I think, a mistake. The most important issue is not how the money is produced but by whom.

The fundamental problem with government money is not that government cannot provide stable money but that it is not always in its interest to do so. Inflation via the printing press is a way in which the government can spend money without collecting taxes. It may also be politically profitable as a device to benefit debtors at the expense of creditors, especially when the government is itself a major debtor. Other forms of monetary instability are often a result of attempts to manipulate economic variables such as the unemployment rate for short-run political objectives.

This suggests that instead of arguing about whether our government should return to the gold standard, we should instead be thinking about whether the government should produce money at all. The idea of private monetary systems may seem odd to us, but such systems have existed before; one example is described by Lawrence White in a book cited in Appendix 2.

The simplest private monetary system is a commodity money produced by a number of private firms. Each firm mints coins of standard weight and sells them. Customers can shift away from a firm that starts producing underweight coins, so the opportunities for such fraud would be rare—or at least rarer than if the government does the coining. Such a system is very much like the competing international monies of the Middle Ages. While those monies were produced by governments, they were sold, for the most part, to customers over whom the producing governments had no control. The governments producing them competed like private firms to induce merchants to use their money; the obvious way of doing so was by maintaining its quality.

In a modern society, another sort of commodity money is also possible: warehouse receipts. Instead of carrying around pieces of gold, one carries around receipts for pieces of gold in storage somewhere. In such a system, unlike a fractional reserve system, every piece of paper is backed by a specific piece of gold—it is a hundred percent reserve system.

The advantages of a system of warehouse receipts over an ordinary commodity system are that it eliminates the wear and tear on the coins and that it permits the use as monies of commodities poorly suited for coinage. Carrying around enough iron to buy an automobile would be inconvenient, to say the least, but carrying around receipts for enough iron would be no more inconvenient than carrying receipts for enough gold. Since the characteristics of the commodity used for money affect how well a commodity system works, expanding the range of possible commodities may lead to a considerable improvement in the system.

Once a private commodity money is established, there are good reasons why a fractional reserve system is likely to develop. By holding only enough reserves to meet its day-to-day needs a bank frees the rest of its assets for other uses; it can lend them out directly or use them to buy interest-bearing assets such as stocks and bonds. The first bank to establish such a system is getting, in effect, an interest-free loan from its customers. Once other banks follow its lead, competition forces them all to pay interest, in money or services, on their deposits. Hundred percent reserve banks, which must charge their customers for the service of holding their money, become an unattractive alternative. The result is a system in which money consists partly of physical commodities (privately minted gold coins) or claims on physical commodities (warehouse receipts) circulating as currency, partly of circulating claims against private fractional reserve banks (bank notes) and partly of non-circulating claims against such banks (checking accounts).

This assumes that the fractional reserve banks can offer depositors a reasonable certainty of being able to get their money back if they want it. Most criticisms of private fractional reserve systems depend on their being either unable or unwilling to do so. It is often argued that such a system is inherently unstable; a run due to rumors of weakness in one bank persuades many depositors to withdraw their money, and since the banking system as a whole has obligations much larger than its reserves the banks are unable to pay and the system collapses.

But even if a bank, or a whole banking system, has obligations much greater than its reserves, it may still be able to fulfill its obligations in full. A bank's reserves are not all of its assets; they are merely the assets held in the reserve commodity. A bank facing a run can sell non-reserve assets for currency, getting back the currency it has paid out to one set of frightened depositors and using it to pay off a second set. One dollar in currency can pay off an unlimited number of dollars worth of deposits, provided that the bank has enough liquid assets to buy the dollar back enough times.

The real problems for such a bank arise either from having assets that are insufficiently liquid, from having total assets that are less than total liabilities, or from having assets whose market value (measured in money) falls in a panic. This last is likely unless the value of the assets is somehow linked to the value of money, since in a panic the money supply falls, the value of money rises, and the money prices of commodities (other than the monetary commodity) consequently fall.

There are a number of ways in which banks can and do protect themselves. One is to hold assets, such as loans and bonds, whose market value is fixed in money rather than in real terms. Another is to start with total assets larger than total liabilities, so as to guarantee to their depositors that even if the bank loses money it can still fulfill its obligations. A historical example is the Scottish banking system described by Adam Smith (and, more recently and in more detail, by Lawrence White); the banks were partnerships and the partners were generally wealthy men. Since they were not protected by limited liability, the partners were individually liable for the debts of the bank. The depositors could lose their money only if the bank's net liabilities exceeded the combined fortunes of the partners. Several of the banks did fail, but in most cases the depositors were paid off in full.

Another alternative for a private fractional reserve bank, and one used by the Scottish banks, is an option clause. The banks issued notes guaranteeing the bearer "one pound sterling on demand, or in the option of the directors one pound and six pence sterling at the end of six months after day of demand." The customer, by accepting such a note, accepts the bank's right to temporarily suspend payment, provided it pays interest during the interval.

Even if private fractional reserve banks can be stable, will they choose to be? Once a bank has built up a reputation for reliability it might pay it to convert that reputation into cash by vastly expanding its deposits without any adequate backing, and then convert that cash from an asset of the corporation to a private asset of its owners and officers, leaving the depositors with a worthless shell.

While such frauds are certainly possible in private banking (and elsewhere in the economy) there is no obvious reason to expect them to be common, especially in a modern economy with well-developed institutions for generating and transmitting information on the financial condition of firms. If such a problem did develop in a private system, one consequence might be a preference by depositors for banks that were not protected by limited liability.

Two further arguments are sometimes made for why money creation cannot be private; both, I think, are mistaken. The first is that competition is impossible since without a uniform money every transaction requires the intervention of a money changer. But this argument confuses standardization with monopoly. It is certainly convenient for the monies of different firms to exchange at a ratio of one to one, just as it is convenient for nuts made by one firm to fit bolts made by another, but this does not require that all money, or all nuts and bolts, be made by the same firm. The obvious way to arrange for standardization is for the different banks offering fractional reserve monies to use the same commodity in the same units.

If all banks make their money (whether notes or deposits) redeemable in grams of gold, for example, then all monies should exchange at one for one (or five or ten to one in the case of different denominations). The only exception would be the money of a bank believed to be financially shaky. Such money would sell at a discount; the resulting inconvenience would greatly reduce the demand for it, providing an incentive for banks to be careful of their reputations.

A second argument against private banking is that, since money can be produced costlessly, it always pays a private bank to produce more of it. There are two errors here. The first is not recognizing that in order to produce money that people will accept, a bank must demonstrate its ability to redeem it; that is not costless, and the cost increases with the amount of money outstanding. The second is the assumption that when a bank gets the use of assets by getting people to hold its money, it need not pay for them. In a competitive market the interest paid for deposits would be bid up until it absorbed any excess, so that banks, like other competitive firms, would receive only enough to cover their costs of operation.

What Commodity?

So far I have not discussed what commodity a private system should base its money on. Historically, the most common standards were probably gold and silver. They were well suited for the purpose since they have a high value to weight ratio (making them portable), are easily subdivided and recombined, and relatively easy to measure and evaluate.

But in a modern society none of these characteristics is important, since the circulating medium is not the commodity itself but claims upon it. The disadvantage of silver and gold is that they have very inelastic supplies and relatively inelastic demands; judging by recent history the value of both (in terms of most other commodities) can and does vary erratically even without the additional instabilities that would be introduced by a fractional reserve system based on them.

The ideal commodity backing for a modern system would not be any single commodity but rather a commodity bundle. The bank would guarantee to provide anyone bringing in (say) a hundred thousand of its dollars with a bundle consisting of a ton of steel of a specified grade, a hundred bushels of wheat, an ounce of gold, and a number of other items. The goods making up the bundle would be chosen to make the value of the total bundle correlate as closely as possible with the general price level. While a change in production technology or non-monetary demand might alter the value of one good in the bundle, it would have only a small effect on the value of the bundle as a whole. Since the quantity of such goods being used for monetary purposes would be a tiny fraction of the total quantity of steel, wheat, gold, etc., changes in monetary demand would have a negligible influence on the value of the bundle. So the value of such a money should be stable against both monetary and non-monetary changes.

Such a system would work, in practice, very much like an ideal fiat system in which the monetary authority maintains a stable price level by appropriate manipulation of the money supply. Under a commodity bundle system, if the money supply increased to the point where the bundle was worth more than 100,000 dollars, holders of dollars would turn them in for commodities, bringing the money supply and the price level back down. If the money supply fell so that the commodities were worth less than the money, banks would find that they could issue additional money without any of it being turned in for commodities, and the money supply would rise. The system as a whole would therefore stabilize prices in such a way as to make the price of the bundle (a crude price index) stable at its face value.

The advantage of this system over a government-run fiat system is that it does not rely on the wisdom or benevolence of the people appointed to manage the money supply. It provides a mechanism for making it in the interest of the (private) people controlling the money supply to behave in exactly the way we would want the officials controlling a government fiat system to behave. Since the nature of the reserves in this system makes it unnecessary for the banks to hold any significant quantity of them, such a system is, in effect, a fiat system in which the obligation to redeem the currency in commodities forces the people controlling the money supply to maintain stable prices.

Preference is not Prediction

I have now finished describing what I would like to see. Is it likely to occur? I think not. To go from one monetary system to another involves a difficult coordination problem. I would rather use a poor money that everyone else uses than an ideal money that nobody else uses. I will therefore continue to use the present system unless I can somehow arrange for everyone else to shift at the same time I do. An inflation rate of twelve percent a year corresponds, for an individual holding a hundred dollars in currency, to an implicit tax of a dollar a month. That is a small price to pay for the convenience of using the same money as everyone else—which is why even quite badly run fiat systems continue to be used.

My own opinion is that, even if there were no legal barriers to the use of private money, the existing fiat system would remain in use unless it became very much worse than it now is. For similar reasons, I think it likely that if a private system does come into use it will be based on gold, even though gold is not a very suitable commodity for the purpose. For reasons I have already discussed, it is desirable that banks issuing private money agree on a common commodity standard. It would be very much easier to agree on gold, which has been widely used in the past, than on some complicated commodity bundle, despite the advantages of the latter.

Even if gold is not a very suitable commodity, it does not follow that a private system based on gold is worse than what we now have. Historical experience suggests that while a gold standard may produce either inflation or deflation, it is unlikely to produce as serious an inflation as even a relatively successful fiat system (such as our own) and that the inflations produced by unsuccessful fiat systems dwarf anything that might result from new discoveries of gold. The possibilities for contraction under a fractional reserve system based on gold are more serious; since governments profit by printing money not by burning it, this has rarely been much of a problem under a pure fiat system.

In considering current proposals for monetary reform, it is important to distinguish between a private banking system based on gold and a government-run fractional reserve system linked to gold, such as the U.S. had (in various forms) during much of this century. It is the latter that is usually meant when people talk about "returning to the gold standard." Under such a system the tie to gold puts some limits on the ability of the government to manipulate the money supply and the price level, but it does so at the cost of giving the government an incentive to block the free flow of goods and services in international trade as a way of avoiding those constraints.

In the short run, we may well be stuck with government money. But we should abandon the idea that such a system is either desirable or inevitable. Money can and should be produced on the market. Like education, it is too important to be left in the hands of government.

ANARCHIST POLITICS: CONCERNING THE LIBERTARIAN PARTY

There exist, among libertarians who support the existence of the Libertarian Party, two quite different views as to its purpose. According to one, the party exists to gain political power by winning elections; it differs from other parties only in wishing to use that power to eliminate or drastically shrink government. This seems to be the dominant view at party conventions, at least the ones I have attended. While I have not yet heard a libertarian presidential nominee predict victory, several have given the impression that it is only a few elections away.

One difficulty with this strategy is that it may be inconsistent with the internal dynamic of political parties. Before asking whether a libertarian party can win elections, one should first ask why the Libertarian Party is libertarian and under what circumstances it will continue to be libertarian.

A party is not a person. It does not have beliefs; it cannot be persuaded by philosophical arguments. To say that a party holds certain views is an abbreviated way of describing the outcome of the internal political processes of that party—the processes that determine what positions are published as the party's platform and, often more important, what positions are pushed by the party's candidates and acted upon if they gain office.

A libertarian rejects the idea that simply because the government says it exists for the general good, it actually acts that way. He should equally reject the idea that a party that happens to be named 'Libertarian' will automatically continue to advance libertarian positions. To understand what either a government or a political party will do we ought to start by assuming that the individuals within the organization rationally pursue their own ends (selfish or otherwise) and then try to predict from that assumption how the organization will act.

A political party, in order to campaign or even to exist, requires resources. It gets them in two different ways. It receives donations of money and labor from people who want it to succeed because they support its ideology; when a party first starts, that may be all it has. But once it becomes large enough to win, or at least affect, elections, a party also acquires political assets with a substantial market value. The political game is played for control over the collection and expenditure of hundreds of billions of dollars a year. Even a relatively weak player in that game—a party, let us say, that gets five or ten percent of the votes in a national election and holds a few seats in Congress—has favors to dispense worth quite a lot of money.

A political party is driven by two objectives. It wishes to proclaim positions and take actions that appeal to its ideological supporters. But it also wishes to attract as many votes as possible, in order to maximize its political assets, and having attracted these votes it wishes to act in such a way as to maximize its (long-run) income. On some issues these objectives may prove to be consistent. On others they will not.

When I say that a party "wishes" something, I am again employing a convenient abbreviation. Consider a small ideological party, such as the Libertarian Party. Initially, all it has to offer to potential workers, officers, or candidates is the opportunity to achieve their ideological objectives. As long as that is true, its members, officers, and candidates continue to be people whose main objective is ideological, and the party continues to 'believe in' libertarianism.

Suppose the party begins to win elections. It occurs to some people that positions of power within the party may, in the long run, be worth quite a lot of money. Some of the people to whom this occurs may be nonideological—and willing to proclaim any ideology they find convenient. Others may be vaguely libertarian, but with a greater commitment to their short-run private objectives than to their long-run public ones. What these people have in common is their willingness to make a profession of gaining power within the party. In the long run, in the struggle for power, professionals will beat amateurs. It is as certain as anything can be in politics that once a party achieves substantial political power it will eventually swing towards a policy in which ideology is a means—perhaps an important means—but not an end. It will become a vote- and income-maximizing party, taking positions dictated by its ideology when that seems the best way of getting votes—or the volunteer labor and money it requires in order to get votes—and taking actions inconsistent with its ideology when such actions yield the party a net profit, in votes or dollars. We already have two parties like that; I see no advantage to having a third.

I began this essay by saying that libertarians who support the existence of the Libertarian Party hold two different views concerning its function. If the purpose of the party is not to put libertarians in office, what is it?

I believe the answer is that we should learn from our enemies; we should imitate the strategy of the Socialist party of 60 years ago. Its presidental vote never reached a million, but it may have been the most successful political party in American history. It never gained control over anything larger than the city of Milwaukee but it succeeded in enacting into law virtually every economic proposal in its 1928 platform—a list of radical proposals ranging from minimum wages to social security.

We should regard politics not as a means of gaining power but as a means of spreading ideas. That does not mean we should never win an election—a libertarian in Congress, even in a state legislature, might get a lot of attention for libertarian ideas. But we should regard winning an occasional election only as a means—a publicity stunt if you will—never an end. As long as our objective remains ideological we will not have to worry about winning very many elections.

As our ideas spread they will bring votes for libertarian ideas, but not necessarily for the Libertarian Party. We can trust the other parties to adopt whichever parts of our platform are most popular, leaving us with the difficult task of getting votes for a party differentiated from the others precisely by those libertarian positions that most of the voters have not yet accepted.

If this strategy is successful it will, in the long run, self-destruct. If we are sufficiently successful in spreading libertarian ideas, eventually even a consistent libertarian will be able to get elected. When that begins to happen, the Libertarian Party will finally become a major party—and promptly begin to pursue votes instead of libertarianism. The transition may be a little difficult to recognize, however, since at that point pursuing libertarianism will finally have become the best way of getting votes. It is a defeat we should all look forward to.

More realistically, the Libertarian Party can be expected to go the way of other parties long before the population is entirely converted to libertarianism; even a minor party has valuable favors to sell. That is no reason not to support it. Very few things last forever; if the Libertarian Party does something to spread libertarian ideas for another decade or two before succumbing to the temptations of politics, that is a good enough reason to work for it. A container may be worth producing, even if its ultimate destiny is to be thrown away.

When this essay was first written it was an exercise in pure speculation, the application of public choice theory to the Libertarian Party. Some years later, part of my analysis was strikingly confirmed by a minor scandal within the Libertarian Party. The story as I heard it was that a Libertarian candidate for state office had accepted a substantial amount of money from his Democratic rival and used it to run a campaign apparently designed to draw conservative votes away from the Republican candidate.

G. K. Chesterton—an author

REVIEW

From about 1905 to 1925, three of the most prominent popular intellectuals in England were George Bernard Shaw, H. G. Wells, and G. K. Chesterton. Both Shaw and Wells are still considered important figures, but Chesterton is remembered, outside of conservative Catholic circles, only as the author of some early mysteries.

The reason is not the quality of what Chesterton had to say. Those of his views which seem odd to a modern reader are mostly ones he shared with his opponents and with much of the advanced opinion of the time. The positions which distinguished him from those around him, in particular his distrust of socialism, paternalism, and the general philosophical trends of the late nineteenth and early twentieth century, look more and more convincing with every decade that passes.

Shaw and Wells, however wrong and dangerous their visions of supermen and scientific or socialist utopias have turned out to be, were 'left', therefore progressive, therefore significant. Chesterton was not. He was a radical liberal in the nineteenth-century tradition, what would now be called a libertarian—a believer in private property (and its wide distribution) who denied that the only alternatives were socialism or the status quo. As he put it:

"I am one of those who believe that the cure for centralization is decentralization. It has been described as a paradox. There is apparently something elvish and fantastic about saying that when capital has come to be too much in the hands of the few, the right thing is to restore it into the hands of the many. The Socialist would put it in the hand of even fewer; but those people would be politicians, who (as we know) always administer it in the interests of the many."

Chesterton was not a conservative; in one of his debates with Shaw he pointed out that his opponent was spending a good deal of time attacking *"the present system of industrial England. . . . Who except a devil from hell ever defended it. . . ? I object to his Socialism because it will be . . . devilishly like Capitalism."*

That sounds paradoxical; when you have eliminated capitalism and socialism what remains? But to Chesterton 'Capitalism' did not mean private property and individual liberty. It meant what he believed he saw around him—a society dominated, economically and politically, by capitalists, in which most people worked for large companies, bought from large monopolies, and read newspapers controlled by a few millionaires—who were, by a curious coincidence, the friends, supporters, and relatives of the ruling political establishment. He accepted much—perhaps too much—of the socialist critique of the then current state of England, while arguing that the socialists' cure went in precisely the wrong direction.

The response of many of his critics was to claim that Chesterton's ideas were simply out of date. He responded that date was irrelevant:

"We often read nowadays of the valour or audacity with which some rebel attacks a hoary tyranny or an antiquated superstition. There is not really any courage at all in attacking hoary or antiquated things, any more than in offering to fight one's grandmother. The really courageous man is he who defies tyrannies young as the morning and superstitions fresh as the first flowers. The only true free-thinker is he whose intellect is as much free from the future as from the past. He cares as little for what will be as for what has been; he cares only for what ought to be."

Chesterton did not limit his unpopular views to politics. In religion he began his intellectual career as an agnostic of vaguely Christian inclinations, became a more and more orthodox Christian, and towards the end of his life converted to Catholicism. If he had chosen his beliefs with the deliberate objective of offending contemporary intellectual opinion he could scarcely have found two better suited to the purpose than nineteenth-century liberalism and Catholicism. Perhaps what is surprising is not that he is generally forgotten but that his books have not yet been publicly burned.

When I first discovered Chesterton I was already a libertarian. I enjoyed his political essays while being puzzled and intrigued to find him defending, with equal intelligence and persuasiveness, Christian and even Catholic orthodoxy—ideas which seemed as indefensible to me as his (and my) political views seemed to everyone else. It was still more intriguing to learn that he was a Christian not in spite of being a libertarian but because of it. In trying to find a secure basis from which to defend his political position, and indeed his whole view of reality and man's place therein, Chesterton, by his own report, found himself pushed step by step towards Christian orthodoxy. Asked why he believed what he did, he replied: *"Because I perceive life to be logical and workable with these beliefs and illogical and unworkable without them."*

Modern libertarians will find that a strange claim; despite a small minority of Christians, most vocal libertarians today seem to be either agnostics or atheists. So far as my own intellectual experience is concerned, I have not, despite my admiration for Chesterton, become a Catholic or even a theist. I have, however, found myself forced step by step into a philosophical position that might be described as Catholicism without God—the belief that statements about right and wrong are true or false in essentially the same way as statements about physical reality, that 'one should not torture children' is a fact in very nearly the same sense as 'if you drop things they fall'. I will not try to defend that conclusion here, but I think it worth recording as evidence that modern readers, especially libertarians, should take seriously Chesterton's claim concerning the connection between his political and religious views.

In arguing that Chesterton's current invisibility is due more to our faults than to his, I must deal with one serious charge often made against him—that he was anti-semitic. It is, I think, exaggerated but not entirely without foundation. The accusation arises in part from his association with two other writers, his brother Cecil Chesterton and his friend Hilaire Belloc, who may well have been anti-semitic, in part from an accident of Chesterton's personal history, and in part from an important element of his political ideas.

The historical basis was the Marconi Affair, a political scandal in which a number of government ministers made money speculating in the stock of the American Marconi company, apparently taking advantage of inside information that the British Marconi Company was to be awarded a government contract to build a chain of wireless stations. Cecil Chesterton wrote a series of vituperative articles attacking several of the principal figures, was sued for criminal libel, conducted his own defense (incompetently) in the belief that the ability to argue was an adequate substitute for knowledge of the law, was convicted and briefly jailed. Three of his opponents in the case, Godfrey Isaacs, a director of both the British and American Marconi Companies, his brother Sir Rufus Isaacs (later the Marquis of Reading), then Attorney General, and Herbert Samuel, the Postmaster General, were Jewish.

G. K. Chesterton was very much affected by the case, partly because of the threat to his adored younger brother and partly because the attempt by the (Liberal) government to cover up the scandal and squelch dissent was to him symbolic of the abandonment of Liberal principles by the Liberal party. As he put it somewhat later *"more than I ever did, I believe in Liberalism. But there was a rosy time of innocence when I believed in Liberals."* One result is that when villains in G. K. Chesterton's stories are rich and powerful, they are also quite likely to be Jewish.

A more important element in Chesterton's attitude towards Jews was his view of nationalism. He was an anti-imperialist and 'little Englander' who believed that patriotism was an appropriate attitude for small countries, not empires. When Britain attacked and annexed the Boer Republics of South Africa, he was pro-Boer. Later, commenting on World War I, he wrote:

"I myself am more convinced than ever that the World War occurred because nations were too big, and not because they were too small. It occurred especially because big nations wanted to be the World State. But it occurred, above all, because about things so vast there comes to be something cold and hollow and impersonal. It was NOT merely a war of nations; it was a war of warring internationalists."

What does this have to do with anti-semitism? For the answer one must read 'The Problem of Zionism', a 1920 essay which contains both ammunition for attacking him as an anti-semite and evidence that he was not. Its central thesis is that the 'Jewish problem' comes from the fact that the Jews are a nation in exile, so that British Jews, French Jews, or German Jews are not really Englishmen, Frenchmen, and Germans. Ignoring the problem will not make it go away; the solution, if any solution is possible, is to establish a Jewish state.

One difficulty with doing so is that the non-Jewish inhabitants of Palestine view Jews with suspicion, precisely because of national characteristics such as the tendency to be bankers instead of blacksmiths and lawyers instead of farmers, which have resulted from their exile. In order for Israel to work, *"The modern Jews have to turn themselves into hewers of wood and drawers of water. . . . It will be a success when the Jews in it are scavengers, when the Jews in it are sweeps, when they are dockers and ditchers and porters and hodmen."* Chesterton recognized that this was precisely the ideal of some of the Zionist settlements; commenting on the collision between the anti-semitic stereotype and the Zionist ideal, he wrote *"It is our whole complaint against the Jew that he does not till the soil or toil with the spade; it is very hard on him to refuse him if he really says, 'Give me a soil and I will till it; give me a spade and I will use it.' It is our whole reason for distrusting him that he cannot really love any of the lands in which he wanders; it seems rather indefensible to be deaf to him if he really says, 'Give me a land and I will love it.' "*

It is an extraordinary essay; the best, perhaps the only, way to understand in what sense Chesterton was either anti- or pro-semitic is to read it in full. It is easy to extract chunks which appear anti-semitic, such as his half serious suggestion that Jews be freed from all legal restrictions save one, the requirement that they dress like Arabs in order to remind themselves and their hosts of their essential foreignness. It is equally easy to find passages that could have been written by a Zionist. I found his assertion that Jews are foreigners in the countries where they live, which seems very odd to an American, less shocking than I might have precisely because I had heard it first from European Jews.

Such arguments sound somewhat different from an outsider, yet I think it would be hard to read the essay with an open mind and not end up admiring Chesterton for his attempt to deal honestly with what was and is a difficult problem. And it is worth noting that he applied the same principles to himself. His eventual decision to convert to Catholicism was a decision to identify himself with a group viewed, by most Englishmen, as alien and suspect. He was defending the same principle—the idea that national groups should be themselves and not poor imitations of someone else—when he criticized Indian Nationalism for being "not very Indian and not very national"—in an article read by a young Indian student named Mohandas K. Gandhi.

What most sharply distinguishes G. K. Chesterton's writing from that of most other ideological writers, before and since, is its essential sanity and good humor. His ideological opponents, even the villains of his fiction, are neither devils nor fools but fellow human beings, in many ways admirable, whose views he thinks mistaken. In both his debates and his novels the ultimate objective is not to destroy those who are in the wrong but to convert them.

APPENDIX 1
SOME NUMBERS

THE ACTUAL EFFECT OF THE GRADUATED INCOME TAX

	1955	1960	1965	1970	1975	1980	1984
Personal Income Tax Collected (*in billions*)	$ 29.6	$ 39.5	$ 49.5	$ 82.9	$124.5	$ 250.3	$ 301.9
Taxable Income Reported (income minus exemptions) (*in billions*)	128.0	171.6	255.1	401.2	595.5	1,280.0	1,701.4
TAX COLLECTED/INCOME REPORTED							
Average Tax Rate Collected	23.1%	23.0%	19.4%	20.7%	20.9%	20.0%	17.7%
Tax Rate on the Lowest Bracket	20	20	16	14	14	14	11
Tax Rate on the Highest Bracket	91	91	77	70	70	70	50

Sources: For 1955–65 *Historical Statistics of the United States, Colonial Times to 1970*, pp. 1110–11
For 1970–84 *Statistical Abstract of the United States, 1987*, p. 304

THE INCIDENCE OF ALL TAXES BY INCOME: 1977

Income Class	under $3,000	$3,000 to $3,999	$4,000 to $4,999	$5,000 to $5,999	$6,000 to $6,999	$7,000 to $7,999	$8,000 to $9,999	$10,000 to $11,999	$12,000 to $14,999	$15,000 to $19,999	$20,000 to $24,999	$25,000 and over	Total
Tax Federal Taxes as a Percentage of Income	22.2	17.4	17.5	18.1	19.3	19.2	21.0	21.6	21.6	21.9	22.1	25.4	22.1
State and Local Taxes as a Percentage of Income	29.7	19.9	17.6	16.5	16.2	15.4	14.9	14.1	13.2	12.7	12.1	11.5	13.5
All Taxes as a Percentage of Income	51.9	37.3	35.2	34.6	35.5	34.5	35.9	35.6	34.7	34.6	34.2	36.9	35.7
Percentage of Families in Income Class	9.0	5.5	4.6	4.7	4.4	4.2	7.8	7.3	10.4	14.8	10.6	16.7	100.0

Source: Tax Foundation, Inc., *Allocating Tax Burdens and Government Benefits by Income Class, 1972–73 and 1977* (Washington, DC, 1981), pp. 25, 28–9

DISTRIBUTION OF INCOME AMONG FAMILIES
Percentage of Total Income Received

Rank of Families by Income Received	1913	1920	1929	1934	1941	1947	1955	1960	1965	1970	1975	1979	1981	1985
Top 1%	15.0	12.3	14.5	12.5	11.4	8.5								
Top 5%		22.1	26.1	24.9	21.9	17.5	16.8	15.9	15.5	15.6	15.5	15.7	15.4	16.7
Top Fifth						43.2	41.0	41.3	40.9	40.9	41.1	41.6	41.9	43.5
Second Fifth						23.1	23.4	24.0	23.0	23.8	24.1	24.1	24.4	24.2
Third Fifth						17.0	17.7	17.8	17.8	17.6	17.6	17.5	17.4	16.9
Fourth Fifth						11.8	12.2	12.2	12.2	12.2	11.8	11.6	11.3	10.9
Lowest Fifth						5.0	4.8	4.8	5.2	5.4	5.4	5.3	5.0	4.6

Sources: For 1913–65 *Historical Statistics of the United States, Colonial Times to 1970,* pp. 293, 302
For 1970–85 *Statistical Abstract of the United States, 1977–1987*

Percentage of National Income From Different Sources

Type of Income	1900–09	1920–29	1945–54	1960–69	1975	1985
Compensation of Employees	55.0%	60.5%	65.5%	71.1%	73.6%	73.5%
Proprietors' Income	23.6	17.6	15.6	10.0	9.7	7.9
Rental Income of Persons	9.1	7.6	3.8	3.3	1.0	0.2
Corporate Profits before Tax	6.8	8.2	14.1	12.4	9.1	8.7
Net Interest	5.5	6.2	0.9	3.2	6.5	9.7

Sources: For 1900–69 *Historical Statistics of the United States, Colonial Times to 1970,* p. 236
For 1975, 85 *Statistical Abstract of the United States, 1987,* p. 427

My competition

The following books, articles, periodicals, and organizations may be of interest to those who wish to pursue the subject matter of this book a little further. I take no responsibility for the views of these authors and they take none for mine. There may be two libertarians somewhere who agree with each other on everything, but I am not one of them.

Most of these are books and articles that I have read, although in a few cases I list a book I have not read by an author whose work I know. Several books, mostly on history, are included on the recommendation of Jeffrey Rogers Hummel, who helped update the references for the second edition; they are identified by his initials. He is also responsible for most of the descriptions of libertarian magazines and organizations.

Fiction

Poul Anderson, 'No Truce with Kings', in *Time and Stars* (Garden City, NY: Doubleday, 1964). A libertarian novelette that plays fair. The bad guys are good guys too. But wrong. You are halfway through the story before you realize which side the author is on.

Robert A. Heinlein, *The Moon is a Harsh Mistress* (New York: Putnam, 1966). Most of his books contain interesting ideas. This one is set in a plausible anarcho-capitalist society; it was one of the sources from which my ideas on the subject developed. A discussion of all the good things about this book would require a long article; some day I may write it.

C. M. Kornbluth, *The Syndic* (Garden City, NY: Doubleday, 1955). A book about an attractive libertarian society (run by organized crime) caught in the stability problem. It is threatened by external enemies and apparently doomed to eventual collapse; any energetic attempt to defend it will make it no longer worth defending.

Larry Niven and Jerry Pournelle, *Oath of Fealty*. (New York: Pocket Books, 1981). Both the authors of this book have some libertarian sympathies; neither is an orthodox libertarian. It is set in the near future and centers around a privately owned arcology—a building the size of a small city, providing its own 'governmental' services to residents. A central point of the book, and one which should be of interest to anarcho-capitalists, is that people protected by a private organization instead of a government will feel for that private organization the same sort of loyalty and patriotism that people now feel for their nation. The arcology is 'us', the government of the city of Los Angeles, where it is located, is 'them'.

Niven and Pournelle have jointly written several other good books that have nothing much to do with libertarianism; I particularly recommend *The Mote in God's Eye* and *Inferno*. 'Cloak of Anarchy', in Niven's collection *Tales of Known Space* (New York: Ballantine, 1975), is an anti-anarchist story that libertarian anarchists should read and think about.

Ayn Rand, *Atlas Shrugged* (New York: Random House, 1957). *The Fountainhead* (Indianapolis: Bobbs-Merrill, 1943). *Anthem*, rev. ed., (Los Angeles: Pamphleteers, 1946). Rand's novels upset some people because the heroes are all handsome and the villains nauseating, with names to match. She did it on purpose; she did not believe art should be realistic and wrote *The Romantic Manifesto* (New York: World Publishing, 1969) to prove it. When someone told her that her work was not in the mainstream of American literature, she is supposed to have replied that "the mainstream of American literature is a stagnant swamp." She has a point.

Eric Frank Russell, *The Great Explosion* (New York: Dodd, Mead, 1962). Bureaucrats from Earth are Putting The Universe Back Together. One of their failures involves an intriguing anarcho-pacifist society. This story may have originated MYOB (for 'Mind Your Own Business').

J. Neil Schulman, *Alongside Night* (New York: Avon, 1987), *The*

Rainbow Cadenza (New York: Simon and Schuster, 1983). Two explicitly libertarian novels. The first describes a libertarian revolt in the near future, the second a society with a male-to-female ratio of ten to one where women are drafted into a prostitution corps.

L. Neil Smith, *The Probability Broach* (New York: Ballantine, 1980), *The Venus Belt* (New York: Ballantine, 1980) and lots more that I have not yet read. His books are sometimes fun; my main reservation is that the good guys are too obviously in the right and win too easily.

Vernor Vinge, *True Names* (New York: Bluejay, 1984), *The Peace War* (New York: Bluejay, 1984; Ultramarine, 1984), *Marooned in Realtime* (New York: Bluejay, 1986; Baen, 1987). These are science fiction novels by a libertarian with interesting ideas. The historical background for the last of the three, which is set in the very far future, includes an anarcho-capitalist society along the general lines described in Part III of this book.

The story 'The Ungoverned', included in the book *True Names and Other Dangers* (New York: Baen, 1987), is set after *The Peace War* and before *Marooned in Realtime*. It portrays an anarcho-capitalist society under attack by an adjacent state. One of the best things about the story is the way in which both anarchists and statists take their own institutions entirely for granted. The failure of the attack is in part a result of its leaders misinterpreting what they run into because they insist on viewing the anarcho-capitalist society as something between a rival state and a collection of gangsters.

Economics

Armen A. Alchian and William R. Allen, *University Economics: Elements of Inquiry*, 3rd ed., (Belmont, CA: Wadsworth, 1972). A good unconventional economics text, entertainingly written.

David D. Friedman, *Price Theory: An Intermediate Text*. (Cincinnati: South-Western, 1986). If you like the book you have just read, you will probably like this one as well. It is intended as a textbook, but could also be used to teach yourself economics. It assumes no previous knowledge in the reader but a considerable willingness to think.

Milton Friedman, *Capitalism and Freedom* (Chicago: University of Chicago Press, 1962). This is a modern libertarian classic and well worth reading.

Milton and Rose Friedman, *Free to Choose: A Personal Statement* (New York: Harcourt Brace Jovanovich, 1980). *The Tyranny of the Status Quo* (New York: Harcourt Brace Jovanovich, 1983). The first of these is the case for a free society, from a slightly more moderate position than mine. The second is largely an explanation of why it is so hard to change the existing situation, even when a candidate like Reagan or Thatcher is apparently elected for the purpose of doing so.

Henry Hazlitt, *Economics in One Lesson* (New York: Harper, 1946). This is reputed to be a good short introduction to economics; I have not read it. *Time Will Run Back: A Novel about the Rediscovery of Capitalism*, rev. ed., (New Rochelle, NY: Arlington House, 1966). The rediscovery of capitalism in a future communist world. It pretends to be a novel. Ignore that, and you will find it an absorbing explanation of why socialism cannot work as well as capitalism and what happens when it tries.

Alfred Marshall, *Principles of Economics*, 8th ed. (London: Macmillan, 1946). This is the book that, more than any other, created modern economics; it was first published in the 1890s and is still well worth reading. The approach to understanding economic efficiency that I use is borrowed, with minor modifications, from Book III, Chapter 6.

Ludwig von Mises, *Human Action: A Treatise on Economics*, 3rd ed., (Chicago: Regnery, 1963). Much is made in libertarian circles of the division between 'Austrian' and 'Chicago' schools of economic theory, largely by people who understand neither. I am classified as 'Chicago'. This is the magnum opus of one of the leading Austrians.

S. Peltzman, 'An Evaluation of Consumer Protection Legislation: 1962 Drug Amendments'. *Journal of Political Economy* September/October 1973. This is a classic example of the use of economics and statistics to measure the effect of government regulation. Peltzman's conclusion was that the particular legislation he was looking at reduced the rate of introduction of new drugs by about half, while having no detectable effect on their average quality.

Adam Smith, *An Inquiry into the Nature and Causes of the Wealth of Nations* (1776; reprint ed., New York: Modern Library, 1937). Usually referred to simply as *The Wealth of Nations*, this is arguably the most influential libertarian book ever written.

Law and Economics

Gary S. Becker and George J. Stigler, 'Law Enforcement, Malfeasance, and Compensation of Enforcers', *Journal of Legal Studies*, 3 (January 1974), 1–18. This article, by two eminent (if somewhat unconventional) economists, introduced the idea of private enforcement of law into the law and economics literature.

Jesse Byock, *Feud in the Icelandic Saga* (Berkeley: University of California Press, 1982). Byock is a historian. While his perspective on the Icelandic system is quite different from mine, his conclusions are very similar.

R. H. Coase, 'The Problem of Social Cost', *Journal of Law and Economics*, 3 (October 1960). This is the article that originated the Coase Theorem and revolutionized the economic analysis of legal rules, in particular rules dealing with externalities.

Richard Epstein, *Takings: Private Property and the Power of Eminent Domain* (Cambridge: Harvard University Press, 1985). Richard Epstein is both a prominent legal scholar and a libertarian. His book argues that the takings clause of the constitution ("nor shall private property be taken for public use, without just compensation"), properly interpreted, imposes stringent constraints on what the government is permitted to do. If, for example, the city government zones my block as single-family residences only, it is taking from me one of the bundle of rights that make up my ownership of my house—the right to rent out part of it. Under Epstein's interpretation of the constitution, it can do so only if it is willing to compensate me for the loss ("just compensation") and only if the benefits of the law are distributed very widely ("for public use"). Since most such government interventions are in fact intended to benefit one group at the expense of another and are politically profitable only for that reason, most of what government now does is, by Epstein's interpretation, unconstitutional. A government bound by his constraints would do very much less than our government presently does.

Part of what makes this book interesting is the intelligence of the author and the sophistication of the argument. He is not merely asserting a constitutional interpretation; he is interweaving lines of argument based on constitutional theory, public choice economics, and political philosophy, in order to support and explain his conclusion.

A critique of Epstein for not going far enough is Jeffrey Rogers Hummel, 'Epstein's Takings Doctrine and the Public-Good Problem', *Texas Law Review*, 65 (May 1987), 1233–1242.

David D. Friedman, 'Efficient Institutions for the Private Enforcement of Law', *Journal of Legal Studies*, June 1984. This is an article of mine rebutting an earlier article by Landes and Posner, itself a response to the article by Becker and Stigler. Landes and Posner claimed to show that a system in which all law was private, so that crimes created a claim against the criminal by the victim rather than by the state, could not be efficient. I claim to show that it can be. What I describe is an anarcho-capitalist enforcement system combined with the present system of courts and laws. Think of it as creeping anarchism. Two more steps and I am home free.

——. 'Private Creation and Enforcement of Law—A Historical Case', *Journal of Legal Studies*, 8 (March 1979), 399–415. A longer and more academic version of Chapter 44.

——. 'Reflections on Optimal Punishment or Should the Rich Pay Higher Fines?' *Research in Law and Economics*, 1981.

——. 'What is Fair Compensation for Death or Injury?' *International Review of Law and Economics*, 2, 1982.

Richard A. Posner, *Economic Analysis of Law* 3rd edn. (Boston: Little, Brown, 1986).

William M. Landes and Richard A. Posner, *The Economic Structure of Tort Law* (Cambridge: Harvard University Press, 1987).

My discussion of the economic analysis of law in Chapter 43 is misleading in at least two ways. It ignores many of the complications one would face in constructing a real law code. It also focuses on the question of what legal rules are economically efficient, while ignoring two other questions of importance: what economics tells us about the consequences of the laws we actually have and what economics tells us about what kind of laws we can expect to have. Posner approaches the subject from a different angle. He argues that there are reasons to expect the common law, the system of legal rules generated not by the legislature but by the accumulation of court decisions, to be economically efficient, and he claims to show that much of the common law in fact is efficient. Both his *Economic Analysis of Law* and the book on tort law by Landes and Posner go into the question of efficient legal rules in much more depth than the discussion in this book.

William Miller, 'Avoiding Legal Judgement: The Submission of Disputes to Arbitration in Medieval Iceland', *The American Journal of Legal History*, 28 (1984). 'Gift, Sale, Payment, Raid: Case Studies in the Negotiation and Classification of Exchange in Medieval Iceland', *Speculum*, 61 (1986). Miller is a law professor who has written extensively on Medieval Iceland. He writes as a legal scholar not an economist, and his conclusions are not always the same as mine.

Public Policy

Martin Anderson, *The Federal Bulldozer: A Critical Analysis of Urban Renewal*, 1949–1962 (Cambridge, MA: MIT Press, 1964). The book that showed what urban renewal does to, not for, the poor.

Leslie Chapman, *Your Disobedient Servant* (London: Chatto and Windus, 1978). A fascinating first-hand account of the mechanics of Friedman's first law—why things cost twice as much when governments do them. The author was a British bureaucrat who tried to reduce the costs of his part of the bureaucracy by modest measures such as not heating buildings that nobody occupied. He succeeded technically, reducing costs by about 35% with no reduction in output, but failed politically; he is no longer a bureaucrat.

Ronald Hamowy, ed., *Dealing with Drugs: Consequences of Government Control* (Lexington: Heath, 1987). (JRH)

Charles Murray, *Losing Ground: American Social Policy 1950–1980*. (New York: Basic Books, 1984). This is a persuasive and controversial book; it argues that the liberal reforms of the Kennedy and Johnson era, especially in welfare and education, had the opposite of their intended effect. While there has been some serious criticism of the author's statistics, the book remains interesting both as a history of what happened and an explanation of why.

Robert Poole, ed., *Instead of Regulation: Alternatives to Federal Regulatory Agencies* (Lexington, MA: Heath, 1982). Poole is the editor of *Reason* magazine and one of the few libertarians I usually find myself agreeing with.

Julian Simon, *The Ultimate Resource* (Princeton: Princeton University Press, 1981). One of the most powerful ideas of recent decades has been the myth of overpopulation, according to which we are on the edge of running out of everything with catastrophic results. Julian Simon has written the best refutation I know of. While I think he occasionally overstates his case—his "ultimate resource" is people, and he seems to believe that the overpopulation scenario is not only false at the moment but virtually impossible—he does a very good job of answering the popular arguments on the other side. In particular, he shows overwhelming evidence that things are getting better, not worse—nutrition, for instance, in the underdeveloped as well as the developed world has been steadily improving—and explains why the simple arguments for imminent catastrophe are wrong.

Thomas Sowell, *Civil Rights: Rhetoric or Reality?* (New York: Morrow, 1984). (JRH)

Richard L. Stroup and John Baden, *Natural Resources: Bureaucratic Myths and Environmental Management* (San Francisco: Pacific Institute for Public Policy Research, 1983). Baden and Stroup, ed., *Bureaucracy v. Environment: The Environmental Cost of Bureaucratic Governance* (Ann Arbor: University of Michigan Press, 1981). (JRH)

Thomas S. Szasz, *Ceremonial Chemistry: The Ritual Persecution of Drugs, Addicts and Pushers*, rev. ed., (Holmes Beach, FL: Learning Publications, 1985). (JRH)

Walter E. Williams, *The State Against Blacks* (New York: McGraw-Hill, 1982). (JRH)

History

T. Anderson and P. J. Hill, 'An American Experiment in Anarcho-Capitalism: The Not So Wild, Wild West', *The Journal of Libertarian Studies*, Volume III, Number 1, 1979. Anderson and Hill discuss the history of the American west as an example of something close to anarcho-capitalism; the theory of anarcho-capitalism they test is drawn from Part III of this book. They describe a wide variety of private institutions by which individual rights were effectively enforced in a society with little or no government. Their conclusion is that the system worked more or less as I predict, and was much less violent than western books and movies suggest. According to their account, only two of the cattle towns ever had as many as five killings in a year; the average (for five towns over 15 years) was 1.5 homicides per year.

T. S. Ashton, *The Industrial Revolution, 1760–1830* (London: Oxford University Press, 1948).

F. A. Hayek, ed., *Capitalism and the Historians* (Chicago: University of Chicago Press, 1954).

Both of these books describe what really happened during the Industrial Revolution and how it got reported by historians.

Ross D. Eckert and George W. Hilton, 'The Jitneys', *Journal of Law and Economics* XV (October 1972), pp. 293–325. This article is the historical background for Chapter 16. It describes the brief flourishing of jitneys in America and how the trolly companies, unable to win on the economic market, succeeded in legislating the jitneys out of existence.

Arthur A. Ekirch, Jr., *The Decline of American Liberalism*, rev. ed., (New York: Atheneum, 1980). The author uses "liberalism" not in its modern sense of democratic socialism in dilute solution but in its old sense of support for freedom—roughly speaking, libertarianism. His book is an overview of the rise and fall of classical liberal views in the U.S. (JRH).

Milton Friedman and Anna Jacobson Schwartz, *The Great Contraction, 1929–1933* (Princeton: Princeton University Press, 1965). How government mismanagement, not any inherent instability in the free enterprise system, caused the Great Depression. This is part of a longer and much more technical work called *A Monetary History of the United States, 1867–1957* (Princeton: Princeton University Press, 1963).

Robert Higgs, *Crisis and Leviathan: Critical Episodes in the Growth of American Government* (New York: Oxford University Press, 1987). Argues that the growth of the U.S. government resulted from opportunistic exploitation of crises such as wars and depressions. (JRH)

Jonathan R. T. Hughes, *The Government Habit: Economic Controls from Colonial Times to the Present* (New York: Basic Books, 1977). (JRH)

Gabriel Kolko, *Railroads and Regulation, 1877–1916* (Princeton: Princeton University Press, 1965). *The Triumph of Conservatism: A Reinterpretation of American History, 1900–1916* (New York: Glencoe Press, 1963). Kolko is a socialist historian who argues, with extensive evidence, that at the end of the nineteenth century and the beginning of the twentieth, capitalism was working fine for everybody except the capitalists, who thought they could make more money by getting the government to intervene in their favor.

James J. Martin, *Men Against the State: The Expositors of Individualist Anarchism in America, 1827–1908* (De Kalb, IL: Adrian Allen, 1953). (JRH)

John S. McGee, 'Predatory Price Cutting: The Standard Oil (N.J.) Case', *Journal of Law and Economics*, 1 (October 1958), 137–69. The classic article showing that the standard textbook account of how Rockefeller established his monopoly is pure myth.

Sheilagh C. Ogilvie, 'Coming of Age in a Corporate Society: Capitalism, Pietism and Family Authority in Rural Wurttemberg, 1590–1740', *Continuity and Change* 1 (3), 1986, 279–331. This is a fascinating article by a libertarian historian, describing how and why liberty was restricted in a pre-industrial society. One particularly interesting point is the causal relation between a welfare state and restrictions on individual liberty. In modern America, an important argument for limiting immigration is the fear that immigrants will go on welfare—a problem that did not exist at the time when we had unrestricted immigration. In seventeenth-century Wurttemberg, welfare was provided at the village level. One result was restriction on inter-village migration. Another was that citizens could be punished for letting their children go fishing when they should have been spending their time learning a trade.

Thomas Sowell, *Ethnic America: A History* (New York: Basic Books, 1981). (JRH)

Lawrence H. White, *Free Banking in Britain: Theory, Experience, and Debate, 1800–1845,* (Cambridge: Cambridge University Press, 1984). The author describes the working of a system in which money was produced by private firms on a competitive market.

William C. Wooldridge, *Uncle Sam the Monopoly Man* (New Rochelle, NY: Arlington House, 1970). The history of private production of such 'governmental' services as delivering mail, building roads, and resolving disputes.

Libertarian Ideology

Walter Block, *Defending the Undefendable: The Pimp, Prostitute, Scab, Slumlord, Libeler, Moneylender, and Other Scapegoats in the Rogue's Gallery of American Society* (New York: Fleet Press, 1976). This is a peculiar book. The author argues that a wide range of what are usually considered undesirable activities are not only permissible but admirable. In some cases he may be right. The book has too much feel of 'I know the conclusion I want to reach, now let's find some arguments for it' to entirely suit my taste.

Karl Hess, 'The Death of Politics', *Playboy* 16 (March 1969), 102–04, 178–185. Reprinted in Henry J. Silverman, ed., *American Radical Thought: The Libertarian Tradition* (Lexington: Heath, 1970), pp. 274–290.

Robert Nozick, *Anarchy, State and Utopia* (New York: Basic Books, 1974).

David Osterfeld, *Freedom, Society, and the State: An Investigation into the Possibility of Society Without Government* (Lanham, MD: University Press of America, 1983). (JRH)

Ayn Rand and others, *Capitalism: The Unknown Ideal* (New York: New American Library, 1966). *The Virtue of Selfishness* (New York: New American Library, 1964). Collections of essays and passages from Rand's books. She had a complete philosophy to sell, of which libertarianism was a part. Many libertarians buy the whole package; that is how some of them became libertarians. I don't and didn't, but find much of value in her writing. Her hard-core disciples are very hostile to the libertarian movement, presumably on the theory that heretics are worse than pagans.

Murray N. Rothbard, *For a New Liberty: The Libertarian Manifesto*, 2nd ed., (New York: Macmillan, 1978).

——.'Law, Property Rights, and Air Pollution', *Cato Journal*, Vol. 2, No. 1 (Spring 1982). This is an article by a prominent natural rights libertarian, trying to deal with the sorts of problems raised in Chapter 41. I find his answers unsatisfactory, but you may wish to read the article and decide for yourself.

John T. Sanders, *The Ethical Argument Against Government* (Washington: University Press of America, 1980). By a political philosopher, for political philosophers, and probably not very accessible to anyone else, myself included.

Morris and Linda Tannehill, *The Market for Liberty* (Lansing, MI: Morris and Linda Tannehill, 1970).

Jerome Tuccille, *Radical Libertarianism: A Right Wing Alternative* (New York: Bobbs-Merrill, 1970).

Jarret B. Wollstein, *Society Without Coercion: A New Concept of Social Organization* (Silver Spring, MD: Society for Rational Individualism, 1969). The Tannehill and Wollstein books were later issued together under the title *Society Without Government* (New York: Arno, 1972).

These books vary widely in orientation and intellectual level. Many cover the same sorts of issues as I do, especially in my third part. If I had found any of them entirely satisfactory, I might not have written this book. The only one I would recommend without reservation is Nozick's book; while I disagree with some of his conclusions, his book is consistently original, intelligent, and readable.

The Libertarian Movement

Henri Lepage, *Tomorrow, Capitalism: The Economics of Economic Freedom* (La Salle: Open Court, 1982).

Norman P. Barry, *On Classical Liberalism and Libertarianism* (New York: St. Martin's Press, 1987).

Jerome Tuccille, *It Usually Begins with Ayn Rand* (New York: Stein & Day, 1971).

The books by Lepage and Barry are sympathetic surveys of libertarianism. Lepage writes as a journalist interested in ideas, Barry as a political philosopher. Tuccille's book is in part a personal reminiscence and in part an inside account of the development of the modern libertarian movement.

Barry is an intelligent and fair-minded scholar and Tuccille an entertaining reporter and storyteller. My main reservation about both is that the parts of their books dealing with the ideas and events I know most about are the parts I find least convincing.

Stephen L. Newman, *Liberalism at Wits' End: The Libertarian Revolt Against the Modern State* (Ithaca: Cornell University Press, 1984). Newman demonstrates how difficult it is to understand and explain a set of ideas when you are absolutely certain that they are wrong. He makes a number of legitimate criticisms of libertarians and libertarianism. But when he finds what seems to him to be a fatal flaw in libertarian ideas, he accepts it as confirmation of what he already knew instead of trying to see if there is some way in which libertarians might deal with it.

Geoffrey Sampson, *An End to Allegiance: Individual Freedom and the New Politics* (London: Temple Smith, 1984). This is the best of the lot. Sampson is a British libertarian (he prefers the term liberal). His book is a thoughtful explanation and critique of libertarian ideas, illuminated by a good many of his own insights.

Barbara Branden, *The Passion of Ayn Rand* (New York: Doubleday, 1986). This is a sympathetic biography of Rand by someone who was close to her. It is interesting more as a portrayal of an extraordinary personality than as an explanation of her ideas.

Miscellaneous

Robert Axelrod, *The Evolution of Cooperation* (New York: Basic Books, 1984). A fascinating discussion, based on game theory and computer simulations, of how and why humans cooperate with each other.

Frederic Bastiat, *The Law* (1850; reprint ed., Irvington-on-Hudson, NY: Foundation for Economic Education, 1950). One of the classic presentations of the libertarian position, written when we were still called liberals. Bastiat is the author of, among other things, a petition from the candle-makers of France requesting protection against the unfair competition of the sun.

Richard Dawkins, *The Selfish Gene* (New York: Oxford University Press, 1976). An explanation of evolutionary biology and sociobiology—the economics of genes. One of the most interesting books I have read in recent years.

Paul Goodman, *People or Personnel: Decentralizing and the Mixed System* (New York: Random House, 1965). Hard to classify. Paul Goodman was not the leftist some leftists think he was; he was a libertarian and an anarchist. His books are variable, with a lot of good ideas.

Friedrich A. Hayek, *The Road to Serfdom* (Chicago: University of Chicago Press, 1944). Hayek argues that a centrally planned economy must lead to totalitarianism.

Sonia Orwell and Ian Angus, eds., *The Collected Essays, Journalism and Letters of George Orwell*. (New York: Harcourt Brace, 1968). Orwell is my favorite political essayist. He was a socialist with libertarian sympathies, who recognized many of the problems with socialism but saw no better alternative. His willingness to discuss honestly the problems in his own position should be a model for all ideological writers.

Alvin Rabushka, *Hong Kong: A Study in Economic Freedom* (Chicago: University of Chicago Press, 1979). (JRH)

Lysander Spooner, *No Treason: No. VI, The Constitution of No Authority* (1870; reprint ed., Larkspur, CO: Pine Tree Press, 1966). Cited in Chapters 6 and 28.

Thomas S. Szasz, *The Myth of Mental Illness: Foundations of a Theory of Personal Conduct*, rev. ed., (New York: Harper and Row, 1974). *The Manufacture of Madness: A Comparative Study of the Inquisition and the Mental Health Movement* (New York: Harper and Row, 1970). Szasz is an interesting writer—a libertarian psychiatrist who profoundly distrusts the psychiatric profession and regards 'mental illness' as a misleading and dangerous metaphor. Here and elsewhere he argues against locking up innocent people just because you think they are crazy.

Anything written by H. L. Mencken. Rothbard called him the joyous libertarian. He was also one of the great essayists of the century. Mencken's style is to Bill Buckley's what Buckley's is to mine.

Some More of My Articles
that You May (or May Not) Find of Interest

'A Libertarian Perspective on Welfare', with Geoffrey Brennan, in *Income Support*, Peter G. Brown, Conrad Johnson, and Paul Vernier, eds. (Totowa, NJ: Rowman and Littlefield, 1981).

'The Economics of War', in *Blood and Iron*, Jerry Pournelle, ed.

'Should Medical Care be a Commodity?' *Rights to Health Care*, George J. Agich and Charles E. Begley, eds., Reidel 1989, forthcoming.

'Comments on Rationing Medical Care: Processes for Defining Adequacy', and 'Comments on "Rationing and Publicity"' in *The Price of Health*, Reidel 1986.

'An Economic Theory of the Size and Shape of Nations', *Journal of Political Economy*, 85 (February 1977), 59–77. My first economics article, and still one of my favorites. I claim to use economic theory to explain the map of Europe from the fall of the Roman empire to the present. Governments are analyzed as firms competing for control over taxpayers.

'Comment on Brody' in *Social Philosophy and Policy* I (1983). This contains my least unsatisfactory explanation of the initial appropriation of land.

'Gold, Paper, or . . . : Is There a Better Money?' Cato Institute Policy Analysis, 1982. This is a longer version of chapter 46.

'Many, Few, One—Social Harmony and the Shrunken Choice Set', *American Economic Review*, 70 (March 1980), 225–232.

Laissez-Faire in Population: The Least Bad Solution. An Occasional Paper of the Population Council, 43 pp. (1972).

Magazines

American Libertarian, 21715 Park Brook Drive, Katy, TX 77450. This monthly tabloid provides the best way to keep abreast of news and gossip about the libertarian movement.

Cato Journal, 224 Second Street SE, Washington, DC 20003. A scholarly libertarian journal more oriented toward public policy.

Critical Review, 532 Broadway, 7th Floor, New York, NY 10012. A high-theoretical quarterly aimed at both libertarian and non-libertarian intellectuals.

Free Life, 9 Poland Street, London W1V 3DG, England. A hard-core if infrequent libertarian magazine published in Britain.

The Freeman, 30 South Broadway, Irvington-on-Hudson, NY 10533. Published by the Foundation for Economic Education (FEE), a venerable promoter of classical liberalism. This monthly publication is free upon request.

Individual Liberty, P.O. Box 338, Warminster, PA 18974. Published by the Society for Individual Liberty (SIL), perhaps the oldest explicitly libertarian organization still in existence. This monthly newsletter contains an assortment of movement news and ideological discussion.

Intellectual Activist, 131 Fifth Avenue, Suite 101, New York, NY 10003. Current events raked over from a rabidly Randian perspective.

Journal of Libertarian Studies, P.O. Box 4091, Burlingame, CA 94011. An interdisciplinary scholarly journal, published by the Center for Libertarian Studies, that has fallen somewhat behind but continues to appear occasionally.

Liberty, P.O. Box 1167, Port Townsend, WA 98368. A bimonthly review "produced by libertarians for libertarians". A publication in which libertarians debate the finer points of their ideology.

New Libertarian, 1515 West MacArthur Boulevard #19, Costa Mesa, CA 92626. Comes out very sporadically—sometimes less than once a year. Among other peculiarities, this publication offers two perspectives not found in any of the other libertarian publications listed: (1) rabid hostility to the Libertarian Party; (2) blind infatuation with science fiction.

Nomos, 727 S. Dearborn Street, Suite 212, Chicago, IL 60605. A bimonthly pitched toward the average libertarian reader.

The Pragmatist, P.O. Box 392, Forest Grove, PA 18922. A bimonthly that challenges the dominant natural-rights thinking within the libertarian movement. In contrast, it is dedicated to a utilitarian approach.

Reason, editorial offices: 2716 Ocean Park Boulevard, Suite 1062, Santa Monica, CA 90405; subscriptions: Box 27977, San Diego, CA 92128. This monthly magazine is one of the longest-operating libertarian publications. It is now devoted to 'outreach', containing mainly factual articles designed to persuade non-libertarians.

Reason Papers, Department of Philosophy, Auburn University, AL 36849. A scholarly libertarian journal that comes out about once a year.

The Voluntaryist, P.O. Box 1275, Gramling, SC 29348. Combines libertarianism with principled pacifism and non-violent resistance. Opposes electoral politics on principle. Also runs historical articles on the American and British individualist anarchist tradition.

Organizations

Advocates for Self-Government, 5533 E. Swift Avenue, Fresno, CA 93727. A grass-roots, chapter-based libertarian organization.

Citizens for a Sound Economy, 122 C. Street NW, Washington, DC 20001. Libertarian lobbying organization. Successor to the Council for a Competitive Economy.

Free Press Association, P.O. Box 15548, Columbus, OH 43215. This is a professional network of journalists committed to questioning political authority. It promotes libertarian journalism with the annual Mencken Awards, given in such categories as best book, best editorial, and best cartoon. Its quarterly newsletter is the *Free Press Network*.

Libertarian Alliance, 9 Poland Street, London W1V 3DG, England. A membership organization which combines internal debate with outreach.

Libertarian Futurist Society, 89 Gebhardt Street, Penfield, NY 14526. For libertarian fans of science-fiction. It publishes a newsletter called *Prometheus* and sponsors the Prometheus Award, given to novels promoting liberty.

Libertarian International, 9308 Farmington Drive, Richmond VA 23229. Includes members from places as far apart as Germany and South Africa. It sponsors annual international libertarian conferences and publishes a newsletter, *Freedom Network News*.

Libertarian Party, 301 W. 21st Street, Houston, TX 77008. In recent years, the LP has been one of the most active libertarian organizations, running candidates for a variety of offices and getting a good deal of publicity. It publishes a tabloid newsletter called the *Libertarian Party News*. There are local parties in nearly all 50 states.

Local Government Center, 2716 Ocean Park Boulevard, Suite 1062, Santa Monica, CA 90405. Research center and clearinghouse on privatization.

National Taxpayers Union, 325 Pennsylvania Avenue SE, Washington, DC 20077. A lobbying organization dedicated to reducing both taxation and government expenditures.

Political Economy Research Center, 502 S. 19th Avenue, Suite 211, Bozeman, MT 59715. Research foundation dedicated to a libertarian approach on environmental issues.

Institutes

Cato Institute, 224 Second Street SE, Washington, DC 20003.

Fraser Institute, 626 Bute Street, Vancouver V6E 3M1, British Columbia, Canada.

Heartland Institute, 55 East Monroe Street, Suite 4316, Chicago, IL 60603.

Independent Institute, 350 Sansome Street, San Francisco, CA 94104.

Institute for Economic Affairs, 2 Lord North Street, London SW1P 3LB, England.

Institute for Humane Studies at George Mason University, 4400 University Drive, Fairfax, VA 22030.

Manhattan Institute, 131 Spring Street, 6th Floor, New York, NY 10012.

Pacific Institute for Public Policy, 177 Post Street, San Francisco, CA 94108.

These institutes promote libertarian work, especially on public policy issues. They publish books and pamphlets, hold conferences, and in some cases provide scholarships or research funding. The Cato Institute also publishes the *Cato Journal*, listed under magazines above.

Sources

Audio Forum, On-The-Green, Guildford, CT 06437. Sells cassette tapes of conservative and libertarian talks, including some of mine. A catalog is available on request.

Free Forum Books, 1800 Market Street, San Francisco, CA 91402. A West Coast libertarian bookstore. Produces a catalog.

Laissez Faire Books, 532 Broadway, 7th Floor, New York, NY 10012. A bookstore specializing in libertarianism. You can order many of the books I list here from them. Their monthly catalog, over 30 pages, listing titles on libertarianism, economics, history, philosophy, psychology, and other subjects, is free upon request.

Liberty Audio and Film Service, 824 West Broad Street, Richmond, VA 23220. Jim Turney, who heads this service, has prodigiously made audio and video recordings of nearly every major libertarian event since 1979. A catalog of his collection has so far never appeared.

Liberty Tree Network, 350 Sansome Street, San Francisco, CA 94104. A libertarian mail-order service which offers not only books and tapes, but also games, ties, T-shirts, and other novelty items. Quarterly catalog, free upon request.

INDEX